Mark Antony drawn up by Cleopatra into the Castle.
See page 30

THE

KINGDOM OF BRASS:

OR THE

HISTORY OF THE WORLD

FROM THE

BIRTH OF ALEXANDER THE GREAT

TO THE

BIRTH OF CHRIST,

INCLUDING THE

HISTORY OF JUDEA DURING THAT PERIOD.

"And another third kingdom of brass, which shall bear rule over the whole earth."

By R. B. BEMENT,

AUTHOR OF SEVERAL WORKS ON ANCIENT HISTORY.

CINCINNATI:
MOORE, WILSTACH, KEYS & CO.
25 West Fourth Street,
1856.

Stereotyped and Printed by
WILLIAM OVEREND & CO.
CINCINNATI.

CONTENTS.

PREFACE.

HAVING personally visited the ground and devoted much time and care to the study of the history of Egypt, and in the preparation of a large work on ancient history, (which was unfortunately lost after it had gone into the hands of the printer,) I determined to prepare a small work embracing only the history of Egypt from the time of Alexander to the beginning of the Christian era, to be called THE LAGIDÆ, or *Egypt under the Ptolemies*. This work had advanced to the time of Physcon, when it became apparent that the history of Egypt could not well be kept distinct from that of other branches of Alexander's vast empire. At that stage the purpose was formed of enlarging the work, filling up a few gaps, and including the four heads of the third beast of Daniel's vision. After much effort, I found it impracticable to avoid an occasional repetition of the same substantial facts, as they affected different governments; but in this respect I believe I have been more methodical than the old authors, although less so than I could desire. I have kept constantly before the mind the connection between the sacred prophets, especially Daniel, and the history to which the prophecies referred. This work has been prepared under peculiar embarrassments. My time has been chiefly devoted to public lectures on ancient history, and it was only at intervals that attention could be devoted to the work. The loss of the manuscripts for the larger work rendered references very inconvenient. Owing to a partial failure of my sight, I have been obliged to employ an amanuensis. Consequently, some difficulty has arisen in filling up gaps, and gliding gracefully from one subject to another. No other writer, so far as I know, has attempted to furnish a connected history exclusively devoted to this period of time, or its harmony with the sacred scriptures. It is therefore hoped that with whatever of defect it may contain, this work may meet with a charitable and favorable reception from the public and the press.

R. B. BEMENT.

INTRODUCTION

TO THE HISTORY OF

ALEXANDER AND HIS SUCCESSORS.

THE unparalleled suddenness of the rise, extension, and dismemberment of the Macedonian empire, was like the unexpected appearance of a magnificent comet, filling the vaulted arch with its dazzling radiance, streaming through the heavens from the western horizon to the verge of the east, then with terrific explosion bursting into four new planets, with many a lesser corruscation, whose meteoric and unsteady lights one by one paled and finally disappeared, leaving the four prominent ones for a time to circle in their eccentric orbit, coming frequently in collision with fearful encounter, then rebounding apart, until the larger brilliant orb of day made its appearance and absorbed all four into its self.

In extent, Alexander's empire embraced more than all that of Nebuchadnezzar. In rapidity of enlargement, it surpassed that of Cyrus. And in many points of comparison it exceeded both, justifying the language of the prophet, "and bear rule over all the earth." This empire, with its subdivisions, is justly called THE KINGDOM OF BRASS. While gold is the appropriate emblem of will, strong, indomitable, successful at home, brass expresses a similar will going abroad to execute its purpose. For this reason, brass is often represented as appertaining to the feet, ready to go forth to execute the will. "His feet were as pillars of brass, as if they burned in a furnace."

The history of Alexander and his successors furnishes a great number of episodes or solitary fragments of history, whose tragical character is of surpassing interest; but clustered together, they exhibit such a brilliancy of sparkling gems as can be gathered no where else in so limited a space of time.

In itself, this history has merit that deserves more attention and careful study than it has usually received. But there is another aspect of this subject that demands our special attention. This period of time was the theme of prophetic vision, and in its elements we find a most complete demonstration of the truth and divine authenticity of the sacred writings.

After a few brilliant visions abounding in rich imagery, representing the future history of four successive great kingdoms, and the final triumph of truth and righteousness, the prophet Daniel drops from the sublime scenery of emblems into plain, literal, and common language, and describes with minuteness these governments in collision, the results of their battles, the regular succession of princes that participated in the history of the third kingdom, and the particular character of each, man by man, as a king of fierce countenance, the raiser of taxes, the vile person, etc., etc.

The history of the Israelites, and especially the Jews, is a subject of much interest to the student of the Bible.

Except the books of Maccabees, which are far from being reliable, but little of their condition from the close of their captivity to the time of Christ, has hitherto been published in the English language, and that little is so merged in the history of others as to be difficult to comprehend, leaving but vague and indefinite impressions upon the mind of the student.

In the following pages an effort is made, after the time of the Epiphanes, to separate partially the history of the Jews from that of the surrounding nations.

It will be seen that after the death of Zedekiah, who was deposed by Nebuchadnezzar, B. C. 588, none of the tribe of Judah reigned over this people.

Authority, so far as any remained in Judea, was lodged in the hands of the high priesthood of the tribe of Levi, and when the kingly form of government was again restored, the crown was placed upon the head of that officer, and not upon a Jew.

If the law-giver did not depart from Judah he was not of that tribe, although he dwelt among them and ruled over them.

Of the ten tribes, often called the lost tribes, the most probable opinion is, that during the captivity all became blended in one nation, under the general name of Jews.

The conquest of so many nations by Alexander at this particular period, was admirably adapted to prepare the way of the Lord; to aid in the early and rapid spread of the gospel of the blessed God. These nations were at that time the most intelligent and energetic people upon the face of the whole earth; they surrounded Judea on all sides; they spoke a great variety of tongues.

The Macedonian supremacy diffused a knowledge of the Greek language through all the different tribes of the family of man.

Before the time of Christ, so extended had become that language that almost every where in the higher circles the Greek was spoken, whereby not only apostles inspired with the gift of tongues were able to address the common multitude, but uninspired ministers of the word could address the rulers and distinguished personages in a large portion of the world.

The subsequent subjection of all to Rome opened also the means of intercommunication between these different nations.

All these must have been by divine arrangement to facilitate the accomplishment of that which the council of heaven had determined, and which the Lord had declared by his servants the prophets.

THE

KINGDOM OF BRASS.

SKETCH OF THE LIFE OF ALEXANDER.

AND as I was considering, behold an he-goat came from the west on the face of the whole earth, and touched not the ground; and the goat had a notable horn between his eyes. DANIEL viii: 5.

THREE hundred and fifty-six years before the birth of Christ, a remarkable personage was ushered into this world from Beecher's preëxistent state, around whose cradle the fates held court, and upon whose decree hung the destiny of many nations as they were to be borne on the bosom of the resistless stream of future time. Alexander the Conqueror was born at Pella, a city of Macedon.

This country comprised the western half of modern Turkey in Europe, while the eastern half of the same country was called Thrace. About 398 years before the birth of Christ, Macedon was governed by King Amyntas, whose wife's name was Eurydice, by whom he had Alexander, Perdiccas and Philip; and by another woman, Ptolemy.

Amyntas died about 379 years before Christ, and his son Alexander took the throne, but perished in war after a reign of one year. The only important event in his administration was, that he delivered his infant brother,

Philip, a hostage into the hands of his enemies, the Illyrians, who soon sent him safely back to his mother.

Perdiccas ascended the throne of Macedon, not without much opposition from his cousin Pausanias. Philip was again delivered to the Thebans as a hostage, where he received an excellent Grecian education, being about ten years of age when he went to Thebes. About ten years later, Perdiccas was slain in battle.

In the midst of confusion in Macedon, Philip, who had escaped from his keepers, appeared suddenly and unexpectedly in the camp of his countrymen, and was at once proclaimed king, to the exclusion of the son of Perdiccas, who was an infant.

For the first four years, Philip only claimed to govern as Prince protector of the infant heir; but in the twenty-fourth year of his age, 360 years before Christ, he assumed the crown.

In his administration he displayed the skill and ability of a discreet politician, a crafty statesman, and an able general. His domestic relations were quite unfortunate. His first wife was Olympias of Epyrus, by whom he had Alexander the Great, and two daughters, Cleopatra and Thessalonica. Olympias was a woman of great energy and decision of character, but most haughty and unloveable in her spirit. Indeed she was a Macedonian edition of Jezebel, but Philip was not another Ahab to submit to her authority. Tired of her evil machinations, Philip divorced Olympias, and married Cleopatra, a Macedonian lady, a niece of Attalus. The nuptials of Philip and Cleopatra were celebrated with great pomp, but before the festival closed they had a regular *family jar.* As we may well suppose, Alexander was in no very pleasant state of mind, to see his mother set aside and another introduced in her place. Attalus drank a toast, and called upon the Macedonians to thank the gods for the prospect of a native prince to heir the throne of Philip. This was an allusion to the fact that Olympias was not a native of Macedon. The words of Attalus fell upon the ear of Alexander like a spark of fire upon a magazine of powder. Seizing a goblet of wine, he furiously dashed it at the head of the insolent nobleman, exclaiming, "Wretch! do you call me illegitimate?" Attalus returned the compliment by hurling another cup at Alexander. The quarrel became general, and cups and wine flew plentifully about the hall. Philip, who had received many wounds in battle, had become somewhat infirm. He arose from his royal seat, and with drawn sword, in wrath advanced across the hall to chastise his son for disturbing the banquet. In his effort, he stumbled and fell to the floor. Alexander, not in the least intimidated, pointed at his fallen father and exclaimed, "A fine king have you to lead the army to war against the Persians, when he can not cross a banquet hall without falling. I will show you in due time who can govern Macedon."

The attendants ultimately separated the parties and ended the present commotion. The little horn of the rough he-goat seen in Daniel's vision had begun to manifest itself. The energy and boldness of Alexander gave foreshadowings of his future career. But this is not the end of this unfortunate jar. There is scarce room to doubt that on that day Philip, great King of Macedon, sold his own life for a trifle. Subsequent events were the offspring of that night's deeds.

Oh, how often do parents forget that children will one day be older and will remember their early wrongs. Some ten years after this occurrence, Cleopatra, not the wife but the daughter of Philip, was married to a King of Epyrus, and a great ceremony was performed in honor of the nuptials. A grand procession marched toward the temple. Philip, walking, dressed in all the gayety of royal robes, in a prominent part of the procession, was stabbed, and sunk dead in the street. The assassin was caught and put to death; but there is no reason to doubt that Olympias and Alexander were the instigators of the murder. Thus perished King Philip, about 336 years before Christ. After having conquered many nations, and won victories in many a battle field, he fell by the stratagem of his own family, and died as a fool dieth.

CHART OF THE FAMILY OF PHILIP.

Brothers—Alexander, Perdiccas, Ptolemy.

Wives and Favorites—Olympias, Cleopatra, Audaca, Philinna, Arsinoe.

Children—By Olympias: Alexander, Cleopatra, Thessalonica. By Cleopatra: Caranus and Europa (both murdered by Olympias.) By Audaca: Cyna, (Eurydice, grandchild). By Philinna a Larissean dancer: Aridæus. By Arsinoe: Ptolemy, King of Egypt.

Arideus subsequently married Eurydice, daughter of Cyna.

Alexander had no sooner ascended the throne of his father, than he began to plan for the invasion of Persia. This had been a favorite topic with his predecessors, none of whom had, however, been able to put their plans into execution. To comprehend the inducement to such an undertaking, we must review a few past events and the then state of the world. Asia Minor, lying between the Black and Mediterranean Seas, was divided into a number of states and provinces, among which were Lydia, Phrygia, Bythinia, Capadocia, Mysia, and Cilicia. These colonies had, in a great measure, been settled by Grecian emigration. The majority of the people spoke a dialect of the

Greek language.. Their manners, customs, literature and religion were Grecian. For a time they had been governed by their own laws, and rulers of their own choosing, but had gradually lost their independence and were subjected to petty kings and local governors, whose avarice and cruelty knew no bounds. The Persian monarchs had subjected these states to their dictation, and appointed satraps as local governors over them who were the mere creatures of the Persian court. It is therefore not surprising that the Greeks, a bold, free and independent people, should sympathise with these brethren in Asia Minor, and that collisions and acts of violence should frequently occur in which Greece and Persia should be found on opposite sides. These events had at an earlier date led Darius and Xerxes to attempt the invasions and conquest of Greece. Their invasions ending in ignominious defeats, had created hereditary hate between the two races. Greece feared Persia and desired her humiliation. Persia detested the free spirit of Greece which was dangerous to her dependencies in that quarter of of the empire. Macedon was indeed an empire of itself, separate from the Grecian states, but it was also originally a colony of Grecian emigration; as among themselves the Greek, the Macedonian and the Epirots are spoken of as distinct nations, but as relating to the rest of the world they are all Greeks. Alexander soon brought all the discordant Grecian elements into one general consolidation and himself at their head. He had ascended the throne of his father in the year 336, being but twenty years of age, and in two years he was prepared to march against Persia. He had in his army a staff of officers, a body of men aged, experienced, grave, and any of whom was capable of taking the entire command of a great expedition and conducting a grand campaign with ability. Most of them were older than himself and had served in the wars of his father;

several of them were persons more or less related to himself. Alexander, in the expedition, was the motive power—the steam-engine; his able officers the engineers—the directors of that power. With the youthful ardor of the ambitious Alexander and the sedate wisdom of Perdiccas Antipater and others, we might expect an energetic war, terminating in triumph.

The Persian empire had now existed about two hundred years from the year 536 B. C. Its authority extended to the great seas of the West. Under its control where Egypt, Palestine, Syria, and Asia Minor, with all that once was Assyria, Babylonia, Media, Parthia and Elimea. But luxury had enervated its monarchs and corrupted its leaders and people, so that Persia, though vast in dimensions, was like an old, feeble, doting man, trembling and ready to fall, yet full of vanity and boasting of its strength. Alexander crossed the straits with an army well disciplined, and inured to toil and hardship, but small in number and almost entirely without funds. They trusted not to their purses but to their swords to obtain supplies. The first battle was fought in the waters and on the banks of the Granicus, where victory after a severe struggle, crowned the standard of the Europeans. About two years were devoted to the conquest of Asia Minor, whose satraps, creatures of the Persian court, resisted manfully but unsuccessfully the invaders, while Darius, for whom they were contending, was still devoting himself to pleasure and debauchery at Susa, not yet having moved to the aid of his dependent provinces. Alexander having subdued all the states of Asia Minor, went into winter quarters at Tarsus, the future birth-place of the Apostle Paul, the locality of the first interview of Marc Antony with the captivating Cleopatra. The next year, 332, was one of great events in the field of Mars: Darius, aroused from his dream, advanced with a large army to check the progress of the Macedonian hero. This army was large only in numbers, not in soldiers. They were a body of proud, conceited, dissolute men, women, and servants, rendered vicious and effeminate by the example and authority of the king; there was great display of riches; silks and tapestry adorned the gorgeous oriental tents, there were cushions and divans, cups of gold and silver and wines to fill them; but these were not the best implements with which to meet a rude and hardy yet well disciplined army of Greece.

Alexander was crossing the mountains of Amanus, which separate Syria from Cilicia, through the gap or pass. When he learned that Darius and the Persian army, having crossed through the northern pass, were now in his rear, he suddenly wheeled, and turning into Cilicia, met and in the famous battle of Issus conquered and entirely defeated the numerous hosts of the Persians. Darius, indeed, escaped with but so few men that little more is heard of him for two years. Alexander now sent forward one of his generals through the pass and down southward on the east of Anti-Lebanon to Damascus, where that officer was so successful as to capture the city, with most of the treasures of Darius which had been deposited there; he also made prisoners of the mother, wife, sister, and other female members of the family of the Persian King. Alexander himself, with part of his army, proceeded along the coast through Phœnicia. On his right the great sea rolled its waves and lashed the shore, here and there wearing into the land, and forming beautiful bays and sheltering harbors where the Phœnicians moored their vessels returning from commercial enterprises, pushed by them into all waters. On his left were the mountains of Lebanon whose highest peaks ascend ten thousand feet above the level of the sea and are capped with perpetual snow. The sides of these mountains are adorned with cedar and fir trees, whose evergreen foliage was an emblem of the unfading laurels of fame which were to repose upon the brow of the youthful hero: between the mountain and the sea is a narrow slope of arable land watered by many a brawling rivulet whose contents leaped from the cliffs and were discharged into the sea below.

But why moves Alexander in this direction? It must be recollected that Phœnicia, except Tyre, had been annexed to Assyria under Shalmanezer, of Nineveh, and in the overthrow of that city had passed to the kingdom of Babylon; then following its fortunes, Phœnicia passed into the possession of the Persians; here also lay all the maritime strength of the enemy. It was, therefore, expedient to secure the coöperation of the Phœnicians, before Alexander could safely proceed in his Eastern enterprise. Beritus, Tripoli, and Sidon gladly threw off the yoke of the Persians, and opening their gates to him, joined the standard of the hero of Macedon. Tyre resisted not so much out of regard for Persia as from a desire for independence; but after seven months siege the proud city of commerce was humbled in the dust and all western Asia was subjected to Alexander.

At the south-east angle of the Mediterranean sea stood, anciently, the city of Gaza. Many a heathen writer refers to the events said to have transpired in and around this spot, when the demigods dwelt upon the earth and mingled in the affairs of men. It is quite uncertain, however, when or by whom Gaza was founded. In the time of Joshua, and for many years afterward, it was in the possession of the Philistines, but ultimately, upon the extermination of that race, it became the property of the kingdom of Judah. In common with the rest of Judah, it became subject to Babylon, and at the fall of that empire, it passed to the scepter of the Persians. Situated as it once was, on the angle of the sea, and commanding the high road from Asia into Egypt, it was ever deemed of great military importance.

It is now governed by a Bey, or Satrap, of the Pasha of Egypt. The modern city of Gaza is situated some miles back from the sea, whether precisely on the spot of the ancient city or not it is hard to determine. All along this coast the sea has in the course of centuries receded far from the ancient land-mark, leaving a long line of sandy beach in many places, so that cities once seaports are left quite remote from the waters. The probability is, therefore, that Gaza has not been removed, but that the sea has deserted it. This city has been the theater of many a bloody strife, both in ancient and modern times.

Darius had placed as governor over Gaza a eunuch by the name of Betis. That class of persons seem to have been favorites with several of the Persian monarchs, yet they were often deceitful, treacherous, and unworthy of confidence, often killing their masters, as in the case of Xerxes and Ochus. To this charge of infidelity, Betis was not obnoxious. The defeat of Darius, the capture of the treasures and family, and the triumph of the enemy, failed to overcome the steadfast attachment of this governor to his sovereign.

Alexander was now marching toward Egypt, and Gaza lay across his path. After the terrible siege and final fate of Tyre, it would not be supposed that Gaza, far inferior in strength, would attempt resistance; yet Betis, and many of the people, true to their lawful sovereign, rejected all overtures of surrender. Alexander besieged the city, but with all the ingenuity and courage of his men, he occupied two months in making a breach in the wall and capturing the city, which was well fortified and abundantly supplied with provisions and munitions of war. Alexander received two wounds in the siege, which greatly enraged him against the governor and his people. He caused two thousand persons to be cut to pieces, and the rest of the men, women and children to be sold as slaves. After insulting Betis for his fidelity to his master, he caused him to be put to death in a most cruel manner. Like Achilles to Hector, he caused holes to be made in the heels of his victim, through which he passed ropes and attached them to a chariot, and dragged the unhappy governor through the streets and around the city until he was dead. All the treasure found in Gaza was sent by Alexander to his mother and sisters in Macedon. However commendable might have been his affection for his relatives, who can excuse this monstrous wholesale robbery and butchery of a whole city for no offense except fidelity to the government under which they were born? The character of Alexander appears at times like an April day: now the sun shines out in loveliness and not a cloud is to be seen; yet before you can walk an hundred yards, the moisture of the atmosphere has condensed into dark clouds, and torrents of rain descend. You fly for shelter, but before you can arrive the storm is past, the sun throws off its veil, and all nature smiles again with cheerfulness. So with the hero of Macedon. We can hardly suppress the emotions of delight, and the acclamations of applause in view of his kind and affectionate treatment of his royal prisoners or other objects of compassion, or we are ready to wish him universal empire for his wise and heroic actions on the field of battle; but before these emotions have subsided, or another page of his history is read, we are shocked at his barbarity toward some faithful officer. Such must be the feelings of every human heart on reading of the massacre of Tyre and of Gaza. Alexander was founding the kingdom of the Leopard, and in this character we must expect to find the bright and dark spots which distinguish that animal.

We must expect to find in him and his kingdom oftentimes the playfulness and the treachery, the affection and the cruelty of the Leopard.

The summer was now passed, and the hero marched toward Egypt, for the overflowing had subsided, and the right season had arrived for strangers to visit the land of the Pharaoh. Egypt, the early land of science, the theme of sacred and profane pens, was not now what it had once been. About 685 years before the birth of Christ, after a period of anarchy, twelve princes had divided and ruled the land; one of them, Psammetichus, by the aid of Greek soldiers, had expelled his eleven associates and established himself sole monarch of Egypt. Under his protection the Greeks found a peaceful home. In the higher circles the Greek language was taught, and began to be much spoken throughout Egypt, while the Coptic gradually declined. The Greek spirit of enterprise was favorably improving the sluggish and exhausted energies of other times. The Egyptians worshiped gods representing the sublime and mysterious powers of nature; to these gods they had erected temples and consecrated images in common with living animals, and representing the elements. A wise and learned priestly class, or caste, had the care of the temples, the sacrifices, and the secret mysteries. The Persians were of a different cast; they worshiped the luminary in the heavens and the sacred fire, his holy offspring. They reared altars on hills, in valleys and in groves, but temples they had none; they repudiated devotion in dark recesses where the light of the sun was not admitted; they abhorred priests, temples, and idols. Cambyses had demolished their temples, rifled their contents, carried off their gods, and degraded their priesthood. The Persian rule had been ever after averse to what the Egyptians would call piety; the country had languished, its revenue had been exhausted, and its fertile plains badly cultivated.

The Macedonians and Greeks were worshipers of idols; they had lords many and gods many; they had temples and images also representing the powers of nature; there were many points held in common between the Egyptian and the Greek; indeed, much of the science and philosophy of Greece had been borrowed from the Egyptian university at Onn. When Alexander approached Pelusium, the Egyptian army was there, as in duty bound to resist him, the enemy of their lawful sovereign, the king of Persia. Alexander sent a messenger to proclaim to them that he had not come to do them harm, but to break the Persian yoke, to restore to Egypt her former glory—her temples—her religion, and her ancient prosperity. This appeal from the commands of a people of similar religion, speaking a language that was common in Egypt, could not fail to be successful, attributing all their misfortunes to the impiety and misrule of the Persians, and desiring again the days when heavenly incense and joyous song should ascend in the sacred edifices. The Egyptians at once opened their hearts and their arms to receive Alexander as their deliverer and benefactor. It was a bloodless victory, and the jewel of Egypt was plucked from the crown of Persia. The army proceeded to Memphis with mirth and joy abounding.

Alexander was a philosopher, a scholar, and a statesman, as well as a warrior. He knew that no small part of Grecian prosperity was owing to her commerce. He had heard of the policy of Solomon, who, by commercial enterprise, had made gold and silver to abound in Jerusalem; he had spent a summer in Phœnicia, whose fame had gone over the world, whose commerce had traversed every sea, and returning home had enriched the coffers of the bold shipmasters. In the recent siege and terrible resistance of Tyre, he had a demonstration of the energy and wealth which commerce confers upon a maritime people. It was now the policy as well as the good pleasure of Alexander to secure the attachment of the Egyptians, so that no reaction or revolution might disturb him when he should be prepared to direct his march toward the heart of the Persian empire. He also foresaw that if Egypt, one of the Persian dependencies, which without resistance submitted to him, should become prosperous and happy under his authority, it must have an influence upon the other nations whom he yet intended to invade and pluck from the Persian land. To his observing eye it was apparent that this land of fertility needed only commercial advantages to make her prosperous; she bordered upon two seas, yet she had almost no harbor and no commerce. The Red Sea was only approachable through trackless deserts; the mouths of the Nile were blocked up by sandbars, hence only small craft, with the utmost difficulty and in the most favorable weather, could approach them along this portion of the Egyptian coast on the Mediterranean.

At a little village called Rhacotis the sea rounded up and formed a tolerable basin, with water of a better depth; nature had here formed a better harbor than at any point on the Egyptian coast; this harbor might be improved and made to answer this purpose. Here Alexander founded a city, calling it after his own name, Alexandria, and invited people from many nations to repair thither.

About one hundred miles west of Egypt is an oasis, a fertile spot in the desert, known as Elcargar. This green spot is about fifteen miles in length, and from two to four miles wide. In the midst of a grove of dates and figs on the western end of the oasis stood an ancient temple devoted to the worship of the god Jupiter Ammon, the principal deity of the ancient Egyptians. These people were greatly devoted to their religious services, and when all Egypt had fallen before the invading Persians, Jupiter Ammon in Elcargar had escaped. In this sacred retreat, a few of the Egyptian priests still resided. To please these priests, and through them to win the affections of the people of all Egypt, was a wise political measure.

Alexander left Rhacotis, and through almost interminable sands made a pilgrimage to the temple of the ram-headed deity in the sacred groves of the lonely retreat. There he honored the priests and offered incense to the deity. He then requested the hierophant to inquire of the divinity through the oracle, the answer to two questions: First, whether he, Alexander, was not the son of the god Jupiter Ammon. This to us may seem an absurd and foolish question, but we must recollect that most of the famous heathen deities had once been men of distinction upon earth. The ambition of kings and conquerors to be called deities at their departure from earth, had once been quite universal; this vanity had nearly ceased before the time of Alexander, but the custom had not been forgotten. It was not, therefore, so unnatural that the Macedonian should desire to be officially and ecclesiastically declared the son of a god. However little he might credit their oracles, it would not only flatter his vanity, but also increase his power and influence over a superstitious people. It was rather a political than a pious device. To this question the subservient priests caused the oracle to respond that Alexander of Macedon was the natural son of Jupiter Ammon, the father of all the gods, and the especial protector of Egypt.

The next question addressed to the oracle was, whether all the accessories to the murder of Alexander's father had been brought to condign punishment. It will be recollected that Philip, the father of Alexander, had been slain in the midst of a wedding procession, and that the assassin had been immediately after slain, and that suspicion was cast upon Alexander himself and his mother, Olympias, as being instigators of the deed. Whether this charge was or was not true, it became Alexander to remove the stain by a real or affected earnestness in punishing the culprits, if any could be discovered. It was natural, therefore, for him to make this inquiry of the oracle, however little he might care for the murder, or however still less he might credit the answer of the oracle. But Alexander had just been declared the son of Jupiter Ammon, not of Philip of Macedon. To the second question the oracle replied that the inquirer, being the son of a god, his father could not die, but was immortal; but for the gratification of Alexander, the oracle would inform him that all the murderers of Philip had made their appearance in the land of the shades. Olympias, the mother of Alexander, still lived. When she heard of his divine pretensions, she wrote to him a mirthful letter, cautioning him to beware lest, claiming to be the son of Jupiter Ammon, he should bring his mother into disrepute for her unchastity and unfaithfulness to king Philip.* Better would it have been for her reputation if she had not herself given other and stronger proofs of her inconstancy than those declared by the oracle on the oasis of the desert.

From the desert, Alexander returned into Egypt, and viewed his new planned city, made some regulations for the government of Egypt, and proceeded with his army into Asia. This was in the autumn of 331 B. C.

---

*In another letter, Olympias cautioned Alexander not to get his mother into difficulty, by exciting the jealousy of Juno, who, by heathen mythology, was the wife of Jupiter Ammon.

In Asia, the usual good fortune attended Alexander. He met and defeated Darius in the famous battle of Arbela, conquered Babylon, Susa, Rasagarda, Persepolis, Ecbatana, and subdued Hyerama, Bactria, India, and many other provinces, and at length returned triumphant to Babylon, having fulfilled the words of the prophet, that the he-goat of the west should stamp the Persians in the ground, and that none could deliver Persia out of his hand. Thus did the kingdom of brass rule over the earth. Darius, the last king of the Persians, was assassinated by his own attendants in the year 330 B. C., and thus ended the empire of the Persians, which had continued from the crowning of Cyrus, 206 years, or from the rise of the Medo-Persian armies 210 years, which may have been the meaning of the angel when he told Darius that the prince of Persia resisted him one and twenty days before the crowning of the prince of Greece, a day sometimes indicating a decade of years instead of a year.

But the little horn was to be broken. Alexander, up to the time of Darius, had practiced great temperance, kindness, forbearance, and chastity, but from and after that time he began to give loose to an imperious temper and sensual indulgence. He now unjustly caused the death of Parmenio, one of his oldest and most faithful generals, and his son Philotas, neither of whom was proved to be guilty of any offense. He assumed the gorgeous dress of the orientals, and had around him a host of concubines. His tables began to abound in luxuries; effeminacy was fast conquering the conqueror of the World. At Babylon he devoted himself so supremely to intemperance and debauch, that he died of a fever induced by excessive use of wine. His death occurred in the year 223 B. C.

FATE OF THE ROYAL FAMILY OF ALEXANDER.

"And when he was strong, the great horn was broken." "And when he shall stand up, his kingdom shall be broken, and shall be divided towards the four winds of heaven, and not to his posterity nor according to his dominion which he ruled." DANIEL.

Twelve princes and princesses of the royal line survived the great hero:

1st. Olympias, his mother, slain by Cassander, 317.

2d. Cleopatra, his sister, a widow, slain by Antigonus, 308.

3d. Thessalonica, a sister, wife of Cassander, slain by Antipater, 294.

4th. Aridæus Philip, a half-brother, slain by Olympias, 317.

5th. Eurydice, wife of Aridæus, slain by Olympias, 317.

6th. Statira, a Persian wife, poisoned by Roxana, 323.

7th. Roxana, a Macedonian wife, slain by Cassander, 311.

8th. Alexander, son of Roxana, slain by Cassander, 311.

9th. Barsina, a Thracian wife, slain by Polysphercon, 310.

10th. Hercules, son of Barsina, slain by Polysphercon, 310.

11th. Antipater, son of Thessalonica, died in prison, 294.

12th. Alexander, son of Thessalonica, slain by Demetrius, 294.

How vain and fruitless are the wild schemes of mad ambition, when unsanctified or unrestrained by a sense of justice. Men of violence, though successful in their enterprises, seldom derive the advantage they propose to themselves. That very success is often destructive to them and their families. Alexander had extended the empire of his fathers over the fairest portions of the earth, but instead of transmitting it to his posterity, their only legacy was treason, murder and extermination.

In the fate of all the kindred of Alexander, modern statesmen and rulers might learn the solemn lesson of the higher law: that the heavens do rule, and what God hath spoken by the mouth of His holy Prophets, he is not only able but will perform.

DEATH OF STATIRA, B. C. 323.

Alexander died suddenly in Babylon, at the age of thirty-three years, and left the family and relatives named in the above list. Statira was a Persian princess of the family of Darius. Alexander the younger, was not born until a few months after his fathers' death. Roxana hoped soon to become the mother of a son who should be heir to the kingdom, and fearing Statira might be in the same condition, and furnish a rival who might mar her own prospects, she removed Statira by inviting her to a banquet, in which that accomplished princess was poisoned, and expired in a few hours. Her death extinguished the royal line of Persia.

DEATH OF ARIDÆUS AND EURYDICE, B. C. 317.

Philip, the father of Alexander, had six wives, or at least, favorites. No mention is made of any other son until after the death of Alexander, when Aridæus came to notice. He was the son of a Larissean dancing woman. Olympias having been divorced, and fearing that this prince might become the rival of her own son, found means to administer to Aridæus, while a child, a dose of poison which, although it did not cause his immediate death, permanently destroyed his senses. He was sixteen years of age when Alexander died.

As will be seen in another place, the generals of Alexander associated Aridæus with the infant son of the hero, and gave them the empty title of kings. After the death of Perdiccas the kings were committed to the custody of Antipater of Macedon; then to his son Cassander. Aridæus married Eurydice, daughter of Cina, and grand-daughter of Philip by another woman.

Polyspercon and Cassander were rivals for the regency of Macedon. To weaken the cause of Cassander and strengthen his own, Polyspercon brought Olympias from Epirus, her native land, into the capital of Macedon where as the mother of the hero and the grand-mother of the infant king, she soon gained adherents, and established herself at the head of government. Had she grown wiser and better by a long and severe experience, and used her authority with moderation and equity, she might have maintained her position, and rendered the close of her life more calm and happy : but born in the midst of tempestuous times, and soured by adversity, she remained haughty, imperious and implacable. She immediately caused the king, Aridæus, to be put to death, and his wife Eurydice, to be thrown into prison. Inveterate against all the branches of the royal family except her own, she sent to the prisoner a dagger, a cord, and a bowl of poison, informing her that she might choose by which of these to end her life, and save the dishonor of a more public execution. Eurydice uttering imprecations upon the head of her murderer, chose the cord, and strangled herself. A hundred of the principal nobility were also executed by command of Olympias. Among these was Nicanor, the brother of Cassander.

DEATH OF OLYMPIAS, B. C. 317.

This monster did not long escape the penalty of her crimes. Being unable to sustain her authority in Pella, she returned to Pydna in Epirus, taking with her Roxana, the infant king, and Thessalonica, her own daughter, with some of her Epirote relations, among others Diedemia, a sister of Pyrrhus the hero. The people of Epirus seemed not to value her presence very highly, although she was a native and a relative of their former king; they may have seen or experienced something of her unloveable temper during her former residence among them. They declared for Cassander, who sent an army against Pydna, and reduced the princess to great distress by besieging the city. Olympias applied to Polyspherеon for relief, and that general, who was in Greece, prepared to march to her assistance; but Cassander was able with one division of his army to continue the siege, while another marched against Polyspherеon, and prevented him from accomplishing anything. The officers of Cassander bribed those of the enemy and frustrated all his purposes. Olympias being entirely unrelieved, was obliged to surrender at discretion.

Alcidæus was then king of Epirus, and was probably a brother of Olympias. He undertook to aid the princess at Pydna, but his officers and army being averse to the war, refused to execute his commands, banished him into exile, and slew nearly all his family. His infant son, Pyrrhus, by the faithfuness of servants, was secreted and safely sent out of the kingdom.

Cassander was desirous to destroy Olympias in a manner that would give the least offense, and save himself from censure. At his instigation the friends of those whom Olympias had caused to be put to death, accused her before the tribune, and obtained a decree of death against her. This court was held in Macedon, and the criminal was condemned unheard and undefended. Whatever may have been her demerits, there was no equity nor propriety in such a proceeding. Cassander, under color of tender regard and a desire to save her life, sent a messenger, who proposed secretly to conduct her by the water to Athens, from whence she might safely retire to foreign lands, and spend the remnant of her days in peace; but his intention was to cause her to perish by sea, and charge the event to the elements, and thus save his own reputation. Olympias aware of his intent, determined to disappoint him. She replied to his messenger that she was the daughter, widow, mother and sister of kings and conquerors; that she would not flee like a vagabond and a slave, but would come to Macedon, and plead her own cause before the assembly of the people. Nothing could be more unfavorable to the ambitious policy of Cassander than the presence of Olympias in Macedon, where the memory of Alexander might rouse the sympathies and the enthusiasm of the people for his mother. He therefore sent two hundred soldiers with orders to destroy her. So noble and dignified did she appear, while energy and majesty flashed from her eyes, that the soldiers quailed before her, and had not the heart to execute their orders, and returned. Cassander then sent a company of the relatives of the noble men who had been put to death by her orders in the affair of Aridæus. These with pleasure obeyed Cassander, and put to death this distinguished princess, whose crimes and varied fortunes form so important a part of the history of her time.

DEATH OF ROXANA AND ALEXANDER, B. C. 311.

Cassander was ambitious to be the sole king of Macedon, but while young Alexander lived he would be deemed a usurper; he therefore sought to dispose of both mother and son. Although emboldened in crime by his success against Olympias, he thought it prudent to move with caution, and test how far his bloody deeds would be tolerated by the people. Under color of greater safety and better means of education for the young king, he caused Roxana and Alexander to be removed to the castle of Amphipolis. They were no sooner there than they were stripped of all the signs of royalty, and treated more as menial prisoners than as princes of the realm. To remove the odium of the murder of Olympias, he ordered a pompous funeral for Aridæus and Eurydice whom she had slain; thus exciting their indignation against his victim, and testifying his sincere regard for the royal family. About this time he sought to strengthen his power by a connection with the royal family; he married Thessalonica, the sister of Alexander the great. Time rolled along, and the good generals were employed in destroying each other. Young Alexander had arrived at the age of twelve or thirteen years. The Macedonians began to demand that the youthful king should appear in public, and take some part in the affairs of state. Cassander determined to rule alone; no time was therefore to be lost. In the castle of Amphipolis, as in a prison, lay the royal widow and the youthful son of the great hero. Thither Cassander sent a confidential agent who caused them both to be privately murdered in the castle. Thus terminated the main branch of the family of Alexander. For the prophet had declared that the kingdom was not for his posterity. The Macedonians had become so accustomed to crime that they seem to have been but little affected by these monstrous murders.

DEATH OF BARSINA AND HERCULES, B. C. 310.

Polyspheroon, the rival of Cassander, although he could not gain the command of Macedon, still held some authority in Greece, where he defended himself against his more successful competitor. Barsina and her son Hercules, to avoid the intrigue of the factions at the capital, had retired to Ephesus, and ultimately united their interests with those of Polyspheroon. After the death of Alexander and his mother, Hercules was the only heir of the hero. Polyspheroon now exclaimed against the monstrous barbarity of Cassander, and put forward the claims of Hercules, calling upon the Macedonians to receive him as their king, hoping thus to aid himself. Cassander crafty and intriguing, saw at once the advantage which this claim would give his rival. He therefore represented to Polyspheron that in raising Hercules to the throne, he would give himself a master; but if Hercules were once out of the way, he might claim for himself the independent government of at least a portion of the kingdom. The old officer was completely deceived, and obeyed the counsel of Cassander. He treacherously murdered Barsina and her son, thus annihilating the strongest influence he had against his rival; and at the same time removing the last obstacle that prevented Cassander from assuming the crown, which he soon did, and then conquered and slew Polyspheron.

DEATH OF CLEOPATRA, B. C. 308.

This princess was the sister of Alexander the great. It was at the celebration of her nuptials with the king of Epirus, that her father, king Phillip, was slain. She had long been a widow; fearing the displeasure of Cassander after the death of her mother, Olympias, she had retired to Sardis, where she was passing her widowhood in contentment; but as she was of the royal race, the aspirants for power sought her influence. Antigonus, the blood-thirsty, then ruled in that part of the world. He did not treat Cleopatra with kindness, and her home began to be uncomfortable. She felt that she was not safe. Ptolemy was then at war with Antigonus. He invaded the states of Asia Minor. In this campaign he became personally acquainted with Cleopatra, and determined to remove her to a place of greater safety; at the same time, thinking it would add to his importance to have her in his party. A correspondence was opened between them. Cleopatra agreed to leave Sardis and meet him at a place appointed. She started; the Governor, a creature in the interest of

Antigonus, aware of what was transpiring, pursued and captured Cleopatra, brought her back to Sardis, and caused her to be poisoned. Under pretense of great indignation at the murder which he had ordered, and to conceal his own guilt, Antigonus repaired to Sardis and put to death all the female attendants of Cleopatra, charging them with the crime. "Justice is fallen in the street and truth can not enter. He that departeth from evil maketh himself a prey."

DEATH OF THESSALONICA. B. C. 294.

After the death of Cleopatra, none remained in whose veins ran the royal blood of Macedon except Thessalonica, the wife of Cassander, the sister of Alexander, and her sons. Cassander died of dropsy. Philip, his eldest son, survived his father but a few months, leaving two brothers, Antipater and Alexander. It will be seen that the elder of these two bore the name of his grandfather on his father's side, while the younger was named after his mother's brother. That fact may have some connection with the mother's partiality. Thessalonica desired Alexander, although the younger, to succeed to the crown. This preference so enraged Antipater that he rushed upon her, and while she entreated him by the breasts that had nourished him, to spare the life of his mother, he plunged the dagger into her heart, and terminated her life, staining his own raiment with maternal blood.

DEATH OF ANTIPATER AND ALEXANDER. B. C. 294.

After the death of Thessalonica, the two brothers engaged in civil war for the crown. Antipater being the more successful, Alexander sought the aid of Pyrrhus, of Epirus, and of Demetrius. The latter was then in Greece at the head of an army. He responded to the call, hastened into

Macedonia and defeated Antipater, who fled to Thrace, was thrown into prison and died in want. Alexander being delivered from the power of his brother, thanked Demetrius for his aid, and desired him to withdraw; but Demetrius had other ends in view. He murdered Alexander and took the government for himself before Pyrrhus could arrive.

They are all gone! The last star of Macedon has descended into a night that knows no morn; and the vision of the Prophet is fulfilled.

"I have seen the wicked in great power, and spreading himself like a green bay tree; yet he passed away, and lo! he was not; yea, I sought him but he could not be found." "The transgressors shall be destroyed together; the end of the wicked shall be cut off."

FATE OF THE OFFICERS OF ALEXANDER THE GREAT.

"For his kingdom shall be plucked up for others, even besides those."
DANIEL, 11 4.

CANOPIED in state, within the palace of Chaldea's great king, lay the mortal remains of him who claimed to be the son of the divine Jupiter Ammon, and aspired to fellowship with the gods. A mortal man, he assumed the airs of a god, and died as a brute. Around that lifeless form stood a group of generals who had aided their late royal master in extending his authority over the human race, from the West to the East.

At Alexander's death, his Empire embraced the civilized and classic lands of Europe — the lofty temples and seats of early science, of Egypt, the cradle of commerce and manufactures, beneath the brow of Mount Lebanon in Phœnicia and Palestine — the variegated lands of Asia Minor — the rich agricultural plains of the once luxurious Assyria, and the wealthy regions of the far East. An indomitable courage and unbounded ambition had enabled the hero of Macedon to fulfil the words of the Prophet, " and bear rule over all the earth." But his kingdom, reared by carnage, was not to remain in his family. By carnage, it was to be given to others, who, by murders, strifes and leopard-like treachery, were to divide it into various fragments and ultimately yield it to " the fourth beast, dreadful and terrible and strong exceedingly."

At first these officers were affected with sincere grief for the loss of him who had led them to victory and glory. Soon however tender affections, usually of transient duration when the object is removed, gave place to thoughts and schemes for their own aggrandizement. Of the generals that surounded Alexander, the following were the most conspicuous: Perdiccas, Eumenes, Neoptolemus, Leomadon, Alcetis, Pithon, Aridæus, Antipater, Cassander, Antigonus, Demetrius, Cartegus, Polysphercon, Alexander, Lysimachus, Seleucus, Philotas, Ptolemy, Nicator and Ophalles.

Eumenes was not a Macedonian, but a native of Thrace. Though a foreigner, he exhibited the most firm attachment to the hero, and after his death, in all the subsequent strifes, cast his lot and his influence on the side of the royal family. For this commendable fidelity, he incurred the hatred of his fellow officers and as we shall see, ultimately lost his life: the too frequent fate of those who, in any good cause, by their skill and industry, reprove the indolent and unworthy. Of the others, except Ptolemy, it may be said they were unwilling to submit to the royal family, yet dared not to trust either of themselves with supreme command, where neither had the right of preference. From the force of circumstances it was determined that the imbecile brother and the infant child of the Conqueror should wear the empty title of Kings, until ambition should find it safe to remove them, which was ultimately done.

The first seven of the generals named above were for a time associated in a faction by themselves. Against this group the others, for some unknown cause, held a grudge. The field of their operations was Syria and Asia Minor. Perdiccas had been appointed Regent, with the care of the Kings. He attempted to establish the amiable and faithful Eumenes as governor of Capadocia and some other northern provinces.

DEATH OF CARTEGUS, B. C. 321.

Some of the other generals, envious of their power, declared war against them. At the head of this movement was Antipater of Macedon; who with Antigonus and Cartegus marched against them with an army. Crossing Europe into Asia, they met and contended with Eumenes; who, with inferior force, possessed far superior skill, and often repulsed his invaders, frequently sparing the life and property of his enemies, when he could have destroyed them. His noble and generous heart desired to do them no more harm than was necessary for his own defense—a generosity illy repaid by his antagonists. After a time the opposing forces met on the plains of Cilicia, and in the battle Cartegus fell wounded and soon expired. Eumenes, although contending against the enemy, was personally a warm friend of Cartegus—a friendship not repaid by the latter. Hearing that Cartegus was mortally wounded, he hastened to his victim—embraced his foe in his arms and wept at his fall. Thus, two years after the death of Alex ander, perished the first of his officers.

DEATH OF NEOPTOLEMUS, B. C. 321.

This officer was at first of the faction of Perdiccas, and had been appointed governor of Armenia. He was sent with an army to assist Eumenes. Antigonus and Cartegus had endeavored to persuade Alcetis, Neoptolemus and Eumenes to desert the cause of Perdiccas and the Kings, and join the other aspirants in the struggle for independence. Alcetis, although a brother of Perdiccas, agreed to remain neutral. Neoptolemus forsook his friends and joined the invading enemy—but Eumenes remained faithful to his charge. Eumenes and Neoptolemus were personal and bitter enemies. It is probable that this fact had something to do with the desertion of the latter. In the battle, when Eumenes found that his former companion in arms but late rival was dead, and would no longer excite his fears, he left his prostrate body and rushed again into the battle, where he met and had a personal encounter with Neoptolemus which resulted thus: "Neoptolemus and Eumenes, who personally hated each other, having met in the battle, and their horses charging with a violent shock, they seized each other, and, their horses springing from under them, they both fell on the earth, where they struggled like two implacable wrestlers and fought for a considerable time with the utmost fury and rage, till at last Neoptolemus received a mortal wound and immediately expired."—(*Rollin*). Some writers say that the death of Craterus occurred in the same battle, subsequent to that of Neoptolemus.

DEATH OF PERDICCAS, B. C. 221.

While these events were transpiring in Cilicia, Perdiccas was marching through Palestine into Egypt to invade Ptolemy, who had been appointed governor. Although the fact is no where recorded, it is presumed that Ptolemy was confederate with the others in the war against the party of Perdiccas; no other cause appearing for this invasion of Egypt. Ptolemy entrenched himself in Memphis, the then capital, on the west of the Nile; and contented himself by acting only on the defensive. Perdiccas encamped on

Destruction of the Army of Perdiccas.—See page 41,

the east of the river, under the brow of the Mocattam Hills, near the spot where now stands Grand Cairo, "the Triumphant." The invading general lost two thousand of his men in a vain and rash attempt to ford the deep rolling river. The army of Perdiccas was composed chiefly of Macedonians and had under its protection the two Kings. The soldiers were exasperated at the sacrifice of their comrades, and the rashness of Perdiccas. After this wanton waste of life, Pithon, who was one of his subordinate officers, with ten others entered the tent of the commander and slew him. This occurred but a few days after the victory of Eumenes, in which perished the two generals whose death we have just recorded, but the knowledge of that event did not reach Egypt until two days after the death of Perdiccas.

The next day Ptolemy, crossing the river, entered the camp of the invaders and in a speech so effectually justified himself that the whole army, not having heard of the good success of their comrades under Eumenes, changed sides, joined the standard of Ptolemy, and offered him the regency of the Kings. This he declined, and that charge was committed to Antipater of Macedon.

ALCETIS,

was slain in battle with Antigonus, B. C. 319.

DEATH OF LEOMADON, B. C. 319.

This officer had served under Perdiccas and by him had been appointed governor of Phœnicia, and continued in power nearly two years after the death of his principal—but Ptolemy claimed that Phœnicia was given to him as a dependency of Egypt. He therefore invaded that country, and sent Nicanor, one of his officers, against Leomadon. The hostile forces met—Leomadon was captured and slain by Nicanor, and his province subjected for a time to the control of Ptolemy.

DEATH OF ANTIPATER, B. C. 319.

This was one of the oldest of Alexander s generals and before that monarch's death had been sent back to take care of Macedon, over which he remained governor to the end of his life. Craterus previous to his death, of which an account is given above, had been associated with him in the government of Macedon, Greece, and Epirus; but after that officer's death, Antipater governed alone. Greece had submitted to Alexander, but after the death of that hero the Greeks declared war against the authority of Macedon. After many and partially successful attempts to subdue them, old Antipater died a natural death, having appointed Polyspercon his successor, with whom Cassander, the son of Antipater, contended for the government.

DEATH OF PHILOTAS, B. C. 318.

Of this officer we know but little, except that he was of the faction of Perdiccas, by whom he was appointed governor of Media, when Neoptolemus was called away to aid Eumenes. Pithon after he had assassinated Perdiccas repaired to the East, where he raised an army, invaded Media and slew the rulers, and for a time took upon himself the government of that country — soon to share the fate of his own victim.

DEATH OF NICANOR, B. C. 317.

This officer, who at one time served under Ptolemy, and, in invading Phœnicia, slew Leomadon, was the brother of Cassander. He was in Macedon when Olympias murdered Aridæus and Eurydice. Nicanor was one of the one hundred nobles whom Olympias caused to be publicly executed on that occasion.

DEATH OF ALEXANDER, B. C. 317.

This young officer was the son of Polyspercon. He contended heroically for his father against Cassander.

Being stationed with his army at Sicyon, where his presence was deemed irksome, the citizens assassinated him.

THE FATE OF ARIDÆUS

is unknown. He was the officer who had charge of the funeral of Alexander, and was one of those who assisted Pithon in the assassination of Perdiccas.

DEATH OF EUMENES, B. C. 315.

After his victory over Craterus and Neoptolemus, Eumenes was continually harrassed by his allied enemies and rivals, who felt that his fidelity to the claims of the Kings, stood in the way of their own authority. He experienced great vicissitudes of fortune, was blockaded for a time in the Castle of Nora, effected his escape—sought and was denied aid from Python of Media, and Seleucus, a Babylonian, and was at last betrayed by his under officers into the hands of his enemy, Antigonus, who ignominiously caused his noble and worthy prisoner to be poisoned. They were personally warm friends and the life of Antigonus, even in war upon him, had been saved by Eumenes; but what is friendship or gratitude, when virtue stands in the way of corrupt and vaulting ambition?

DEATH OF PYTHON, B. C. 315.

This usurper of the government of Media had joined Antigonus in war against the virtuous Eumenes, but after the death of that nobleman, Antigonus thought to wipe out the debt of gratitude by the death of several officers who had contributed to his success. Antigonus therefore put to death Python and several others.

DEATH OF OPHELLUS, B. C. 307.

This officer returning from Babylon with Ptolemy, was appointed governor of Lybia. After a few years he rebelled against Eygpt, and was persuaded by Agathocles, King of Sicily, to engage in a war against the Carthaginians, where he was treacherously assassinated by the very man who induced him to undertake the expedition.

DEATH OF ANTIGONUS, B. C. 301.

After the death of Eumenes, Antigonus, with his son, claimed to govern all Syria. The extent of his territory and the ambition which he manifested, aroused the jealousy of the other great masters. Lysimachus, Cassander and Ptolemy, with their adherents, formed an alliance and made war upon Syria. This conflict, after repeated engagements by land and by sea, was finally terminated in the decisive battle of Ipsus in Phrygia, in which Antigonus was slain. His son Demetrius after the defeat fled into Greece.

DEATH OF POLYSPHERCON, B. C. 299.

This officer served in Macedon under Antipater, who, fearing to trust his son Cassander with power, appointed Polyspheron his successor, which resulted in civil war between the rivals. After having aided in destroying the the royal family, by putting to death Hercules and his mother Barsina, he was slain in battle by Cassander.

DEATH OF CASSANDER, B. C. 297.

This son of Antipater married Thessalonica, the sister of Alexander the Great, whose untimely fate, with that of her children, is given in the account of Alexander and his family. Cassander died of dropsy.

DEATH OF DEMETRIUS, B. C. 286.

This son of Antigonus, after the death of his father, experienced many vicissitudes of fortune; was for a short time king of Athens; at another time, of Macedon; murdered the family of Cassander; married his daughter to Seleucus;

quarrelled with his son-in-law, with whom he engaged in war, was captured and thrown into prison, in Laodicea, Syria, where he died of want.

PTOLEMY SOTER,

died in Egypt of a good old age, B. C. 283.

LYSIMACHUS OF THRACE,

was slain in battle with Seleucus, B. C. 281. He had espoused the cause of Agathocles and Ceraunus.

SELEUCUS NICANOR OF SYRIA,

was the last survivor of Alexander's officers. He was slain seven months after the death of Lysimachus, B. C. 280, by the ungrateful Ceraunus. Surely, "he that taketh the sword shall perish by the sword."

EGYPT UNDER THE PTOLEMYS.

THE LAGIDÆ.

In the service of Philip, king of Macedon, was a distinguished personage by the name of Ptolemy Lagus. From him the Ptolemys of Egypt descended. For this reason, they were called the Lagidæ, and sometimes the Ptolemys. In the army of Alexander the Great, there were about twenty generals of greater or less note; by whom, with bloody strifes, his vast empire was divided. Ultimately, after many of the generals had perished, frequently by violence, four of them became kings in four different countries. Egypt and some bordering countries fell to the lot of Ptolemy Soter, son of Lagus. At the time of Alexander's death, no partitions of his kingdom had ever been settled. For aught that we can discover, one had as good a claim to dominion as another. Most of the aspirants attempted to secure their elevations by the most consummate treachery and despicable assassinations. Several of them were participators in the murder of the heirs and relations of Alexander. Of these bloody deeds, some account has been given in a previous chapter.

Ptolemy took no part in the destruction of the royal family. In no instance do we find him wantonly destroying human life. This, though but negative merit, is great praise when we consider the age in which he lived, and the fact that other thrones around him were swimming in innocent blood. Ptolemy Soter was born in the year 367, B. C.

He was of Greek origin, spoke the Greek language, and was something of a scholar in the sciences of those days. The reign of the Ptolemys in Egypt was the era of the introduction of literature into the land of Ham. Soter had been companion in war with the great Macedonian conqueror until the death of that monarch in Babylon.

Immediately after that event, he repaired to Egypt, where he administered the laws until his death; not at first as king, but while the heirs of Alexander lived, claiming only the powers of governor under the authority of the kings. After years of administration, and after most of Alexander's generals had put on the crown, all the heirs of Alexander having been put to death, Ptolemy also assumed the title of king of Egypt. The most important wars in which Ptolemy Soter was engaged, occurred before he assumed the title of king, and while the other generals were constantly employed in quarrels.

Perdiccas, a general of Alexander, had the care of the young king, and was in Syria with a great army. He with a large force, chiefly Macedonians, entered Egypt from Asia by Pelusium, the point at which Egypt has been so many times invaded. Memphis was, as yet, the capital. There Ptolemy was shut in with his friends. Perdiccas encamped on the opposite shore, near where Cairo now stands, between the two arms of the Nile. No ferry, with latteen sails, was at hand, such as now awaits the traveler to bear him across the turbid stream. The rivers of Macedon and Asia Minor are often shallow and fordable. Alexander had often waded directly through them, and even fought battles when part of his men were standing in the water. Perdiccas had seen and participated in these events. He was an able general—but great men are not always wise; he did not understand, that what was perfectly safe in one country, or under certain circumstances, would be madness in a different condition. He attempted to ford the Nile, above the Rhoda, with his army. The obedient soldiers descend into the water, pressed forward by the indiscreet commander. They attempt to swim. The surges of the water overwhelm them, and they are engulphed beneath its waves. The crocodile sports in the midst of them. Some of the soldiers are drowned, some are devoured by the monsters, and a few retire to the eastern shore. Two thousand perish, and Ptolemy is delivered from present fear. Treason now rears its head in the camp of the invader. The Macedonians are horror stricken at the waste of life, and enraged at the author of it. Pithon, a general, and ten others, enter the tent of Perdiccas and murder him. The next day, Ptolemy quits Memphis and enters the camp of the invader. He addresses them—they hear him with pleasure, and declare for Ptolemy. Thus ends another invasion of Egypt. This must have been in the year, B. C., 321, and two years after the death of Alexander.

In 315, Antigonus had gained the regency of Asia, and was exercising despotic power over the provinces—displacing governors, and committing many acts of cruelty. Seleucus, one of Alexander's younger generals, was at this time governor of Babylon. Being hunted from his office and fearing for his life, he repaired to Egypt and incited Ptolemy to war with Antigonus. Antipater, of Macedon, and

Lysimachus, of Thrace, also engaged in the war. These were then the four kingdoms into which the Alexandrian empire was divided. By looking at the map, it will be seen that the Syrian kingdom was much larger than all the others. It involved all of Persia, and all of the modern Turkish empire except the seacoasts of Palestine and Phœnicia, which were attached to Egypt. It was this magnitude of empire and the ambitious spirit manifested by Antigonus, that aroused the jealousy of his co-generals. Their object, therefore, was to diminish the power of their neighbor. Ptolemy had a greater interest in the war than his confederates. Egypt was a rich valley, and abounded in fruit and grain. It also bordered upon the sea, and had great facilities for commerce, one of the indispensable elements of natural wealth: but Egypt had no forests; she could not furnish the material for ship-building. To her prosperity and the development of her resources, Palestine, Phœnicia and Cyprus were indispensable. They were equally so to Syria and the far East. The mercantile cities at the eastern end of the Mediterranean sea—Tyre, Sidon, Joppa and Gaza, together with the isle of Cyprus—became therefore a frequent bone of contention between the great nations east and north of them. Hence, the five sieges and the ultimate desolation of Tyre.

Antigonus, expecting an attack from the other princes, marched into Palestine and conquered most of Ptolemy's possessions there. But Tyre resisted, and was besieged fifteen months; after which the city surrendered to Antigonus, nineteen years after its destruction by Alexander. Antigonus now removing the seat of war to Asia Minor, Ptolemy sails and attacks Cyprus, in 313. The island submitted to him. Ptolemy then proceeded to Syria and Cilicia—gained some provinces, took great spoils and prisoners, and sent them into Egypt.

THE TRAGEDY OF PAPHOS.

The island of Cyprus anciently contained nine cities. Over each of these cities, a king presided. There were thus nine kingdoms on an island, not larger than so many counties in Ohio. It must not be understood that these kingdoms were independent nations. In times previous to the Christian era, there were multitudes of kings and kingdoms, all of which were tributary and subject to some foreign and general empire; the relations of these petty kingdoms to some superior authority, was much like that of the States of the Union to the general government at Washington. Such was the condition of the nine kingdoms of Cyprus. Seldom independent, often not united among themselves, but tributary sometimes to Phœnicia, to Babylon or to Persia, and sometimes forming part of the empire of Macedon, of Syria or of Egypt. The island often changed masters, after the death of Alexander the Great. In 312 B. C., Ptolemy, governor of Egypt, and Antigonus, governor of Syria, were at war. Cyprus had been given to Ptolemy, in the partition of the Macedonian empire. Antigonus had taken possession of it; but Ptolemy had regained it, and required of all the rulers an oath of allegiance to him. Nicocles, king of Paphos, with the others, had acknowledged his dependence upon Ptolemy. Some time after, he fancied he would be better suited with Antigonus for a master, and entered secretly into an allegiance with that governor. The fact came to the knowledge of Ptolemy. The island was at his control, and the traitor was at his mercy. Ptolemy had been a mild governor; a protector, not a destroyer of his people. It was on this account that he had received the name of Soter (saviour). I do not recollect another example in which he took the life of an enemy, except in the regular course of war. But if Nicocles be spared, his other rulers might be tempted to follow his example. Nicocles was clearly guilty of treason, and had forfeited his life. There are times when a sickly sympathy for a wrong-doer is not tenderness—is not mercy; there are occasions when rigor on the part of government is the highest mercy and kindness to society at large, when forbearance toward the wrong-doer, though congenial to the tender feelings of humanity, would be cruel injustice to multitudes, and, instead of diminishing, would add to the sufferings of the human family.

To spare Nicocles would have been offering a reward for treason, and would have filled the empire with scenes of horror and bloodshed. Ptolemy saw all this. Filled with kindness and regard for all his subjects, he could do no less than order his rulers in Cyprus to destroy Nicocles. This, to them, was a painful duty. They were fellow officers with the victim—they ruled on the same island—they were his neighbors—yet they dared not disobey the great governor of Egypt. Knowing that Nicocles must die, they go to him, explain his condition and their embarrassment, and request him to destroy himself; a very modest request, indeed. But Nicocles had none to help him, no means of escape. A wide sea rolled between him and Antigonus. Oh! what thoughts! what agitation filled his mind! he might now have understood what it was to find no place for repentance, though he sought it carefully and with tears. He grants the request of Ptolemy's officers; retires to his chamber, and by his own hand ends his life. But did the evil stop here? Domestic relations in royal families are usually held together by public ties. The roots of affection that in humble life twine around the heart and by sweet restraining tenderness bind the members of a family into one bond of life, seldom have a vigorous growth in king's courts; the glitter of royalty, the schemes of ambition, and the interests of faction so often disturb the soil of affection that its tendrils die, or at least do not mature the sweets of perpetual love. To this there are some exceptions. In the midst of the arid sands of royal and princely hearts, where no rains of pure love descend, and no genial plants of domestic felicity thrive, there are occasional oases. Connubial, parental and filial affection do sometimes, in isolated spots appear on the page of history even in royal courts. An example of this is found in the unfortunate family of Bactriana, the brother of Xerxes the great. Another is found in the palace of Paphos. Nicocles had a family — wife, children and brothers. Ptolemy had with his usual generosity ordered that the utmost care and respect should be paid to the members of the royal household. How nobly this exhibited the tender and humane spirit of the ruler of Egypt. How it contrasted with the eastern ruler, his predecessor, who both in Egypt and in Persia so often in the most cruel manner put to death the women and children for the real or imaginary offense of the husbands or the fathers. But would the affectionate wife of Nicocles forget her lord in the midst of the courtiers of Egypt? Ah, no! the fond heart suddenly and violently separated from the object of tender regard, found no solace in the attentions of a stranger. The Queen could not survive the death of her lord. Calling the entire royal family around her she exhorted them not to survive the king, with a dagger slew her children, then plunged the bloody weapon into her own bosom. The princes set fire to the royal palaces and sought and found death in the flames. While we, at this distance of time, look back and admire the constancy and affection of the royal family of Paphos, when all the greater courts around them were filled with strife and turmoil, we can not but regret that the religion of Jesus of Nazareth had not dawned upon that island and upon the mind and heart of those disconsolate princes, giving them hope that though their sorrows were great, they need but endure them for a time and then enter into an eternal rest. In the time of affliction how needful is the blessed Gospel of peace.

SIEGE OF SALAMIS.

312 B. C., Ptolemy had taken the island of Cyprus from Antigonus, governor of Syria, at that time the most powerful of all Alexander's successors. In 305,. Antigonus directed his son, Demetrius, who was then at Athens, in Greece, to besiege and try to recover possession of Cyprus. The hostile fleet was soon seen hovering around the island, and threatening its ports and harbors. At length Demetrius landed with a large army and encamped near Salamis, one of the principal cities of Cyprus. Menelaus, a brother of Ptolemy, was there with an army to defend the place. After some delay, the forces of Salamis were marched out to meet the invader. Demetrius engaged them, and a severe battle was fought, but Menelaus was defeated. One thousand of his men were slain, and three thousand more taken prisoners. He retreated into the city, and strengthened the walls, gates, and other fortifications of Salamis, presuming that Demetrius would take advantage of his late victory and attempt to besiege the city. A courier was dispatched over the sea to inform Ptolemy that the island was besieged and the first battle lost—that Salamis and all Cyprus were in danger, and that help was needed. The call was heard and the aid dispatched. But time is requisite for the fleet to leave Egypt and arrive at the seat of war. Demetrius after carefully examining the defenses of Salamis, and the number of his foes, was not disposed to attack the city at first, but sent to his father, in Syria, from whom he received a vast amount of iron, and timber, and artists. He then commenced building prodigious battering rams, heliopoles,

Seige of Salamis.—Burning of the Engines of Demetrius.—See page 53.

and other besieging apparatus. All being prepared, he commenced his attack upon the walls of the city. They tremble, they break, they fall before the engines of the invaders—a great breach is made, the engines rest for the night, the weary officers retire to their tents to seek repose, intending in the morning to renew the attack, and if possible, force their way through the gaps already made, into the city. So they sleep quietly. Hark! a sound is heard. Their slumbers are broken. They awake. A bright light is shining upon the tents, the banners, the camp. Their great engines are all on fire. The besieged within the city, fearful of the fate of to-morrow, had collected dry material, and with dexterity had hurled them from their walls against the engines below; then with long poles and torches of pitch had set them on fire. The camp of Demetrius was roused. With much effort they extinguished the fire, but not until the engines were materially damaged.

Grey dawn appears, and the besiegers intend to-day, sword in hand, to force a passage into Salamis. How little do mortals know what a day or an hour may bring forth. The morning fog slowy rises, the bright sun throws his glorious rays across the water, and reveals, to the surprise of the beholder, the fleet of Ptolemy, consisting of one hundred and fifty vessels, lying off the harbor.

Oh how joyous within the city was the light of that morning. Say, joy! thou effervesence of faith; hope! thou gilded bird, when wilt thou fold thy pinions that mortals may overtake thee? Not till the dark valley of the shadow of death be passed—then shalt thou rest thy wing, and perch upon the anchor within the veil. Then and only then shall hope become fruition. Reader, did you ever observe with a joyous heart the bright morning sun? No cloud was there. You rejoiced in the prospect of a day beautiful to the close. But, alas! the sky gathers haziness, clouds deepen darker, thunder rolls, and ere the setting, a disturbed heaven pours forth its floods; night sets in gloomy as the shades of Erebus. Such have I often seen, and such in the path of life have I experiencd. Such was the day to Salamis; brightly opening, we shall see how it closed.

Undismayed by the fire of the night or the fleet of the morning, Demetrius prepared for an attack upon the newly arrived enemy. Ptolemy communicated with Menelaus and desired him to annoy the fleet of the enemy in the rear while he assailed them from the open sea. But Demetrius left a few vessels at the mouth of the harbor, which completely shut up what ships Menelaus had, so that they could not come into action. With the rest, though far inferior in number, he sailed out and attacked those of Ptolemy; he had also arranged his land forces along the shore to protect any of his men that might have occasion to swim to the land.

But Menelaus being already besieged in the city, could not afford the same protection to Ptolemy's men. By the fury of the attack, the vessels of Demetrius were able to break through the center of Ptolemy's line of battle, and after a severe struggle victory remained upon the side of Demetrius. All Ptolemy's household, women, children and rich furniture were taken by the conqueror, but having been himself treated with great kindness on a former occasion by Ptolemy, who had captured his family at the siege of Gaza, he restored all the family and treasures of Ptolemy, who immediately abandoned Cyprus to its fate, and sailed for Egypt. Menelaus, thus abandoned, immediately surrendered Salamis with all its inhabitants to Demetrius.

The number of captives taken by these successive victories was about seventeen thousand soldiers, besides the sailors. What became of the prisoners of war? They were all engrafted into the army of the conqueror. Thus it mattered little to the soldiers which conquered. They fought as readily on one side as the other. This indifference in the masses will in part explain the sudden reverses of fortune in the wars of ancient times. After the victories of Salamis, Antigonus and his son Demetrius assumed the title of kings, a precedent which was soon followed by the other great generals of Alexander.

The year after the siege of Salamis, Antigonus conceived the plan of entirely subverting Ptolemy, and annexing Egypt to his already vast empire. Accordingly he advanced through Palestine with an army of one hundred thousand men, to Gaza.

Demetrius was on the coast with a fleet of vessels of war. A few years before Gaza had been taken from them and Demetrius had suffered a great defeat; but Ptolemy had again lost these possessions. While the army of Antigonus crossed the desert and approached Pelusium, Demetrius sailed around the coast to the mouth of the Nile. But here he was unable to effect a landing. The storms shattered many of his vessels; while Ptolemy had taken great care to fortify all places of landing. At the same time sickness, desertions, and death, were rapidly diminishing the number of Antigonus' men. The entire expedition was a failure and Antigonus and Demetrius returned to Assyria disheartened. Ptolemy had but little trouble with his neighbors after the retreat of the Assyrians. The remainder of his days were devoted to science and the improvement of his country. But the ambition of Antigonus and Demetrius now effectually aroused the three great princes of the world against him. Cassander of Macedon, Lysimachus of Thrace, and Ptolemy of Egypt determined upon his overthrow. Ptolemy seems to have had less to do in these wars than the others. He however regained his possessions in Phœnicia. Seleucus, governor of Babylon, now began to attract more attention. He was with the others instrumental in the entire ruin of Antigonus, who was slain in the battle of Ipsus and his dominions chiefly given to the Seleucidæ. The history of their affairs belongs however to Syria rather than to Egypt.

B. C. 285, Ptolemy Soter resigned the crown to his son Philadelphus, and two years after died, in 283, being eighty-four years of age; having governed Egypt nineteen years as Governor and twenty as King.

CORONATION OF PTOLEMY PHILADELPHUS.

Ptolemy Soter was now becoming an old man. While in the army of Alexander, in the East, he had a female favorite who accompanied him in those expeditions. It was the female who, at the feast of Alexander in Persepolis, proposed to illuminate the festival by burning the palace. After the death of the Macedonian, when Ptolemy was established as governor of Egypt, he seems to have abandoned her, according to the usual custom of princes, and entered into legitimate matrimony. He married Eurydice, a Macedonian lady, the daughter of old Antipater, and sister of Cassander, afterward king of Macedon. The bride came into Egypt in great splendor, attended by a lady of honor, named Berenice, a widow, who had a son, Magus. This son was made governor of Lybia, where he afterward plotted a rebellion. After a time, Ptolemy became equally or better pleased with Berenice, the attendant, than with Eurydice, his proper queen. He therefore married the widow. By both of these wives he had several children, whose fraternal quarrels fill a bloody page of history.

By Eurydice, he had Ptolemy Ceraunus and Lysandra:

these were the elder children. By Berenice, he had Philadelphus and Arsinoe. Perceiving that he would not long be able to administer the affairs of his kingdom, and desiring to settle the heirship to the crown himself, he called a council to deliberate upon the succession. His prime minister was Demetrius Phalarius, who had once been king of Athens, but had been expelled, and had fled to Egypt, a refugee, where he had become an able, faithful, and much beloved officer. Demetrius recommended that the usual course should be preserved, of declaring the oldest son the heir to the throne. As an additional reason for this course, it was shown that this heir was, by his mother, descended from the royal family of Macedon; while the children of Berenice, though noble, were not, on the mother's side, of kingly descent. This council, if followed, would have given the crown to Ptolemy Ceraunus.

It is a fact, of almost daily occurrence, that a second wife, of less honorable connections, will exert a greater influence over a husband than the first, even though the husband is aware of the fact, and tries to guard against it. He often finds himself under an influence which he feels and condemns, and yet can not resist. Berenice had found means to supplant Eurydice, and to establish her son in Lybia. She now succeeded in overthrowing the council of the ministry, and obtaining a decree that Ptolemy Philadelphus, her own son, should succeed Soter, to the exclusion of the children of Eurydice. Accordingly, B. C. 284, and two years before Soter's death, Philadelphus was crowned, and associated with his father in the government.

This coronation was the most splendid pageant ever recorded on any page of history. It presents a view of the extensive complicated mythology of the polytheism of both Greeks and Egyptians. It also exhibits the abundance of wealth and luxury which had accumulated in

Egypt, under the wise and prudent administration of Soter. I will transcribe from Rollin an account of the ceremony, with occasional remarks of my own.

The procession began with a troop of sileni; some habited in purple, others in robes of deep red. Their employment was to keep off the crowd and clear a path. Next to the sileni came a band of satyrs, composed of twenty, in two ranks, each carrying a gilded lamp. A satyr is a fabulous being, with wings upon its head and feet. They were supposed to meet and dance by night among the ruins of deserted cities. The word sometimes referred to a class of men, dressed in a style to imitate the fabulous satyr. They were dancers, jesters, fun-makers; about what we would now call clowns. The lamps referred to their night revelries; the wings were intended to represent the levity of dancing, but might, perhaps, more appropriately signify that their heads were empty, and their feet expeditious to run away from their creditors. In this instance, although not so intended, it very appropriately represented that all kingly parade and ostentation of dignity were but mere buffoonery and empty show. These were succeeded by victories, with golden wings, carrying vases partly gilt and partly adorned with leaves of ivy, in which perfumes were burning. Their habits were embroidered with figures of animals, and every part of them glittered with gold. No writer has given us the signification of this group, if it had any. I will venture, therefore, an appropriate interpretation, although I do not know that Philadelphus, if he were to arise from the dead and read my comments, would feel himself flattered by them. The victories signify the conquest of kingly government over mankind—quite as often over the life, liberty, property, soul and body of their own subjects, as that of their foreign foes. "Their dress was adorned with figures of animals." I have often had occasion to remark, that most human governments are organized animals, sustaining themselves by animal force in a brutal manner. Most of them have been blood-shedding, flesh-eating beasts and birds. This very coronation was of a king over one of the heads of that kingdom, which, by the Spirit of the living God, had been revealed to Daniel as a great spotted leopard.

These figures of animals, therefore, truly represent Egypt under the Ptolemies, whose general career was one of animal gratification, both ferocious and voluptuous. The burning of incense may justly represent the grateful pleasure with which the world ever applauds successful bad deeds; and the golden adornings bespeak the insatiable avarice of monarchs, who, by victory, rob their fellows to enrich themselves.

After these came a double altar, nine feet in hight, and carved with a luxuriant foliage of ivy, intermixed with ornaments of gold. It was beautified with a golden crown, composed of vine leaves, and adorned on all sides with certain white fillets.

After victory cometh the crown and the altar of incense, not to the righteous Ruler of the universe, but to the successful tyrant, who, by the wreath of ivy, signifies his desire for immortal fame.

A hundred and twenty youths advanced next, clothed in purple, each of them bearing a golden vase of incense, myrrh and saffron. They were followed by forty satyrs, wearing crowns of gold, which represented the leaves of ivy; and in the right hand of each was another crown of the same metal, adorned with vine leaves; their habits were adorned with a variety of colors.

What could this signify? May it not imply, that after victory cometh the crowning of the conqueror; then the youth who succeed him, imply the next generation; and then those satyrs, wearing and also carrying crowns, signify that hereditary monarchs transmit the crowns of energetic predecessors to light, empty-headed, dancing satyrs and fools, for successors. If this was not the intended signification when Philadelphus was crowned, it is about the sum of what history has verified.

In the rear of these marched two sileni, arrayed in purple mantles and white dresses: one wore a kind of hat, and carried a golden caduceus in his hand; the other had a trumpet. Between these two was a man, six feet in hight, masked and habited like a tragedian. He also carried a golden cornucopia, and was distinguished by the appellation of the year. The cornucopia signifies plenty, or the products of the year; but, in this connection, it may signify that the tragedian in disguise and the empty title of king, with no intrinsic merit, or the imitation of what one is not, brings abundance to the ruler, who, instead of being the benefactor, is the robber of his people.

This person preceded a very beautiful woman, as tall as himself, dressed in a magnificent manner, and glittering all over with gold. She held in one hand a crown, composed of the leaves of the peach tree, and in the other hand a branch of palm. She was called Penteteres. This, we are informed, referred to the feast of Bacchus, which was celebrated in the beginning of the fifth year; a festival in which women, wine and debauchery abounded: a fit accompaniment of royal courts, showing the debasing nature of intemperate authority.

The next in the procession were the genii of the four seasons, wearing characteristic ornaments and supporting two golden vases of odors, adorned with ivy leaves. In the midst of these was a square altar of gold. This is more rational, as it represented the work of the Creator in the seasons of the year, furnishing the means of subsistence, without which kings could not luxuriate. But having obtained the good things which Providence had furnished, instead of gratitude and a discreet use we see folly again triumphant. A band of satyrs appeared, wearing golden crowns fashioned like the leaves of ivy, and arrayed in red habits. Some bore vessels filled with wine, others carried drinking cups.

Immediately after these, (buffoons and wine-bibbers), came Philiscus, the poet and priest of Bacchus, attended by comedians, musicians, dancers, and other persons of that class.

Two tripods were carried next, as prizes for the victors in the athletic combats and exercises. One of these tripods, thirteen and a half feet in hight, was intended for the youths; the other, which was eighteen feet high, was designed for the men.

A car of an extraordinary size followed these. It had four wheels, was twenty-one feet in length, and twelve in breadth, and was drawn by one hundred and eighty men. In this car was a figure fifteen feet in hight, representing Bacchus, in the attitude of performing libations, with a large cup of gold. He was arrayed in a robe of brocade purple which flowed down to his feet. Over this was a transparent vest of saffron color, and above that a large purple mantle embroidered with gold. Before him was a great vessel of gold, formed in the Lacedæmonian fashion, and containing fifteen measures, equal to one hundred and thirty-five gallons. This was accompanied with a golden tripod on which were placed a golden vase of odors, with two cups of the same metal, full of cinnamon and saffron. Bacchus was seated under the shade of ivy and vine leaves, intermixed with the foliage of fruit trees, and from these hung several crowns, fillets and thyrs with timbals, ribbons and a variety of satiric, comic and tragic masks. In the same car were the priests and priestesses of that deity, with the other ministers and interpreters of mysteries, dancers of all classes, and women bearing vases.

This was a grand pantomine of Bacchanalian revelry, not unlike those which occur in our day, where may be seen wine, gay clothing, men and vile women.

Next marched along the Bacchantes. These were the wives, sisters and daughters of Bacchus. Their hair was disheveled, their heads were crowned with serpentine yew, vine and ivy; in their hands they grasped either knives or serpents. This is a just representation of the frantic and wretched condition of the female members of a Bacchanalian family, whose heads and hearts are stung with anguish, and whose hands grasped serpents or weapons of destruction. Next moved along a car twelve feet in breadth, drawn by sixty men. Here rode the the statue of Nysa, the nurse of Bacchus; when sitting she was twelve feet high; she was clothed with a yellow dress embroidered with gold, over which was another short dress. By the aid of invisible machinery this statue arose apparently without aid, and poured milk into a golden cup, again seating itself. The head was covered with a golden crown wrought in the form of leaves of ivy, from which hung pendant clusters of grapes, composed of various gems. In the left hand was a thyrsus adorned with ribbons. The whole image was covered with a deep shade, formed by a blended foliage; a gilded lamp hung at each corner of the car.

What does Nysa mean? She is the nurse of Bacchus; she is the promoter of intemperance; she is the embodiment of the liquor trade; she rises without help and pours forth her poisonous fluid, and unceasingly pushes her infernal traffic. She is crowned with gold; she acquires wealth by her occupation, although she blesses no one; her car is drawn by a multitude of men. It was lighted by gilted lamps, for she nurses Bacchus chiefly in the night season.

Let us go a step farther back, from the liquor dealer to the liquor manufacturer, for we are now following up the stream.

Next came a car thirty-six feet long and twenty-four wide, drawn by three hundred men, bearing a wine press thirty-six by twenty-two and a half feet, which was full of grapes. Six satyrs expressed the juice from the grapes by dancing upon them to the sound of the flute, while they sung Bacchanalian songs, corresponding with their employment. Silenus, the catch-fly, was the chief of this band. Streams of wine flowed from this chariot as it passed along. Behind this followed another car of the same size, drawn by six hundred men; it contained a wine vat of immense size, made of leopard skins sewed together. This vessel contained three thousand measures, or twenty-seven thousand gallons of wine, which it poured forth in streams as it passed along. Then came the vessels for storing and for drinking the ardent fluid. This last car was followed by one hundred and twenty satyrs and sileni, carrying pots, flaggons, and large cups full of gold. They may truly represent the retailers, coming to the manufacturers to replenish their stock. Then came another car drawn in like manner, by six hundred men, bearing a silver vat which could contain five thousand four hundred gallons; this vessel was wrought with chased work; figures of animals adorned the rims, the handles and the base. Next appeared two cars, on each of which rode an enormous silver bowl, eighteen feet in diameter, and nine in hight; the top was studded with jewels, the bottom being concave, reposed upon several silver animals, the central ones being a foot and a half high, and the others being of less size. Next came ten great vats and sixteen other vessels, the largest of which contained two hundred and seventy gallons, and the least forty-five gallons. There were also ten caldrons, and twenty-four vases with two handles, standing upon two salvers; two silver wine-presses on which were placed twenty-four goblets; a table of massive silver, eighteen feet in length, and thirty that were sixty feet long; one silver tripod whose circumference was twenty-four feet, and three smaller ones of less value, adorned with precious stones in the middle.

Then came eighty delphic tripods, all of silver. These were small; they were accompanied with twenty-six ewers, sixteen flagons, and one hundred and sixty other silver vessels, the largest of which contained fifty-four gallons, and the smallest eighteen.

Then came vessels of gold. Four of these were Lacedæmonic and were crowned with vine leaves; two were Corinthian vases, whose rims were embellished with the figures of animals; these contained seventy-two gallons. Then a wine press on which stood ten goblets; then two vases containing forty-five gallons, and two that held eighteen gallons. There were also twenty-two vessels for keeping liquors cool, the largest of which contained two hundred and seventy gallons, and the smallest about nine gallons; there were four very large golden tripods, and a golden basket, in which to place the golden vessels. This last was enriched with jewels, and was fifteen feet in length; it was divided into partitions one above another. Figures of animals above three feet in hight were carved upon it. Two goblets and two glass bowls with golden ornaments, two salvers four cubits in diameter, and three of less size, ten ewers, an altar four feet and a half high, and twenty-five dishes, made up the complement of golden vessels on these cars.

After all this display of treasure to be used in wine-bibbing, marched sixteen hundred boys, dressed in white garments, crowned with ivy or pine. Two hundred and fifty of them carried golden vases, four hundred of them had silver vases, and three hundred carried liquor coolers. These were followed by another company, bearing large drinking vessels, twenty of which were of gold, fifty of silver, and three hundred variegated. There were several tables six feet in length, each one supporting some object of curiosity. On one was represented the bed of Semele, with the clothing lying upon it; some of golden brocade, and others adorned with precious stones.

It would be impossible to follow this procession through, in the exact order, on account of its great length and tediousness. We will not, therefore, do more than mention some of the most prominent objects. In one car, thirty-three feet in length and twenty-one in breadth, which was drawn by five hundred men, was represented the god Mercury, with a golden caduceus in his hand, and clothed in splendid raiment, standing by a deep cavern, from which issued out and flew about pigeons, ring-doves, and turtles, to whose feet were fastened little bands, that they might be caught by the people. From the cavern issued two streams, one flowing with milk, and the other with wine. Around this fountain stood the nymphs, with crowns of gold.

The representation of the expedition of Bacchus into India, constituted an imposing portion of this procession. The statue of this god was eighteen feet in hight, arrayed in purple, and wearing a golden crown, intermixed with ivy and vine leaves. In his hand, he held a long golden thyrsus. His feet were shod with sandals of gold. He was mounted upon an elephant, upon whose neck was seated a satyr, above seven feet high, crowned with gold, wrought in imitation of pine branches. The satyr was in the attitude of blowing a trumpet, made of a goat's horn. Upon the elephant's head was an ivy crown of gold, and all of his trappings were of the same precious metal. Bacchus was followed by five hundred young virgins,

6

clothed with purple dresses and golden girdles; one hundred and twenty of these wore crowns of gold. They, in turn, were followed by one hundred satyrs, armed with silver and copper weapons, not unlike the knights errant of the days of chivalry. Next came five troops of crowned sileni and satyrs, mounted on asses, harnessed with gold and silver.

Then came a long train of chariots, drawn by beasts, twenty-four by elephants, sixty by he-goats, twelve by lions, six by wild goats, fifteen by buffaloes, four by wild asses, eight by ostriches, and seven by stags. The drivers in these chariots were young lads, dressed like charioteers, wearing broad-brimmed hats. Other smaller boys rode with them, having tiny weapons of war, and clothed with mantles embroidered with gold; accompanying these were other cars, drawn by camels and mules, carrying tents resembling those of the Barbarians.

Within these tents were women of India and other nations, in the dress of slaves. These cars also carried immense quantities of incense, saffron, cinnamon, ivys and other odoriferous spices.

Another group was composed of a large band of Ethiopians, armed with pikes. One company of them carried six hundred elephants' teeth, and another two thousand branches of ebony, while a third carried sixty cups of gold and silver, with a large quantity of gold dust.

Two hunters, carrying gilded darts, marched at the head of two thousand four hundred dogs, gathered from India, Arcadia and the interior of Asia. One hundred and fifty men supported trees, to which were fastened birds and deer. Others carried cages, in which were parrots, peacocks, turkey-hens, pheasants, and a great number of African birds. Then came one hundred and thirty Ethiopian sheep, three hundred Arabian sheep, twenty sheep of Eubœa, twenty-six white Indian oxen, eight Ethiopian oxen, one white bear, fourteen leopards, sixteen panthers, four lynxes, three small bears, a cameleopard, and an Ethiopian rhinoceros: quite a caravan of animals, and far more appropriate than human beings to wait upon Bacchus.

Next came the drunken god himself, a second time, wearing a golden crown, with leaves of ivy. He was represented as fleeing from the wrath of Juno, and hiding at the altar of Rhea. By his side stood Priapus, wearing a similar crown. Juno was there, wearing a golden diadem. The statues of Alexander and Ptolemy, with similar crowns of gold, were in the group. Near to Ptolemy stood the image of Virtue, crowned with golden olive branches, and also another image, representing the city of Corinth. Near by them was a great vase, filled with cups of gold, and a large golden bowl, which contained forty-five gallons. Several women, richly arrayed, wearing crowns of gold, and each bearing the name of some Grecian city or island, followed this car of Bacchus. In one car was carried a golden thyrsus, one hundred and thirty-five feet in length, and a silver lance, ninety feet long.

In one portion of the procession were horses and wild beasts, including twenty-four lions, of prodigious size. Moreover, there were numbers of cars containing a great number of statues of the kings and deities. In one group were six hundred men, one-half of whom played on gilded harps, while the others sung the chorus. Near at hand were two thousand bulls, all of the same color, adorned with collars and crowns of gold.

Such was the representation of the great expedition of Bacchus into India.

It was followed by a procession of Jupiter and a great number of other deities; and, last of all, that of Alexander the Great, whose image, standing between Victory and

Minerva, was placed in a car and drawn by elephants. Several thrones of gold and of ivory, with crowns and horns of the same metal, accompanied this procession. One of these thrones was that of Ptolemy Soter, which supported a golden crown of the weight of ten thousand pieces of gold, equal, in value, to about twenty-five thousand dollars.

In this procession were carried three thousand two hundred crowns of gold, and an almost infinite number of golden vessels, of various forms and sizes, for various purposes. Four hundred chariots were required to carry the silver vessels, and twenty for the golden ones, while the spices alone filled eight hundred chariots.

This grand coronal procession was guarded by an army of fifty-seven thousand six hundred foot, and twenty-seven thousand horse.

If the foregoing facts were not well attested by authentic historians, who flourished shortly after the time, and some of them at the very time, and had every facility for obtaining correct information, we could not credit the account. Where could so much gold have been obtained? How could such unbounded magnificence be supported?

The reader may judge that some of my remarks and explanations, in the foregoing account, are frivolous, or too severe. I acknowledge that some of them are fanciful; but it is a truth, that these pompous Bacchanalian displays were the forerunners of that spirit of intemperance which, in after times, diffused itself among the mass of the people, and produced, in our days, the great evil of which we complain. Rollin makes the same reflection in the following words: "But what can we say, when we behold a sacred procession and a solemnity of religion converted into a public school of intemperance and licentiousness, calculated only to excite the most shameful passions in the spectators and induce an utter depravity of manners, by presenting to their view all the instruments of excess and debauchery, with the most powerful allurements to indulge in them, and that under the pretext of paying adoration to the gods. What divinities must those be that would suffer, and even exact, so scandalous a pomp in their worship?"

TROUBLE IN THE KITCHEN DEPARTMENT OF MACEDON AND THRACE, B. C. 280.

Thrace had been governed by Lysimachus, one of the generals of Alexander, ever since the partition of the empire. He was, therefore, one of the four heads of the third beast to which Daniel refers. Macedon had, of late, been added to his kingdom. His capital was Byzantium, the modern Constantinople.

Ptolemy, king of Egypt, had several wives, and by them many children. Agathocles, eldest son of Lysimachus, had married Lysandra, a daughter of Ptolemy, and Lysimachus himself, although an old man, about the same time married Arsinoe, another daughter of the same king — half sister of his daughter-in-law. Both sisters were soon mothers, and each became jealous and anxious that the crown should descend to her children, to the exclusion of the other. In Egypt, the same difficulties were brewing. Ptolemy had two sons, Ceraunus and Philadelphus. These were half brothers, and own brothers to the sisters in Thrace. Arsinoe, the young queen of the old king of Thrace, was the daughter of the youngest of the wives of Ptolemy, as was also Philadelphus. But as we have seen in the history of those kings, the elder son of the elder mother was set aside, and Philadelphus succeeded to the throne of Egypt; while Ceraunus fled to the court of Lysimachus, to his sisters. The two queen mothers in Egypt were constantly promoting discord between their daughters in Thrace. The arrival of the fugitive, Ceraunus, caused Arsinoe, the young step-mother and queen, to suspect that the half brother and sister would unite their interests against herself and children. Without waiting for any evidence of wrong on their part, she resorted to the usual device of step-mothers, that of inflaming the father's mind against his own children. The old doating Thracian, so enamored of his youthful wife, and the children of his declining years, listened to Arsinoe, who artfully represented to the king that his oldest son was tired of waiting for his father's death; that he had conspired to dethrone and murder him, and that the lives of Lysimachus, herself and children, were in such imminent danger as to admit of no delay. The deceived old king drank in this story as so much truth, and, without the least inquiry, caused his son to be thrown into prison and murdered. Thus, although perfectly innocent, perished the legitimate heir to the throne, through the intrigue, jealousy and infernal machinations of the harem. Oh! what good a woman can accomplish; what evils she often does produce; which will preponderate when women's rights prevail? What fearful forebodings must have spread the pall of gloom over the princes at the court of the Bosphorus. The eldest son of Egypt's king had fled from the younger; while, by the intrigue of the younger mother, the younger son was crowned by the partial father; the eldest son of the Macedonian court was murdered by the too partial monarch, at the instigation of the mother of the younger members of the royal family. Together they mingled their sighs, their fears, their plans for the future. Ceraunus, the fugitive; Lysandra, the sister and widow of the murdered prince, with her children, and Alexander, a brother of the late victim, dare no longer remain in Thrace, where an old dotard wears the crown, but a sister administers authority — a sister, artful, cunning, implacable, infernal, whose hands were stained by the blood of her step-son. Let us listen to the conversation of the mourning group: "But where may we fly? who will shelter us? who dare protect us? Our father's throne in Egypt is filled by Philadelphus, the hater of our mother and of us, the brother of the bloody Arsinoe, of whom we are now in fear; the throne of our grand-father of Macedon is united to that of this hateful Thrace. Nor are there any in the family of Cassander who can aid us — let us away to Seleucus." And to Seleucus, king of Syria, the whole party fled, and were cordially received with open arms. His residence was, at that time, at Antioch. Will old Lysimachus, after the murder of his son, and the abandonment of the children of his earlier years, come down quietly and in peace to his grave? Ah, no! the Most High God rules in the nations of the earth, and is not unmindful of the doings of his representatives. It may have been the rashness, rather than the malignity of Lysimachus, that caused him to murder his own son; but he that is too weak to be just, ought no longer to be king. Many of his faithful officers were shocked at his barbarity, and deserted their post. These following the fugitives, presented themselves at Antioch. Let us away after them to Syria. "Seleucus, the great king of the East, behold us, desolate, sad, forsaken, and forlorn; the children of your fellow generals in the army of the conqueror; by your love for your associates in arms in your youthful days, we beseech you, remember our wrongs; avenge us and restore us to our home, where slumber your grateful loves. Besides, what advantage it will be to you. Awake, O youthful ambition! arouse ye, powers of other days, and extend the empire of Seleucus, that his name may descend by the side of Alexander the Great." The fugitive officers join in this effort. Seleucus determines upon a war with Lysimachus. These were now the only two surviving generals of Alexander. A mighty army was raised; Seleucus, in person, led the host, and soon Asia Minor, which had belonged to Lysimachus, was added to the kingdom of Syria. Sardis resisted, but was soon captured. The old Thracian now began to move. He led an army across the Hellespont, and in Phrygia met his enemy. A severe battle was the result, and Lysimachus was slain, his kingdom transferred to the monarch of Syria and all the East, and the blood of his royal son avenged.

Thus ended the year 281, B. C. For the successes and enlargement of his empire, Seleucus received the title of Nicator, the Conqueror. Arsinoe, the murderer, the Jezebel of the times, the instigator of all these ills, still lives to receive, in due time, the just reward of her bloody deeds. Seleucus, who was himself a native of Macedon, from which his public duties had separated him ever since the commencement of the expedition of Alexander, now desired to make his native land the home of his old age. In all these recent movements, Ceraunus had accompanied him. This exile now began to cast his longing eyes upon the lands over which his mother's ancestors had once reigned. Ambition fired his soul, and destroyed all those generous, noble feelings of gratitude toward his benefactor, which he should have cultivated. Seleucus was intending to proceed to Egypt to dethrone Philadelphus, and crown Ceraunus, whom he deemed the rightful heir. But that ungrateful vagabond would rather be an independent king, than feel a sense of obligation to any surviving monarch for his elevation. He therefore undertook to wipe out the debt, by the murder of his benefactor. Ceraunus assassinated Seleucus in the year 280 B. C., and seven months after the death of Lysimachus. Thus perished the last general of Alexander of Macedon.

Ptolemy Ceraunus, half brother of Philadelphus, king of

Egypt, was crowned king of Macedon. By his mother, he was the grandson of Antipater, the oldest of Alexander's generals. His two cousins, Antipater and Alexander, sons of Cassander, had been some time dead. He now proposed marriage to his half sister, Arsinoe, the widow of the late Lysimachus. She was the mother of two youthful sons by her former husband, on whose account she had embroiled the kingdom in the recent wars, and we are now about to see the fruit of her intrigues. Ceraunus professed the most ardent affection for her; urged her to marry him, and promised great things: but the real motive of all his conduct was the desire to remove every possible claimant to the throne. Incest, at that time, was not uncommon with the princes of the East. This near relationship was no obstacle in the mind of the widow, who herself had married the father of her own brother-in-law. But Arsinoe remembered her own guilty conduct toward him and all the family. She had learned the character of Ceraunus, in the murder of Seleucus, his benefactor, and she recollected that he who now sought her hand in marriage was the rival and enemy of her own brother, Philadelphus, of Egypt. She therefore declined, delayed and deferred the union as long as possible, but ultimately yielded her assent to the marriage, which was celebrated with great pomp, and many demonstrations of mutual attachment. Ceraunus expressed the greatest regard for his two youthful step-sons. All this was a farce. The wedding is over. Now, Arsinoe! now is the time of retribution. Thou hast caused the murder of thy step-son, and God will reward thee doubly. The party had proceeded to Pella, the ancient capital of Macedon. Here Ceraunus ordered his guards to enter the apartment of the young princes — the one about sixteen and the other twelve years of age. They fled to their mother, and while she attempted to shield their bodies with her own, she beheld the ruffians, in obedience to the order of the king, plunge their daggers into her sons. Their blood drenched all her garments! Oh! where was then the spirit of Agathocles, who, for their sake had been murdered? Where was the spirit of Lysimachus, who, by the unjust murder of his own true and faithful oldest son, had brought all these calamities upon his household. Arsinoe, in ragged and bloody garments, was driven into exile to linger out a useless and jealous life, in prison and in want, and Ceraunus is king without a rival. Who shall avenge the crime of the usurper? None of the generals of Alexander yet survive; Philadelphus has more on his hands than he can do, and these are not the subjects of prophesy. Hear, oh Heaven! and forgive him not. Let him not descend in peace to the grave; let not his children possess the throne after him.

About this time came on the famous invasion of the Gauls, who, after disturbing Macedon and Greece, ultimately planted a colony in Asia Minor, called Galatia, to whom Paul wrote one of his epistles. Against this western host Ceraunus marched, with vain, pompous and blasphemous boasting. The two armies met; the Macedonians were defeated and cut to pieces. Ceraunus was wounded, taken prisoner, and his head cut off, which, upon a pike, was presented to his friends. Righteous are thy judgments, Oh Lord God Almighty; who shall not fear thee? Thus perished Ceraunus, whose name signifies the thunderer. If women are soon to bear rule over the world, as some are prophesying, I do hope and pray that their cunning, intriguing, managing administrations will being forth better fruit than those of Eurydice and Berenice, wives Ptolemy, or Lysandra and Arsinoe, their mischief-making daughters, the princesses of Macedon and Thrace. Ceraunus was succeeded by Melagar Sosthenes, Antigonus Gonatus, son of Demetrius, Antigonus Doson, Philip and Perseus; then came the Roman sway.

PTOLEMY PHILADELPHUS, B. C., 265.

Another Kitchen Cabinet—The Scene in Lybia.—West of Egypt along the shore of the great sea, were the famous gardens of the Hesperides, described in the songs of the ancient bard. Here the Lybian desert had been reclaimed by industry and art. Groves of fruit trees and pleasant gardens smiling with roses in deepened plats of ground, rewarded the efforts of the husbandman. Here dwelt the Lybian. Near at hand were the Cyrenians, the descendants of a Greek colony. These were the people, and this the theater of those petty wars, which resulted in the ruin of Pharaoh Hophra many years before. Lybia and Cyrenia had been united to Egypt, and with that country had become part of the Great Macedonian Empire, and were subject to the authority of Ptolemy Soter. This king had married several wives, one of whom, Berenice, a widow, had a son, Magus, who, at his mother's request, was appointed satrap of Lybia and Cyrene, in which office he continued after the death of Soter, Philadelphus being his younger brother by the same mother. Magus had married Apame, the sister of Antiochus Theos, and the grand-daughter of Seleucus, who was assassinated by the ungrateful Ceraunus. Ambitious of kingly honor, Magus rebelled, threw off the authority of his brother, Philadelphus, and assumed the independent crown of those provinces of which he was before but the governor. To sustain his present position, he thought he must also subvert the government of Egypt. He therefore marched an army toward Alexandria, relying upon the co-operation of his father-in-law, Soter, king of Syria. Philadelphus marched out of his capital to receive his rebellious brother; but Magus now heard of an insurrection in the rear, and therefore began a hasty retreat, to quiet matters at home.

Philadelphus prepared to harrass the retreating army of

Magus; but while thus occupied, a new thunder cloud arose in the heavens, and threatened to pour a tempest upon Egypt. About four thousand of the Gauls, who had invaded Macedon and slain Ceraunus, had been taken into the service of Philadelphus. Just in the heat of this pursuit of Magus, these foreigners rebelled against Egypt, and Ptolemy was obliged to face about and meet this new foe. In the sequel the Gauls were completely annihilated, by being decoyed into an island of the Nile, where they were so closely guarded, that they either died of starvation, or were slain by each other. Magus had thus time to quiet matters at home, and prepare for another invasion of Egypt. Antiochus of Syria was to make another attack on the other side, so that by dividing the forces of Ptolemy, they hoped to triumph over him; but that monarch had sufficient sagacity to discover and derange their plans. His navy so harrassed all the coast of Syria, that Antiochus could not invade Egypt, and without him the Lybian king feared to attempt it.

After a time, Magus being an old man, desired to negotiate for peace. The women were the wire-workers. Berenice, the daughter of Magus, was to be given in marriage to Evergetes, the eldest son and heir to the crown of Philadelphus. Lybia was to be the dowry of the bride, and the war to cease. (B. C., 258). The nuptials were not immediately consummated. The next year old Magus died, after ruling Lybia fifty years. At this time Antiochus Soter, of Syria, died, and was succeeded by Theos.

Apame, the widow of Magus, was not disposed to surrender the crown and kingdom so quietly to Egypt, especially as she had a brother on the throne of Syria to support her claims. She therefore sought to break up the nuptial arrangement. She sent to Macedon, and invited Demetrius, a nobleman, to visit her court, to whom she promised Berenice in marriage. The new guest and intended son-in-law, arrived at the gardens of the Hesperides; a new shuffling of the cards takes place. Apame becomes enamored of Demetrius, and instead of giving him Berenice, she is herself married to him. Demetrius desired the kingdom, but cared but little for either of the ladies. He assumed the reigns of government, and treated the daughter and officers of State with so much insolence, that a conspiracy was formed against them. Berenice herself led the conspirators to the door of her mother's apartment, where entering, they slew Demetrius upon the bed of Apame, although she endeavored with her own body to shield him from their weapons. Apame was sent to her brother in Syria; and Berenice repaired to Egypt, where she, according to the treaty of her father, soon became the wife of Ptolemy Evergetes, 256 B. C., and eight years before her husband became king. This is the queen whose golden hair became a constellation in the heavens. What amiable and lovely things ladies become when clothed with power and inducted into all the intrigue of courts.

SELEUCUS NICATOR, B. C., 300.

After the battle of Ipsus, in which Antigonus was slain, the vast empire of the Macedonians was again divided, but the boundary was not materially different from that of the former division.

Seleucus had been governor in Babylon, from which place he had been expelled. He had instigated the war against Antigonus, and became king of all Syria, which term, at this time, embraced a large portion of Alexander's conquests, in Asia. Rollin thus speaks of it:

"The dominions of this province are usually called Syria, because Seleucus afterward build Antioch, in Syria, and made it the chief place of his residence, in which his successors, who, from his name, were called Seleucidæ, followed his example. It includes not only Syria proper, but the vast and fertile provinces of upper Asia, which constituted the Persian empire. Seleucus had exercised some authority in the provinces for twenty years previously, but did not receive the crown, nor was he acknowledged king until the death of Antigonus. After this event he reigned another twenty years. As far as is known to us, the kingdom flourished under his administration. He built several cities, among which were Antioch, Seleucia and Apamia. A very unusual domestic affair occurred in the latter part of his life. According to the custom of the eastern provinces, Seleucus had a number of wives; among others was Stratonice, a young and beautiful girl. The eldest son of Seleucus was Antiochus, afterward called Soter. This son became deeply enamored of his step-mother, Stratonice, but owing to the relation she sustained to his father, he dared not reveal his wishes, and fell sick from the disorder of his mind. His physician discovered the real malady, and represented the case to his father, who so ardently loved his son, that he resigned his queen, and she became the wife of Antiochus. We may wonder at the readiness of his father to sacrifice his interest for his son, but it must be recollected that Seleucus was at this time about eighty years of age, that he had other wives, and that Stratonice was still young and unsuitable for him. Soon after this event occurred the war of Seleucus with Lysimachus, of which an account is given in the history of Ceraunus the ingrate.

"This prince had extraordinary qualities; and without mentioning his military accomplishments, it may be justly said that he distinguished himself among the other kings by his great love of justice, by a benevolence and clemency that endeared him to the people, and by a peculiar regard for religion. He had also a taste for polite literature, and made it a circumstance of pleasure and glory to himself to send back to the Athenians the library which Xerxes had carried away, and which he found in Persia. He accompanied that present with the statues of Harmodius and Aristogiton, whom the Athenians honored as their deliverers."

ANTIOCHUS SOTER, B. C. 310.

This was the oldest son and successor of Seleucus the great. Notwithstanding his marvelous love for his stepmother, whom he married, he had other wives and children, who figure on the pages of history. Among others Apame, who was the wife of Magus of Lybia, and the mother of Berenice, the wife of Ptolemy Evergetes.

An account of the intrigue and wars of which she was the ruling cause, is given in the life of Ptolemy Philadelphus. Another daughter of his was Laodicea, of whom an account is given in the history of Evergetes.

Why Antiochus should have been called Soter is not very apparent, for he neither saved his country, nor did any other very worthy deed. Three events in his history constituted the record of his administration. First: Antigonus, son of Demetrius, of whom we have so often spoken, claimed the throne of Macedon. Soter also claimed it, by virtue of his father's conquest at the time of the affair of Ceraunus. The rivals purposed to determine the title by force of arms. Bythinia was at this time governed by a king Nicomedes. This kingdom was situated just south of the Black sea, and lay almost immediately between Syria and Macedon. Nicomedes had lent his aid and influence to the party of Antigonus against Antiochus; for this reason the king of Syria first marched against Bythinia, but the forces were so nearly equal in strength, that little was done, and both parties remained inactive for a time, during which negotiations were in progress, which resulted in a peaceful settlement of the question.

Stratonice, the beloved wife of Antiochus, had a daughter,

Phila, by her first husband, Seleucus. This daughter was the half-sister as well as step-daughter of the king of Syria. Phila became the prize in this new arrangement. She was given to be the wife of Antigonus, and her dowry was to be whatever claim Soter might have, more or less, to the kingdom of Macedon. This arrangement was finally consummated, and the throne of Macedon remained in the family of Antigonus for a long time.

The army of Antiochus now turned their arms against the Gauls, who had invaded and desolated Bythinia. In this war the Syrians were quite successful, and compelled the Gauls to keep within the borders of Galatia. (These Gauls were a band of those adventurous barbarians by whom Ceraunus was slain).

Let us reflect upon the satisfactory result of war. Seleucus, Ptolemy, Cassander, and Lysimachus had united all their strength, and in war had sacrificed an untold amount of human life and happiness, to destroy and exterminate the family of Antigonus and Demetrius, in order that they might occupy their thrones in quiet, and trust not them to their children. In the sequel we see that it resulted in the destruction of the families of Lysimachus and Cassander, neither of whose thrones remained in the permanent possession of their descendants. But the grand-son of their enemy, by Phila, the daughter of Seleucus, one of the confederates, was at last firmly seated upon the throne, and transmitted it to his posterity. And such is usually the result of ambitious wars. The very opposite of the end intended is the invariable result; while the friend of peace secures permanent prosperity. Surely he that taketh the sword shall perish by the sword.

Another small kingdom of Asia Minor now comes under our view in the history of the times. Pergamos, a city with a small territory, had belonged to Bythinia, and had been subject to Lysimachus of Thrace. But taking advantage of the distracted state of affairs at the time of the death of Lysimachus, Arsinoe and her two sons, and finally of Ptolemy, Seleucus threw off the yoke of Thrace, while its governor, Philetærus, under favor of Seleucus, assumed the crown, and ruled as an independent sovereign.

Rollin thus speaks of Philetærus: "He served Lysimachus very faithfully in this post for several years; but his attachment to the interest of Agathocles, the eldest son of Lysimachus, was destroyed by the intrigues of Arsinoe, the younger daughter of Ptolemy Soter, as I have formerly related; and the affliction he testified at the tragical death of that prince caused him to be suspected by the young queen; and she accordingly took measures to destroy him. Philetærus, who was sensible of her intentions, resolved upon a revolt. He succeeded in his design, by the protection of Seleucus; after which he supported himself in the possession of the city and treasures of Lysimachus; being favored in his views, by the troubles that arose upon the death of that prince and that of Seleucus, which happened six months after. He conducted his affairs with so much art and capacity, amid all the divisions of the successors of those two princes, that he preserved the city with all the country round it, for the space of twenty years, and formed it into a state which remained for several generations in his family, and became one of the most potent states of Asia. He had two brothers, Eumenes and Attalus; the former of whom, who was the eldest, had a son named also Eumenes, who succeeded his uncle, and reigned twenty-two years.

"Philetærus died about 263 B. C. As he left no children, Antiochus Soter now sought to take advantage of his death, to annex Pergamos to the kingdom of Syria. This was the second event in the public life of Soter. He invaded Pergamos, but his army was met by another, under the command of

Eumenes, a nephew of Philetærus, who defeated Soter with a great slaughter. Chagrined and disgraced by this defeat, he returned to Antioch, in no very agreeable frame of mind, to perpetrate the third act in the tragedy of his reign. Soter had a son by one of his wives, whose name has not been transmitted to us. Whether he was really guilty of any offense, it is difficult for us now to determine. It is quite possible that Stratonice, to favor her own son's interest, intrigued against her step-son, and charged upon him some act of disorder, produced, perhaps, by herself; but whatever was the fact, Soter, who had received so signal a mark of kindness from his own father, had no compassion for his son, who, being accused of producing some commotion during his father's absence, was ordered to be put to death. Another son of Soter, by Stratonice, was hereupon declared heir to the throne of Syria. After this inhuman act, Antiochus Soter died, and was succeeded by

ANTIOCHUS THEOS, B. C. 260.

Little can be said of this monarch, which has not already been given in the history of Philadelphus and the Lybian war with Magus, whose wife, Apame, was sister of Theos. Antiochus Soter had a daughter, Laodicea, half sister of Theos, to whom he was married some time before he assumed the crown, and by whom he had two sons, one of whom succeeded him on the throne. The first and most important event in his reign, occurred soon after he ascended the throne. Miletus, an island on the coast of Caria, belonged to that province, and was subject to the kings of Egypt. Ptolemy Philadelphus had appointed one Timarchus governor of all these provinces; but the faithless governor threw off his dependence, and assumed the government for himself. He made Miletus the seat of his kingdom. For some reason, Ptolemy had not reduced his revolted subjects, and Timarchus ruled with such terrible severity that the inhabitants, to get rid of him, applied to the king of Syria for aid. He immediately marched, with an army, for their relief. He took Miletus, and slew Timarchus. It was for this deliverance the people of Miletus conferred upon this monarch the title of Theos, which signifies god. The other events of his life are recorded in the history of Egypt, and are chiefly the divorce of Laodicea and marriage with Berenice, the subsequent divorce of Berenice and restoration of Laodicea, and the death of Theos by poison, administered by Laodicea.

While Antiochus Theos was engaged in a fruitless war with Egypt in order to favor Magus, to whom he had married his sister, Apame, a rebellion of a serious nature broke out in another quarter. That portion of his eastern provinces which, in the earlier periods, was called Persia, was now called Parthia. Over these provinces Theos had placed a governor, Agathocles; by his cruelty and mismanagement, this individual caused a revolt. The governor attempted some violence upon a boy, whose brother, to avenge the wrong, rebelled against the governor, slew him, and raised himself to power. Being successful, he established a new kingdom of Parthia. This was about 250 B. C. Bactriana was another province which once belonged to Persia, had been subdued by Alexander, and added by him to the kingdom of Syria. Over this province Theodotus had been appointed governor. About the time of the Parthian rebellion, Theodotus assumed the crown of Bactriana, and became an independent king.

Theos was so fully occupied with his needless war with Ptolemy Philadelphus, that he had no leisure to subdue these revolts. At length, after all the war was done, he made peace with Egypt, by marrying Berenice.

PTOLEMY EVERGETES, B. C. 247.

But out of a branch of her roots shall one stand up in his estate, which shall come with an army, and shall enter into the fortress of the king of the north, and shall deal against them, and shall prevail:

And shall also carry captive into Egypt their gods, with their princes, and with their precious vessels of silver and of gold; and he shall continue more years than the king of the north.

So the king of the south shall come into his kingdom, (of Syria), and shall return into his own land. DANIEL xi: 7, 8, 9.

ON the death of Ptolemy Philadelphus, domestic troubles of a most tragical character broke out at Antioch, resulting in a fearful fate to the royal family.

It must be borne in mind, that Antiochus Theos had divorced his wife, Laodicea; had married Berenice, the daughter of Philadelphus, and had declared her children heirs to the throne. This whole arrangement had been consummated purely as a matter of political interest, and not from any disregard for Laodicea, nor any affection for Berenice.

As soon as it was known at Antioch that Philadelphus was dead, Theos divorced Berenice, and restored Laodicea. Ungrateful for this favor, and fearing future changes in the mind of the fickle king, Laodicea poisoned Theos. She also attempted the murder of Berenice and her child, but the victim fled with her babe to Daphne, where they were soon after murdered by the agents of Laodicea.

Almost the first act of Evergetes, after ascending the throne of his father, was an attempt to rescue his sister, now a prisoner at Daphne.

Several of the states of Asia Minor assisted in this effort; but, before aid could arrive, Berenice and her child had perished. Evergetes determined on revenge. He prosecuted vigorously the war already commenced against Seleucus, the son of Theos who had succeeded to the throne of

Temple of Daphne.—See page 84

Syria. Laodicea was captured and publicly executed, in retaliation for the murder of the unhappy Berenice. All Syria was distracted — the provinces of the north restored to the crown of Egypt, and the provinces of Syria, on the Euphrates and Tigris, were plundered and devastated. Thus bitterly did Laodicea lose her life, and Seleucus much of his kingdom and treasures, by their rash and unjustifiable cruelty toward Berenice, and thus were the words of the prophet fulfilled, "and shall enter into the fortresses of the north, and shall deal against them, and shall prevail."

Evergetes, in this expedition, took a vast amount of treasure, and, among other things, many of the gods of gold and silver that had been carried into the East by Cambyses, the Persian; these he brought back into Egypt, and restored to the temples. The Egyptians rejoiced to see this restoration, in their bigotry supposing that the presence of their ancient deities would restore their land to its ancient glory and prosperity. In the overflowing of their joy, they conferred upon the king the title of Evergetes, which signifies benefactor.

It is probable, that to please the people and maintain himself quietly in possession of his throne, Evergetes paid a visible respect, and conformed to the external ceremonies of the pagan worship of Egypt. Kings are not always more exempt from the necessity of courting public favor, than the rulers of so-called republics. Ptolemy had retreated from the late Syrian war sooner than he intended, on account of an insurrection at home; but the restoration of the gods seems to have composed all the discordant elements.

It is hardly probable that Evergetes had any real confidence in the so-called divinities of Egypt. He must have read the Jewish Bible, which had been translated into his native language, by order of his father.

He had also called at Jerusalem, presented offerings, and worshiped in the holy temple in that city, as he returned from this Eastern war. Evergetes seems to have partaken somewhat of his father's love of learning.

He added much to the valuable library, previously collected at Alexandria. This place was fast becoming the most learned city in the world.

A little romance, of a domestic nature, occurred in the royal family about this time. The wife of Ptolemy was Berenice of Lybia, of whose marriage, and the effort of her mother to prevent it, an account is given in the history of Philadelphus. Berenice seemed greatly attached to Evergetes. When he set out on this Syrian expedition, she grieved and feared he might meet with some ill fortune. She made a solemn vow, that if her lord returned in safety, she would consecrate her hair to the gods in gratitude for his deliverance.

From the monuments of Egypt, as well as from history, we learn that the Egyptians were exceedingly proud of a good head of hair. The offering, therefore, of Berenice, was no inferior sacrifice. Evergetes returned in safety and prosperity; the pagan vow was performed, the golden locks of Berenice were shorn, solemnly consecrated to the gods, and deposited in the temple of Venus, on the island of Cyprus. By some unknown accident, this hair was lost, and Ptolemy became angry at the priests. To pacify and please the king, priests, astronomers and poets got up a fiction that the sacred hair of Berenice had been transported to the heavens, and had become a constellation of stars. Berenice was flattered, Ptolemy was pleased, and the careless priests were saved. Ever since that time, a certain group of stars has been known by the name of the hair of Berenice. May it not be that, from this pagan consecration the Church of Rome formed the custom of cutting off the hair of the nuns when about to take the vail? The following story is related of Evergetes, in reference to the revenue derived from the Jews, which, if true, must have been about this time:

It appears that the Jews, in common with other provinces, paid an annual tribute to the government of Egypt, for which they were inadequately repaid by a partial and imperfect protection. Judea had been without a king ever since the great captivity under Nebuchadnezzar. The duties of government were performed by the High Priest, whose office was filled at that time by one Onias, who, through carelessness, had neglected to collect and pay over the revenue.

Ptolemy construed this neglect into an intended insult. He therefore sent Athenion to demand the payment of the arrears, and to threaten Judea with an invasion.

Little of importance is known of Evergetes, after the Syrian war, except that he enlarged his library, and extended his empire by conquest on both sides of the Red Sea to the straits of Babelmandel; he, however, lost Lybia and Cyrenia, the dowry of his wife. These were taken from him by Demetrius, king of Macedon. After a reign of twenty-five years, he died, 222 B. C. Seleucus C. had died several years before, a prisoner in the East. Evergetes was much older than Seleucus, having been named before the king of Syria was born; thus he "continued more years than the king of the north." Daniel xi: 8.

In the latter part of his reign, occurred a great earthquake on the island of Rhodes, which destroyed a large portion of the city, and prostrated the famous brazen colossus, one of the seven wonders of the world.

With Evergetes departed all the virtuous and noble qualities of the rulers of Egypt. The Ptolemies that succeeded, were devoted to sensual delights and acts of treachery and cruelty, until the termination of the race. Several of them were, however, subjects of prophesy.

Let as now leave the land of the Nile, and repair again to Antiochus Seleucus, the successor of Theos, who had been greatly perplexed and disheartened by the invasion of Evergetes. He had been unable to save his mother from execution, or his country from devastation. When he learned that Evergetes was returning into Egypt, he gathered an army to continue the war, and succeeded in regaining some of his northern provinces.

He now called upon his brother Hierax, to aid him in the war against Egypt. Antiochus Hierax was the younger son of Theos and Laodicea. He was called Hierax from his fierceness, like a hawk. He was at this time about fourteen years of age, and readily responded to the call of Seleucus, not from fraternal feelings, but from motives of personal aggrandizement. A large army was collected in the northwest, ostensibly to invade Egypt, but really to secure to himself the throne of Syria. Ptolemy, however, suddenly concluded a truce with Seleucus, for the space of ten years, *which he did not live to terminate.* Hierax had previously some authority in Asia Minor, but Seleucus had promised him the government of all the provinces, as a reward for the intended service against Ptolemy. Having now, however, come to terms with that monarch, and no longer needing his brother's services, he declined bestowing the promised authority. This furnished the youthful hero a pretext for war. Seleucus saw that no alternative was left but to fight his brother. He therefore crossed Mount Taurus, and passed into Galatia, where a battle was fought near Ancyra.

Now Theos' sons their arms unite,
To try the field again;
With Egypt's crown they boast to fight,
T' avenge their mother slain.

How soon, alas! fraternal love
Is changed to direst hate—
Against each other now they move,
And seal impending fate.

Few domestic quarrels have been more fruitful of evil than those of Syria, in the time of Seleucus Callinicus. The death of his father, Theos, of his mother, Laodicea, and his step-mother, Berenice and child, have already been recorded. Now the two brothers meet in deadly strife on the plains of Galatia. The first result of the battle was that Seleucus, the king and older brother, was completely routed and his hosts dispersed by the young hawk; yet this victory brought no great advantage to the young hero.

Galatia, where the batle was fought, was at this time chiefly occupied by a band of those Gauls, to whom allusion has been previously made, and by whom Ptolemy Ceraunus had been slain in Macedon. Many of these Gauls had been employed in the army Hierax. After the battle, these people, supposing Seleucus was slain, thought to take advantage of the disturbed state of affairs, and benefit themselves. They therefore commenced a war upon Hierax. To pacify them, he gave up to the Gauls all the spoils of victory, and granted them an independence from his authority. Just at this juncture, a new actor appeared in the field. Eumenes, a prince of Pergamos, learning the disturbed state of affairs, suddenly marched an army into Galatia, and commenced a war upon both parties, relying upon their divisions for his success. So sudden and unexpected was this invasion, that although the forces of the Galatians and of Hierax united, they were defeated, and all Asia Minor was thus opened to Eumenes. Hierax was completely routed, and after being the sport of fortune for the space of twelve years, ultimately fled to his father-in-law, Ariarathes, king of Cappadocia. There he became so troublesome to his friends, that the king determined to destroy him. Fearful of his impending fate, he next fled to Egypt for protection, to that very king against whom he had taken up arms. Ptolemy, the well known enemy of his house, caused Hierax to be thrown into prison, where he lingered several years. He ultimately effected his escape, but was murdered by a band of robbers, as he was fleeing out of Egypt, B. C. 226. Thus perished one of these brothers, who so early in life displayed so much energy and courage.

Eumenes, the conqueror of Hierax, after his victory in Galatia, might have made himself master of all Asia Minor, but instead of improving his advantage, he abandoned himself to intemperance, and soon died of debauch.

MACEDON.

Let us once more return to Macedon. We have before related the death of the ingrate Ptolemy Ceraunus. He was succeeded for a short time on the throne, by his brother Melaga, of whom little is known; soon after this one Sosthenes possessed regal authority, but who, or what he was, we are not informed. About 256 B. C., Antiochus Soter, son of Seleucus I., and grand-father of Seleucus II., and Hierax and Antigonus Gonatus, were rivals for the throne of Macedon. This Gonatus was grand-son of the Antigonus, a general of Alexander, who so often fought against Ptolemy Soter. He was the son of Demetrius, the great machine builder, who conducted the siege of Rhodes and of Salamis, and, who coming to aid Alexander, the son of Cassander, robbed him of the throne of Macedon. The rivalship between the two aspirants was finally compromised, by the marriage of Gonatus with Phila, the daughter of Seleucus I., and half-sister of Antiochus Soter.*

---

* This Phila was the daughter of Stratonice, who, from being the stepmother, became the wife of Soter.

Thus, in Syria, marriage begins and ends in war, while in Macedon, strife begins and ends in wed-love. Antigonus Gonatus lived to be about eighty-three years of age, and ruled in Macedon thirty-four years. He died about 241 B. C., and just about the time that the two brothers in Syria were going to battle.

Antigonus Gonatus was succeeded on the throne of Macedon, by his son Demetrius, who reigned ten years. He made himself master of Lybia and Cyrenia, which had been for a long time dependent upon Egypt. Demetrius married the sister of Hierax, but subsequently divorced her and married Phthia, grand-daughter of the king of Epirus.

Where was Seleucus, the other brother, about this time?

After endeavoring to quiet the disturbed state of affairs at home, Seleucus undertook to reclaim his eastern provinces of Parthia and Media, which, during the war with Ptolemy Evergetes and with his brother, threw off the yoke of his authority. In his first attempt he entirely failed, and abandoned the enterprise in a dishonorable manner. Discord at home also having broken out anew, necessitated his hasty return to Antioch.

Subsequently he again attempted the enterprise, and was taken captive by the Parthians, with whom he remained a prisoner, until the time of his death. His captivity was, however, made comfortable by all the attention which the king of Parthia could bestow. He died in consequence of a fall from a horse.

Attalus, king of Pergamos, successor of Eumenes, taking advantage of the distracted state of Syria, was fast making himself master of all Asia Minor. Against him, it was therefore determined to declare war. Seleucus Ceraunus marched an army across Mount Taurus, and entered Phrygia. Here sedition arose in the camp, and the king was poisoned. Thus ended the expedition, and the life of Seleucus III., after a reign of four years. He died on the same day with Ptolemy Evergetes, and was succeeded by Antiochus the great. Achaeus attended the king on this expedition, and avenged his death, by the execution of his guilty murderers.

Seleucus Callinicus had previously married a wife by the name of Laodicea, whose brother Andronicus, one of his most important generals, had been taken prisoner by Ptolemy Evergetes, and carried into Egypt. After many years of confinement, he was delivered to his son Achaeus, in the year 219, B. C. Seleucus left two youthful sons — Seleucus who succeeded to the throne — and Antiochus, afterward called the Great Seleucus III. Antiochus was afterward called Ceraunus, the thunderer, although no action of his rendered him worthy of any fame. They are all gone: Theos, Laodicea, Seleucus and Hierax, Gonatus and Demetrius, Ceraunus, the Berenices, and Evergetes. Their lives have been constant exhibitions of family quarrels, wars, bloody treasons, and fratricides. O could these quarrels with their bones be buried in the earth, then would there be hope for the next generation. Was it so? The next chapter will tell us.

SYRIA AND EGYPT.

But his sons (the sons of Seleucus Callinicus) shall be stirred up, and shall assemble a multitude of great forces: and one (Antiochus the Great) shall certainly come, and overflow, and pass through, (Celosyria, Ptolemias and Galilea): then shall he return, and be stirred up, even to his fortress. (Seleucia).

And the king of the south (Ptolemy) shall be moved with choler, and shall come forth and fight with him, (at Raphia), even with the king of the north: and he (Antiochus) shall set forth a great multitude; but the multitude shall be given into his hands, (into the hands of Ptolemy).

And when he hath taken away the multitude, his heart shall be lifted up; and he shall cast down many thousands. Daniel xi: 10, 11, 12.

A NEW troupe of actors are on the stage; a new generation

of things have arisen. These princes had witnessed the follies, the quarrels and the tragical fate of their predecessors, yet they appear not to have acquired wisdom or instruction by the bloody lesson. Evil examples are soon imitated, and even excelled; while good ones make but a slight impression, and are soon forgotten.

Ptolemy ascended the throne of Egypt in the same year that Antiochus the Great succeeded his brother in Syria. The title of Philopater, lover of his father, was bestowed upon him ironically, for he was suspected of poisoning his father to death. The old feuds between the fathers were revived by the sons. In the partition of the empire of Alexander, the island of Cyprus and the coast of Phœnicia and Palestine were given to Egypt. This was a desirable arrangement, as Egypt, although situated upon the sea, favorably for commerce, had not timber for ship-building, which these provinces could supply; on the other hand, Syria and the East comprehended a large territory and vast resources. But the contiguity of these possessions annoyed the rulers of Antioch, and became the subject of a hereditary quarrel, which lasted until the two governments were overcome and merged into the all-absorbing power of Rome.

ANTIOCHUS THE GREAT, B. C. 222.

For the king of the north shall return, and shall set forth a multitude greater than the former, and shall certainly come after certain years with a great army and with much riches. DANIEL xi: 13.

THIS distinguished monarch was the sixth of the Seleucidæ. He was the grandson of Theos, who was poisoned by the jealous queen, Laodicea. He was the third son of Seleucus Callinicus. Antiochus was born at Antioch about 237 B. C. At his father's death, he was sent to Seleucidas, in Babylonia, to be instructed in the wisdom of the Eastern Magi, and his elder brother, Seleucus Ceraunus, ascended the throne of Syria. The reign of Ceraunus was short and inglorious. Having marched into Asia Minor to subdue a rebellion, the king was poisoned by his subordinate officers, and Antiochus, being but fifteen years of age, was immediately recalled from Babylonia to ascend the throne. The events of his administration may be arranged under six divisions:

1. The campaign to subdue Molo and Alexander, in Mesopotamia and Babylonia.

2. The famous wars with Egypt, under Philopater and Epiphanes.

3. A war with his revolted cousin, Achæus.

4. The great expedition in the East, and the conquest of Armenia, Parthia, Bactriana, and many other provinces.

5. A war with the Romans; and

6. The loss of his life, in attempting to rob the temple of Elymas, in Media.

Success or failure in the pursuits of life, often depend upon the right estimate of character. In declining years, we are too suspicious and distrustful; in early life, too simple and confiding. Many of the indiscretions and failures of young men, which are called crimes, are the results of generous impulses, and a too ardent and confiding friendship. Happy are they whose errors, in this respect, are discovered sufficiently early to teach them lessons of prudence and caution; then may those failures be the best of teachers. Energy and decision of character in middle life, crowning efforts with triumphant success, are often the fruits of early and bitter lessons.

Antiochus was a type man, representing a large class of men, simple, confiding, ardent, yet ambitious, in youth; next perplexed and harassed, well nigh overwhelmed by misplaced confidence; then relying upon self, energetic, efficient, cautious, successful, in manhood; and, at last, having learned to disregard the opinions and feelings of all others, by some bold misstep terminating a splendid career. Antiochus ascended the throne of his brother, a simple, ardent, confiding youth. He immediately procured the appointment of a set of officers to share with him in the administration of authority, expecting the affairs of government to glide down like a gentle stream. In this expectation, he was fated to be disappointed. The following is a programme of the most important officers: Hermias, prime minister; Epigenis, commander-in-chief of the army; Apollophanes, king's physician; Achæus, governor of Asia Minor; Molo, governor of Media; Alexander, governor of Persia; Xeon and Theodotus, generals.

Achæus immediately repaired to Asia Minor, conquered Attalus, and subdued all those provinces which had revolted from the crown of Syria. The ultimate fate of that noble officer, I have given in a subsequent article.

Hermias, the prime minister, was a vain, haughty, conceited man, entirely selfish in all purposes, implacable toward all, and destitute of the requisite qualifications for his station. Having no goodness in himself, he could endure none in his officers, yet he had the success to gain the entire confidence of the youthful king. This, for a time, was the misfortune of Antiochus. Hermias was as a millstone suspended about the neck of the government, and, until it was cast off, nothing could prosper.

Molo and Alexander were brothers. After having received insult and abuse from Hermias, they repaired to their stations. What were their thoughts and consultations on the way? Must it not have been something after this fashion? "Our king is a simple-minded boy, and can afford us no protection in our new homes. The prime minister is a haughty tyrant; we can expect neither favor nor friendship from him; the government of Syria must soon be in a distracted state by his counsel. Why should we be dependents of a ruined state, the servants of a mere boy, and the victims of a tyrannical prime minister? Would it not be more glorious to shine for ourselves?" Alexander and Molo had no sooner reached their posts, than they threw off the yoke of Antiochus, and assumed to be independent kings of their respective provinces.

Epigenis was a man of skill and experience, and sound judgment, capable of giving good counsel to his king. He was the ablest general of his time; for these good qualities, he was the special object of hatred to Hermias. The old war between Egypt and Syria, though for a time suspended, was not terminated. Ptolemy Philopater had just ascended the throne of Egypt. When the news of the revolt of Molo and Alexander reached Antiochus, the young king was perplexed. The ablest officers and wisest nobles in Syria, were convened in council to deliberate. Two questions were submitted to the council: first, shall the government proceed immediately to war with Egypt for the recovery of the provinces south-west of us; or, secondly, shall we proceed immediately against the rebellion in Media and Persia. These were questions of war, and the discreet commander of the army, whose judgment ought to have been respected, was the first to speak in the council. He represented to the king that a revolt was much easier quelled in the first outbreak, than after the rebel had time to fortify himself, acquire experience in his new station, and accustom the people to his government. He therefore advised the king to proceed immediately in person to the East, and recover his revolted provinces, to which he had an indisputable title, rather than waste time in an uncertain war with a neighboring nation, then at peace with him. Hermias interrupted the speaker even before his argument had closed. Hermias was a coward, as men of haughty insolence generally are; he knew that he had himself been the primary cause of this revolt. If the king marched to the East, he would have to accompany the army, and should he fall into the hands of Molo, his reception would not be very civil. He was desirous to keep out of harm's way. Should any event in the war result in an interview between the king and his revolted subjects, the evil conduct of the prime minister might come to the knowledge of Antiochus. Hermias therefore spoke decidedly against the king's proceeding to the East, and advised immediate war on the possessions of Ptolemy. This council was held in the year 221 B. C.

The advice of Hermias prevailed. Part of the troops, under Xenon and Theodotus, marched eastward, to carry on war with Molo, while the king himself, with the rest of the army, moved on toward Celosyria. The prime minister sought, by every possible means, to keep the young king occupied in pleasures and trifles, that he might the better usurp the entire management of the government. To this end he had induced him to an early matrimonial arrangement with Laodicea, daughter of Mithridates, king of Pontus. It was at Seleucia that he met the bride, and celebrated the nuptials with great joy.

In the midst of this conviviality, news was brought from the camp of war. Molo and Alexander had united their forces, had met those of the king, had beaten his generals, and driven his army from the field. The eyes of Antiochus began to be opened; he saw that he had committed an error in following the advice of his minister of pleasure, rather than that of his wise and experienced commander of the army; yet he had not decision enough to shake off the parasite. He now proposed to lay aside the enterprise against Celosyria, and march against the rebels. Hermias persisted obstinately in opposing this decision. The king vibrated between two extremes; on the one side was sound judgment, manifest duty and interest, and on the other the bad advice of an unworthy counsellor, the intensity of the youthful love of pleasure, and the unwillingness to offend an officer that ministered to that pleasure. When we consider the age and experience of Antiochus, we are not surprised to see which end of the scale preponderated. Hermias declared that it became kings to march in person against kings, and send their lieutenants against rebels. Antiochus yielded to the opinion of his prime minister, greatly to the regret of his other officers. We shall soon see the sad result. A body of troops was again sent to the East, to assist those already there in subduing the rebels, while the king in person marched against Celosyria, where Theodotus, the Egyptian governor, met and defeated him, driving his army quite out of the country. Of this invasion and defeat, an account is given on a subsequent page, in the history of Ptolemy Philopater. The army in the East was committed to the care of Xenates, a man of no military experience, and possessing no merit, except that of being a great favorite of the prime minister. The other officers in the East were commanded to subject themselves to him. Raised so suddenly to a high pitch of honor, he became haughty and abusive toward his subordinate officers. His movements were marked with impudence, and he would receive no council. He marched across the Tigris, and fell into an ambuscade, where himself and all his army were cut to pieces. The king having returned to Antioch from his fruitless expedition against Celosyria, and having heard of the destruction of his army in the East, once more called a council of war. It would seem that three defeats had begun to open his eyes. In this council, Epigenis modestly remarked that it would have been best to have marched against the rebels at first to prevent them from fortifying themselves, as they had now done, and that, for the same reason, they ought now, with all expedition, to devote their whole care and study to this war, which, if neglected, might terminate in the entire ruin of the empire, as by the late defeat Babylonia and Mesopotamia were opened to the enemy. Hermias raged, reviled and abused the wise counsellor; he urged the king not to lay aside the Celosyrian scheme, declaring that the wisdom and firmness of the king would be brought into disrepute. The council were ashamed, and Antiochus, for once, was displeased with the advice of his prime minister. To march with the utmost speed against the rebels, was the almost unanimous resolve. Hermias finding that all resistance would be in vain, came over on the other side, and was most actively engaged in preparations for the war. The army assembled at Apama, the general place of rendezvous.

When we consider the warlike character of the reign of the two preceding monarchs, Seleucus Callinicus and Seleucus Ceraunus, the three recent defeats and the marriage banqueting of the present administration, we are not surprised that the finances of Syria were in an embarrassed state. Indeed, we are surprised that the whole nation had not become bankrupt. Honors and favors are abundantly showered upon ministers of war and ministers of voluptuous pleasures, while nothing is said about ministers of finance, boards of trade, committees of manufactures or presidents of agricultural societies. Hence the treasuries of Syria were exhausted.

The country, however, still possessed wealth. In a country possessing so mild and bland a climate — so productive a soil, yielding every variety of fruit and grain, and rich mines abounding in precious metals, as those of Syria — a little industry can not fail to produce competency to its inhabitants, if not oppressed by a tyrannical government. The army were prepared to march from Apama, when a sedition arose among the soldiers. They had been dragged through one campaign after another, and had received no pay; they refused to proceed further and endure more fatigues, until their just demands were answered. Antiochus had no money. He was perplexed and disheartened. This is a not uncommon state of mind with young men, who have entered an important enterprise without the necessary experience: little obstacles appear like mountains, and they become discouraged and abandon further efforts. Antiochus in later years, and with more experience and a better acquaintance with himself, would have felt and acted quite differently. Hermias availed himself of the king's embarrassment to gain entire control over him, and accomplish his own purposes. He promised himself to pay the demands of the soldiers, and relieve the king from his embarrassment. But, while making this promise, he desired the king not to take Epigenes on this expedition. What could the king do? He must either grant the request of his favorite minister, and commit the most rank injustice toward his officer, or, for want of funds, abandon the entire expedition, and probably lose his throne and kingdom. Hermias represented to the king, that as Epigenes had disagreed in council, it would be dangerous to have two such men in the army. Thus taking advantages of his own fault, he asks that the good counsellor be dismissed, in order that the acknowledged bad counsellor may be retained. The king yielded to the advice of his minister, and ordered Epigenes to return to Apama. So the soldiers were paid, and the army advanced. The officers were frightened into silence by the fate of their comrade, and dared not complain; while the soldiers were pleased with a prime minister through whom they had received their pay. Perhaps the king never troubled himself to inquire how the prime minister had relieved him. But the careful student in history will ask, from whence came the funds to pay these soldiers? They were gathered from the people of the land by the prime minister, by the most terrible injustice and extortion. The whole country groaned under his oppression, yet none dared to inform the king of the wrongs that were practiced.

As the army moved toward the Euphrates, the mind of Hermias must have been ill at ease. Should the campaign prove unsuccessful, the responsibility of the failure would rest upon him for having given bad advice in the onset, and for having expelled an able general from the army. He had left an enemy in the rear. Perhaps, in some outbreak of popular enthusiasm, that officer might be elevated to power, and himself brought to punishment for his offenses. He therefore resolved upon the destruction of Epigenes. A conspiracy was formed between him and Alexis, governor of Apama, for this purpose. A servant of the general is bribed. A letter, purporting to be from Molo, thanking him for the late disturbance and suggesting how he could raise an insurrection, was slipped among his papers. Alexis then paid a visit to Epigenes, and asked him if he had not received a letter from Molo. The old veteran replied that he had not, and was indignant at the suspicion of such a thing. The governor informed him that he had orders to examine his papers, which was accordingly done, and the forged letter was found. Epigenes, by the governor's orders, was immediately put to death, and the letter sent to Antiochus in the camp. "The righteous perish and no man layeth it to heart." The simple-minded king, on the receipt of the letter, had no doubt of its genuineness, nor of the guilt of this faithful officer. But most of his council at once suspected the trick, though, through fear of the prime minister, they dared not tell him of it.

Antiochus now, with all his forces, crossed the Euphrates, and, the season having expired, put his army into winter quarters. Thus ended the year 221 B. C.

On the return of the spring, the army crossed the Tigris and compelled Molo to come to an engagement, in which his army was defeated and cut to pieces. So terribly was Molo disheartened, that he committed suicide. Neolas, another brother of the two rebels, fled from the army to Persia, to Alexander, who was also in arms against Syria. There they abandoned themselves to despair, on account of the late defeat, and after having put to death their mother, wives and children, destroyed themselves, rather than fall into the hands of the implacable Hermias. Thus easily were the affairs of Antiochus re-established in the East, and the people quietly submitted to his authority. To fill the cup of pleasure, about this time, a messenger arrived, giving information that the queen had given birth to a son.

Hermias, not content with all his other evil deeds, now conceived the idea of murdering the king. He reasoned thus: If Antiochus were out of the way, the infant being heir to the throne, would be put under the care of the prime minister, who would thus have the entire government in his own hands for a long period of time. His insolence had already rendered him odious to all men. The people were crushed under the avarice and cruelty of his tyrannical rule, yet no one dared to inform the king of the oppression under which his people groaned. Although Antiochus suspected that all was not right, and began to be in fear of his own prime minister, yet with whom to consult or what to say or do, he knew not. His lords and nobles were afraid to counsel him, though they saw his perplexity. At length Apollophanes, his physician, having occasion to meet the king alone, informed him of the state of the country, of the terrible wrongs and outrages practiced by the prime minister, and of the fear of his noble and faithful officers to inform him, lest they should experience the cruel revenge of Hermias, as others had done. He told the king that it was evident that Hermias had some evil design toward him, and warned him to remember the fate of his brother, and beware. The king heard, believed, and was alarmed. Apollophanes assured him that there was no time to be lost. The king was thankful that he had one good and faithful adviser. A plan of action was immediately devised to get rid of this dangerous minister. Accordingly, the king, with a very few attendants, retired a little distance from the army, upon the pretense of being in ill health. He required Hermias to accompany him, but without his attendants, as the king required quiet and retirement. Then taking a solitary walk with him, he caused Hermias to be assassinated, on which account were great rejoicings, both in court and camp. The whole realm rejoiced at his fall. In Apama, this rejoicing burst out into acts of violence, for the populace ran together, and in a tumultuous manner stoned to death his wife and children. Thus retaliation becomes so often the aggressor, and wrongs re-echo wrongs again. The king and his army soon returned to the capital.

Antiochus had been deceived and abused by his prime minister. His faithful subjects had been oppressed, and some of his best officers put to death, and he knew it not, for he was a boy and the tool of a designing man. But he had learned a lesson, and was a boy no longer. From this time, he was a man of decision; he placed full confidence in no one; he examined every thing, and deliberated every question for himself. While he took counsel of others, he exercised his own judgment. He observed carefully the character and conduct of all his subordinate officers, and held them to a strict account. He was kind and paternal to all his people, and protected them in their rights. He was energetic and persevering in his ambitious enterprises, and although sometimes defeated, was generally successful in his campaigns. This character was undoubtedly developed by the misrule of the infamous Hermias.

In 219 B. C., Antiochus had before him two great enterprises. The first of these was the recovery of Celosyria and Palestine, which he attempted, and which ended in the battle of Raphia. Of this expedition and its results, I have given an account in the history of Philopater. The other enterprise was the reduction of Achaeus, who had rebelled against him. This expedition was commenced in 216 B. C., and its results are given in a separate article, under the title of Achaeus.

THE WAR IN CELOSYRIA AND PALESTINE.

The first year after Antiochus ascended the throne, his counsellors advised him into a war with Philopater, for the possession of these provinces; he marched against Celosyria, where Theodotus, an Aetolian officer, under Ptolemy, governed. This faithful officer defended the province, repulsed the invaders, and compelled Antiochus for the present to abandon the war. While these things were transpiring in Asia, Ptolemy was reveling with his profligate courtiers, in Alexandria, leaving the care of his provinces to his faithful subjects. Theodotus had done well for his king, but the licentious court persuaded Ptolemy to believe that he might have done better. This heroic officer was summoned into Egypt, to be tried for cowardice and misconduct. Here, after suffering insult and contempt, abuse and reprimand, and threatened to be beheaded, he was at last acquitted and sent back to his post. What can be expected from a government where profligacy runs rampant, and faithfulness is rewarded with scorn and abuse? Who will be faithful to Philopater in his next emergency? Theodotus had seen the imbecility of the king, and the corruption of the court. He was disgusted with Egypt, and although modest and unambitious, and willing to be a subordinate, he chose to serve a worthier master. Alas! how many causes suffer, and are brought to the verge of ruin, by the abuse of its best friends.

Rollin thus speaks of the influence of this visit to Egypt, on the mind of Theodotus; "The luxury and effeminacy of the whole court, to which he had been an eye-witness, hightened still more his indignation and resentment. He could not bear the idea of being dependent on the caprice of so base and contemptible a set of people. And, indeed, it would be impossible for fancy to conceive more abominable excesses than those in which Philopater plunged himself during his whole reign; and the court imitated but too exactly the example he set them. It was thought that he had poisoned his father, whence he was, by antiphrasis, surnamed Philopater. He publicly caused Berenice, his mother, and Magus, his only brother, to be put to death. After he had got rid of all those who could neither give him good counsel nor excite his jealousy, he abandoned himself to the most infamous pleasures, and was solely intent on gratifying his luxury, brutality, and the most shameful passions. His prime minister was Sosibus, a man every way qualified for the service of such a master as Philopater, and one whose sole view was to support himself in power, by any means whatsoever. The reader will naturally imagine, that in such a court, the power of women had no bounds.

Theodotus could not bear to be dependent on such people, and therefore resolved to find a sovereign more worthy of his services. Accordingly, he was no sooner returned to his government, than he seized upon the cities of Tyre and

Ptolemais, declared for king Antiochus, and immediately dispatched the courier to invite him thither.

The next year, Antiochus again commenced war upon Egypt. Evergetes in the preceding reign, twenty-seven years previously, had taken the city of Seleucia, at the mouth of the Orontes, some twenty miles below Antioch, and established an Egyptian garrison in it. Antiochus was annoyed by having a foreign fortress at the seaport most convenient for his own capital. Having determined upon a war with Philopater, he marched against Seleucia, besieged and took the city, and expelled the Egyptian garrison. He next invaded Celosyria.

This is a rich tableland, lying between the ridges of Lebanon and ante-Lebanon; its extent north and south is about three hundred miles, and to the east about two hundred and fifty miles, and lies in latitude from thirty-three to thirty-four degrees north. It has a very fine climate, and is watered by a number of small streams, one of which forms the Leontes, which, issuing through the mountains, empties into the sea at Tyre. In this district are still to be seen the splendid ruins of Balbeck. Against this province, the present campaign was directed. Theodotus, the Egyptian governor, still held possession.

His experience during the preceding year, and the ingratitude of Philopater, were not lost upon him; he therefore notified Antiochus, that upon his approach the province should be surrendered to him, which was accordingly done, and Egypt lost a valuable territory by its abuse and ingratitude toward an able officer.

Nicolaus was in the vicinity with an army; he, however, was unwilling to desert his Egyptian master; he laid siege to Ptolemais, guarded the pass of Mount Lebanon, and somewhat harrassed the Syrians, but was ultimately compelled to abandon all the posts along the coasts. Ptolemais, Tyre and

Damascus, with military stores and munitions, and forty vessels were lost to Egypt. Antiochus contemplated invading Egypt immediately, but it being the season of the overflowing of the Nile, he postponed this expedition; he, however, spent the autumn in attacking the Castle of Dora, near Mount Carmel. Nicolaus had fortified the place, and offered such a resistance that the Syrians were unable to take it. A truce for four months was agreed upon, and Antiochus returned to Seleucia, and put his army into winter quarters. Theodotus was made governor of all the places taken in this campaign. Thus ended the year 219 B. C.

Antiochus was contemplating a war with Achæus, a revolted subject in Asia Minor, and was therefore desirous of peace for the time being, with Ptolemy; on the other hand, Philopater, who had not in person entered the field, but had left all to his generals, was unprepared at present, to continue the war. The four months of truce were exhausted in fruitless efforts to conclude a treaty of peace; not that either contemplated peace — they only wished to gain time. The points in debate were, how much and how many territories in Asia were given to Egypt in the great partition, and how much was reserved to Syria. The spring came and nothing was concluded; the war, therefore, recommenced.

THE BATTLE OF RAPHIA.

Nicolaus, the Aetolian, had the command of the Egyptian army, and Perigenes of the navy. Provisions were sent to Gaza, where all the army made a rendezvous. From thence Nicolaus proceeded along the coast to Mount Lebanon, and seized all the passes through which he supposed Antiochus must cross, intending from his advantageous position, to stop him. The fleet also sailed along the coast of Palestine and Phœnicia.

The enemy were not idle. The Syrian fleet, commanded

by Diogneius, came out to meet the Egyptians on the sea, while Antiochus put himself at the head of the land forces. A battle was fought on the sea and on the land at the same time, and but a short distance apart. At sea neither party gained any great advantage, but on land the enemy entirely routed Nicolaus, and drove him to retire to Sidon, after having four thousand of his soldiers either killed or taken prisoners. Perigenes and the Egyptian fleet also collected at Sidon.

Antiochus surrounded the place, both by sea and by land, intending to besiege the city; but finding it a difficult task, he sent his fleet into Tyre, and marched his army across the mountains into Galilea, where all the region round about that sea and in Gilead, on the east of Jordan, submitted to his authority.*

The winter coming on, nothing more was attempted that season. Thus ended the year 218 B. C., and Ptolemy, through his indolence, had lost every engagement. Still he devoted himself to sensuality, and while his court abounded in profligacy, left the defense of his country to his officers.

In the spring of 217, Philopater seemed to wake up from his carousal, and stir up like a lion aroused for the conflict. He put himself at the head of his army, and crossed over the short desert of Shur, with seventy thousand foot soldiers, five thousand horsemen and seventy-three elephants, with all the munitions of war. He encamped at Raphia, between Rhinoconuna and Gaza, and determined to await the arrival of the foe, who was advancing. Antiochus marched against him with a superior force of seventy-two thousand footmen, six thousand horsemen and one hundred and two elephants, and encamped at first about a mile and a half from Philopater, but afterward he came within three-quarters of a mile;

---

* This was the district occupied originally by the tribes of Reuben, Gad and Manasseh.

here the two armies reposed for some time. Skirmishes occurred daily between squads and individuals of the opposite parties, who met in their foraging to obtain wood and water.

Theodotus, the Aetolian, thought this a good opportunity to avenge himself on Ptolemy, for the insult offered some years before. Favored by the darkness of the night, he stole into his tent and attempted his assassination. Ptolemy was absent, and Theodotus, by mistake, slew his physician, supposing him to be the king, and then effected his escape.

At length the two kings resolved to try the results of a battle, force against force; and dreadful was the conflict.

"The two kings rode from one body to another, at the nead of their lines, to animate their troops. Arsinoe, the sister and wife of Ptolemy, was not content with exhorting the soldiers to behave manfully, before the battle, but did not leave her husband even during the engagement. The issue of it was, that Antiochus at the head of his right wing, defeated the enemy's left. But while hurried on by an inconsiderate ardor, he engaged too warmly in the pursuit. Ptolemy, who had been as successful in the other wing, charged Antiochus' center in flank, which was then uncovered, and broke it before it was possible for that prince to come to its relief. An old officer, who saw which way the dust flew, concluded that the center was defeated, and accordingly made Antiochus observe it.

"But though he faced about that instant, he came too late to amend his fault, and found the rest of his army broken and put to flight. He himself was now obliged to provide for his retreat, and retired to Raphia, and afterward to Gaza, with the loss of ten thousand men killed, and four thousand taken prisoners. Finding it would now be impossible for him to maintain himself in that country against Ptolemy, he abandoned all his conquests and retreated to Antioch, with the remains of his army." —*Rollin.*

On arriving at home, Antiochus hastily sent an embassy, desiring conditions of peace, for he feared a revolution among his own people, who, since this defeat, had lost confidence in him. Peace, by treaty, was now restored, and all Celosyria, Phœnicia and Palestine, returned to their old masters, the Egyptians. Had Ptolemy been possessed of any ambition or energy, he might have taken advantage of his late victory, and extended his empire, and so subdued Syria as to have saved his kingdom from further trouble in that direction; but he cared more for luxury and effeminate pleasures of idleness, than for the toils of the camp. Perhaps this is not to be regretted; if princes will destroy somebody, they may as well destroy themselves and their corrupt associates, by intemperance, as their neighbors by war. It is questionable whether it is not better for mankind to have lazy, intemperate kings like the boy-king of the frogs in the fable, than to have kings, serpent-like, active and ambitious, who, in war shed a vast amount of blood. The inhabitants of these Asiatic provinces preferred to be subjects of Egypt rather than of Syria, and hastened with presents to pay submission to Ptolemy.

The reason for this preference is not very apparent; for their partiality the Jews sometime afterward suffered severely.

"Ptolemy now made a trip through the conquered provinces, and visited their most important cities. At first he was quite pleased with Jerusalem, made oblations, and bestowed considerable gifts upon the temple, and offered sacrifice to the God of Israel. From the book of Maccabees we learn that he was not content with entering the outer court, to which alone the Gentiles were admitted, but was determined to enter into the temple, even to the holy of the holies, to which none but the high priest alone was permitted to enter; the whole body of the priests and the Levites assembled to oppose the design, while the air was rent with wailing, and all the places were filled with lamentations, lest their holy temple should be defiled. This resistance but increased the curiosity of Ptolemy, to see what was to be seen. He therefore pushed his away through the guard of the Jews, and was about to enter the most sacred retreat, when he was smitten of God with sudden terror, which so paralized him that he was carried off half dead. On account of this accident which had befallen him, he became exceedingly exasperated toward the whole Jewish nation, and left their city, threatening them with his vengeance. The next year he commenced a serious persecution against the Jews, especially those of Alexandria, whom he endeavored to compel to worship the Gods of Egypt." —*Rollin.*

It is highly probable that Ptolemy had some difficulty with the bigoted, obstinate Jews, at Jerusalem, but it is hardly credible that the entire story, as above related, is true; it is probably a Jewish fiction.

How fickle and inconstant the public mind! The Egyptians, who were well acquainted with the effeminacy of Ptolemy, did not expect success in the war. They were, therefore, surprised and confounded at his great victory at the battle of Raphia; yet upon reflection, they murmured that he did not prosecute more vigorously the war, after gaining so great an advantage. These murmurs at length grew into an open rebellion, about 212 B. C., so that Ptolemy, in closing the war with Syria that he might enjoy ease, drew upon himself a civil war at home, which, after a time, was quieted. I am not aware that the particulars of this civil war have been made a matter of record.

Let us now look a little more closely into the court of Egypt. Ptolemy had married his own sister, Arsinoe, who is also called Cleopatra.[*] From and after the triumphant victory at Raphia, he abandoned himself more entirely to sensuality, and his associates were the most corrupt and licentious. Agathoclea, his concubine, her brother, Agathocles, and their mother, ruled the king in every thing. Day after day passed in dissolute banquets, and night after night in the vilest debauches. Instead of attending councils of State, and of projecting measures for the good of his people, he played upon instruments and presided at concerts; instead of bestowing offices of trust upon men of integrity and experience, he permitted the vilest women to dispose of all employments and posts of honor in the government. The prime minister was Sosibus, a corrupt old officer, who had been in power from the early days of Ptolemy Philadelphus, and, with advancing years, had grown the worse and not the better man; his highest ambition was to please, by obeying the commands of a corrupt prince and his vile courtezans, however unjust these commands might be. Arsinoe, the king's wife, who had, with him, endured the fatigues of the camp, and contributed so much to his success in the battle of Raphia, had no influence in Ptolemy's court; grieved to see her place supplied by another, and herself treated with disrespect, she could do no less than complain. To hush these complaints, the king directed Sosibus to get rid of her; who ordered one Philammon to assassinate her, which was accordingly done. The people at length became enraged at so many acts of cruelty, and especially this last. They compelled Sosibus to resign his office, which was conferred upon Hepolemus, a

[*] About this time, the Romans sent a deputation to Ptolemy and his queen, with presents which indicate the rude and simple state of society at Rome at that time. The presents consisted of a robe, a purple tunic, and an ivory chair; and, to the queen, of an embroidered robe and a scarf.

young man who had signalized himself in the army. He continued to hold the office of prime minister until the death of Ptolemy Philopater; but he possessed neither talent nor experience requisite for his station. He was easily corrupted by flattery, and was puffed up with pride and haughtiness at his exaltation. Following the example of all around him, he abandoned himself to profusion, luxury and intemperance.

Debauchery and excess had quite worn out the constitution of Philopater, which was naturally vigorous. He ascended the throne in the twentieth year of his age, and after a reign of seventeen years died, 204 B. C., and was succeeded by his son, Ptolemy Epiphanes, then but five years of age.

ACHÆUS.

This young, heroic and unfortunate prince was the son of Andromachus, brother of Laodicea, the queen of Seleucus II., (Callinicus). Andromachus was himself a prisoner in Egypt. When Seleucus III. (Ceraunus) ascended the throne of his father, Syria was in a distracted state, and impoverished by unsuccessful wars with Egypt and the Eastern provinces. Ceraunus was young and inexperienced just at this time, and, encouraged by these misfortunes, Attalus, king of Pergamos, and successor of Eumenes, the conqueror of Hierax, not content with the bounds of his own kingdom, was extending his empire all over Asia Minor.

Young Ceraunus and his counsellors found it necessary to check the progress of this revolution, or they might soon expect to see him, like Hierax in the preceding reign, aspiring to the throne of Syria. An army was collected, and the king, accompanied by his cousin, Achæus, crossed Mount Taurus, and marched into Phrygia. Ceraunus was without funds, and the army without pay. Misfortune in this fallen world is oftener punished than crime; and honest poverty invites bold, bad men to the commission of evil deeds. Two of the officers, Nicanor and Apaturus, conspired and poisoned Ceraunus, whom the soldiers despised because he could not pay them. Achæus, being a man of energy and decision, might now easily have made himself their master, and ascended the throne of Syria. Indeed, the army offered him the crown; but, true and faithful to his trust, he quelled the insurrection,* executed the murderers of the late king, and bestowed a crown upon Antiochus, the young brother of Ceraunus. We shall see, in the sequel, how his cousin rewarded him for his fidelity.

Antiochus, at this time, was not fifteen years of age; he had been sent by his brother, at the beginning of the war, to Seleucia, in Babylonia, to be educated, where he was when his brother died. Achæus having sent an officer and part of the army to see the youthful heir fully and safely established on the throne, retained the rest and toiled to reduce the provinces of Asia Minor to the authority of Syria, in which he was entirely successful; compelling Attalus to confine himself to his original kingdom of Pergamos.

This very faithfulness was the primary cause of his ruin. It was manifest to all, that Achæus had done a great and good service to the young king. Antiochus was surrounded by a most wicked, dangerous set of ministers and nobles, whose ill advice had cost him many a loss. These false-hearted wretches, to make a show of faithfulness, and at the same time to disparage a man whose superior fidelity and ability were a rebuke to their idleness and worthiness, began to accuse Achæus of aspiring to make himself king of all those provinces of Asia Minor which he had reclaimed,

* To comprehend a position of these States, it is desirable that the reader should look upon a map of this region. In a history of Asia Minor, I have given a more full account of these internal wars.

and of which he was, by appointment, the governor. They accused him of secret correspondence with Ptolemy, with whom Antiochus was at war. How dangerous it is to be more zealous, or more faithful, in any cause than one's fellows. Here is the secret of all the intrigues in political circles. Here is the weakness of all civil government, that the worthy and the faithful can not be endured by the evil and the indolent, and are therefore, like Daniel, cast into the lion's den.

It is only in times of extreme poverty and danger, that good and true men can share in government, when there is nothing to share but suffering and danger. We have sometimes thought the government of these United States an exception; but we are fast learning that men and governments are the same everywhere. When our government was struggling for existence, or contending with a mighty foe, good men endured the hardships, did the service and blessed the nation: but now, in our pride and fullness, a good man may as well leap into the den of lions as to ask any favor of government; even the few good men who have been placed in office, not by the government, but by the people of their own district, are treated with obloquy and contempt, while the corrupt, bloated, idle villains, who hold places and do nothing, or that which is worse than nothing, are favored and exalted to the skies. Alas! the same spirit and the same results are but too manifest in our ecclesiastical organizations. The men of indolence and small capacity receive large support, and are held in favor, while the truly active, industrious and faithful are sure to be contemned and crowded out of place.

Achæus was, undoubtedly, innocent of all these charges when they were first preferred. His fidelity to the youthful king, whom he might have destroyed, ought to have been a sufficient pledge for his innocence. The evil counsellors of Antiochus prevailed, and Achæus was destined to fall. Apprised of this decision, it is not surprising that the governor of Asia Minor and the saviour of the king of Syria should be deeply sensible of this ingratitude, and should conclude that his former generosity had been bestowed upon an unworthy object.

When Syria was in trouble, he saved her; when she was in prosperity, she aimed to destroy him. Had this prince been kindly treated, he might and would have been of great use to Antiochus in his subsequent extremities; but being unjustly accused, and at the point of ruin, he had but the alternative either to submit and die in his innocence, or resist, and thus commit the crime with which he had been charged. As many others have been, he was driven to become an enemy; he chose to save himself, if possible, or perish in the attempt. He therefore assumed the crown, and caused himself to be proclaimed king of Asia Minor, B. C. 219.

THE BYZANTINE WAR.

The city on the beautiful island of Rhodes, situated near the coast of Asia, was occupied by a free, independent people, mostly devoted to commerce; they sought to maintain peace, while the nations around were engaged in war. Thus Rhodes became rich through the folly of her neighbors. The Rhodian commerce extended into the Black Sea. A great amount of trade was carried on with the Bythynians, whose country lay on the south of that sea, and in the north-west corner of Asia Minor. Both nations were enriched by this commerce, and sustained friendly relations with each other.

Ever since the death of Lysimachus, in the war with Seleucus and Ceraunus, Thrace had been dismembered: a large part of its territory had been merged in that of Macedon.

Bythynia and some other districts formed independent governments; where now stands Constantinople, the proud capital of the Turks, then stood Byzantium. This city and a little territory in the vicinity, constituted a distinct kingdom. Being situated on the strait that connects the two seas, it commanded the pass; so that, without their permission, no vessel could enter the Black, then called Euxine Sea.

The power of the Byzantines formed a check upon the trade of the neighboring nation, and about the time of Ptolemy Philopater, in Egypt, of Antiochus the Great, in Syria, and of Achæus, in Asia Minor, that is about 219 B. C., the Byzantines thought to exercise this power which her position gave her. She permitted no vessel to pass or repass the Hellespont, but upon the payment of a heavy tribute into her treasury. This led to the Byzantine war. Rhodes and Bythynia refused to pay the unreasonable demand, declared that the seas were made of God, and were free; and united in a war against the city of the straits. With an enemy on each side of her, cutting off her supplies, Byzantine found herself in the straits, indeed. Her rulers, therefore, found means to engage Achæus on their side. Bythynia and Rhodes were perplexed to see the greatest captain of the age join with their foes, against what they deemed to be their natural rights. The Bythynians, an agricultural people, were discouraged, and almost ready to abandon the effort; but the Rhodians, a commercial people, immediately thought of finance, and determined to drive a bargain. A singular article of commerce was devised, and brought into market to change the fates of war. Rhodes had great trade with Egypt, and was on the best of terms with Philopater. In Alexandria lay Andromachus, the father of Achæus, a prisoner, taken by the father of the present Ptolemy in a war against the father of the present

Antiochus. The Rhodians sagaciously saw the advantage, and represented to Ptolemy, that when Andromachus was taken prisoner he was fighting for Syria, but that now his son was the most dangerous foe of this country. Ptolemy was himself not at peace with Antiochus; to restore Andromachus and aid Achæus, was but to aid himself against Syria. At the same time the friendship of Rhodes was of great value to him in his possession of Cyprus and Phœnicia. The advantage was seen to be mutual. Achæus had more to fear from his cousin Antiochus, than from all other foes; it was therefore his interest to be at peace and on good terms with Ptolemy; but neither had seen these advantages until the commercial Rhodians had pointed them out to the opposite parties. Achæus and Egypt were enemies merely from habit, not from any motives or policy. A bargain was concluded, and the two were ever after friends. The Rhodians receive the prisoner, Andromachus, and deliver him to his son Achæus, who deserts the Byzantines, aids the Bythynians and the Rhodians, and compels the city of the Straits to permit the vessels to pass and repass undisturbed. Here again is another among the unnumbered examples of the power of foreign commerce to bless the nations, sheath the sword and lull the elements of strife into peace and tranquility.

The war of Antiochus with Ptolemy, kept him employed until after the battle of Raphia, and the year which followed, so that he was not prepared until the year had elapsed to disturb Achæus, who, during the time had fortified himself, and made preparations for the threatened invasion, which commenced in 216, B. C. Antiochus passed Mount Taurus, as his brother and father had done before him, to subdue Asia Minor. He concluded a treaty of peace with Attalus, king of Pergamos. Their forces uniting, were successful against Achæus, and after various battles, compelled him to retreat into Sardis, where he shut himself up and was closely besieged by the united forces, for the space of one year. Skirmishes, however, and small battles frequently occurred between the contending forces. At length the city was taken by a stratagem of Lygonus, an officer of Antiochus, and Achæus, with a number of soldiers, was closely surrounded in citadel or fortress, where they still resisted and refused to surrender. Ptolemy Philopater had made a treaty with Achæus, and was now disturbed to see him so closely besieged. He therefore directed Sosibus, his prime minister, if possible to relieve him or effect his escape. In the court of Ptolemy was a man by the name of Bolus, a Cretan by birth, famous for his intriguing, cunning, craft and falsehood, as indeed are all the Cretans. "The Cretans are always liars, evil beasts, and slow bellies." — Titus i: 12.

To Bolus, Sosibus applied, to know if he could not effect the deliverance of Achæus. The Cretan promised to do the required deed, and received ten talents in advance, as compensation, with promise of much more if successful.

His plan was as follows: He had an intimate friend and near relation in the army of Antiochus, Cambylis, another lying Cretan, and captain of a band of Cretan guards, who at that time had command of a fort just back of the citadel, where Achæus was confined. By the aid of this friend, he expected to let Achæus escape on that side. Bolus repaired to Sardis, found his friend Cambylis, and explained the nature of his mission. As they were working for pay, they were hired to deceive; they little cared which party they deceived or which they betrayed, so that they were well paid for the fraud. The liars therefore proceeded to Antiochus, and explained the whole affair to him, who offered them a still greater reward to finish their work in a little different manner. Bolus then repaired to the citadel, where, by means of letters from Sosibus, and other friends of Achæus, he gained complete and perfect confidence of the unfortunate prince, and led him out to the department of captain Cambylis. The confiding and deceived Achæus was delivered up to Antiochus, who ordered him to be immediately beheaded. Thus ended the war of Achæus, and thus by the order of Antiochus, perished a great man to whom that monarch was in debt for his crown and kingdom. It is unsafe to do good to kings and prince, for they are ever desirous to wipe out the recollection of their obligation by the destruction of their benefactors. I can not agree with Rolin that this was a just fate of a rebel against his king—it was a rebellion of a king against his subject. Achæus was driven to take up arms in defense of himself and his rights against an ungrateful monarch. The day of righteous retribution will overtake him, as the reader will learn in the the ultimate fate of Antiochus.

EGYPT—PTOLEMY EPIPHANES, B. C. 207.

The great centers of attraction in the life of Epiphanes, were at Antioch, in Macedon and in Greece, while Egypt became secondary in importance. The record of a few events only comprises the history of Egypt during his reign.

When Ptolemy Philopater died, worn out by excesses, his court was still filled with the corrupt creatures who had continually surrounded him, ministered to his dissipation, and thus hastened him out of the world. How, in what state of mind, or in what manner he expired, is not known; no one being present except his infamous concubine, Agathoclea, her brother and mother, who had entire possession of the king's person, and of the infant heir, whose mother had been previously assassinated. They concealed for a time the fact of the king's death, until they could provide for themselves, by purloining the money, jewels and other effects in the palace. These they carried off and concealed, and then coming forward with the child, announced his majesty's death, and declared that the late royal father, in his expiring moments, had committed the darling son to the care of Agathoclea, during his minority. They implored the people to protect them against the prime minister, Hepolemus, who, they asserted, was preparing to destroy the child, and usurp the crown. They proposed to introduce witnesses to prove the treason. The object of all this false show with regard to the infant, and false accusation against the prime minister, was that they, by having the care of the young king might still sustain in power, and hold the reins of government during the minority of the prince, who was now but about five years of age. The people saw too plainly the artifice and iniquity of these corrupt creatures. Instead of destroying the prime minister, as they had hoped, the king was taken out of their hands and put upon a throne, in the Hyppodrome, and Agathocles, his sister and mother were brought before him; then as if by his orders, were immediately put to death, and their bodies dragged through the streets, and exposed to every possible indignity; all their friends were also executed.

Upon this summary process Rollin remarks: "The usual and just end of those unworthy favorites, who abuse the confidence of their sovereign and oppress the people, but which does not effect the reformation of those who resemble them."

I do not entirely agree with that author in this reflection. It is true that this is the usual fate of such persons. When multitudes have been long oppressed by wicked creatures in power, and when their wishes and rights are set at defiance, they feel deeply indignant, and if ever the power of retaliation returns into their hands, they over-act and hurl a terrible revenge upon their unjust rulers. Such an exhibition of revenge is seen in the first revolution of France, in the rising of the masses against their titled, corrupt and oppressive nobility. Such by an inevitable law of human destiny, will ultimately be the fate of the rulers of our own land, should they, forgetting their high and responsible position, be induced by intrigue and management, to sell the liberties of this country, and set at defiance the will of the whole people. Wo worth the day when a righteous retribution shall overtake an oligarchy of oppressive rulers. But I can not agree with Rollin, that this was a just fate of these corrupt courtesans. They had erred—who caused them to err. The king, theman clothed with power, sustained by that people who now revenge the victims of that same government, which, in this very act, they were attempting to repudiate. It still remains true, that the people are responsible for the form, and must suffer for the faults of their government. If the government of this land shall set at defiance the wish of the great mass of the people, and rob them of their liberty, it will be by the instrumentality of the people themselves, who, by wilfully adhering to clans and parties, clothe corrupt men with power, and thus furnish the weapons of their own destruction. What good could result by the barbarous execution of all their friends, or dragging their dead bodies through the streets? Certainly none to the victims, and Rollin himself admits that others like them are not reformed by such fate. Would it not have contributed more to the morality, peace and prosperity of all others, if these creatures had been silently removed from the possibility of doing further harm, and some check devised upon the then forming government, to prevent the repetition of such flagrant abuses.

A little specimen of woman's rights authority was exhibited about this time. Queen Arsinoe, it will be recollected, had some years before been assassinated, and this Agathoclea had occupied the king's bed in her place. The queen had been attended by ladies of honor who were greatly attached to that unfortunate princess, and who grieved for her cruel fate. About the time of the death of Agathocles and friends, Philammon, the murderer of Arsinoe, who had been absent to Cyrenia, returned to Alexandria. These ladies of honor having heard of his return, determined on revenge, and took advantage of the excited state of affairs. Collectively they repaired to the house where he was, and broke open the door, and with clubs and stones beat him to death. Was this just? What had he done? He had assassinated the queen, but it was by an order of the prime minister, at the command of the king. Had he not then just the same authority for his act that any sheriff has when he executes a convict either publicly or within the walls of a prison?

In either case it is murder by authority. Can one murder justify another? Indeed, every assassin who is hired to murder acts by the authority of some one or more, possessed of power. How great a power it requires to constitute righteous authority to take life, it is impossible to determine.

The young king for the time being was committed to Sosibus, a son of the former minister of that name. At this time Philip was on the throne of Macedon, and Antiochus the Great still reigned in Syria. When these monarchs heard of the death of Philopater, and that he had left only an infant heir to the throne, they entered into an agreement for the ruin of the kingdom and a partition of the inheritance. In the language of Nicolas, the sick man was dead, and they were for attending the funeral. Philip was to have Cari, Lydia, Cyrenia and Egypt, while the king of Syria was to have Palestine, Celosyria and Cyprus, with Cilicia. Antiochus immediately took possession of Celosyria and Palestine, without opposition or hindrance; but Philip was so occupied with war in other directions, that he never found time to take possession of his share of the spoils.

New actors now appear on the stage—the fourth beast of

Daniel is rising out of the sea—Rome began to interest herself in the affairs of Greece and Macedon. Being annoyed by some of the movements of Antiochus, they were determined not to permit Egypt to fall into his hands. They therefore spread the mantle of their protection over the infant king. Æmilianus, a Roman consul, proceeded to Egypt, regulated affairs in the best possible manner, and appointed one Aristomenes prime minister, and to have the care and education of the king. This officer had long been in Egypt, had acquired great experience, and now administered the government with diligence, prudence and fidelity.

Aristomenes immediately set about the recovery of Palestine and Celosyria. The Ætolians of Greece were, in these days, esteemed the best soldiers in the world. They were accustomed to sell their services to other nations. Scopas, one of their generals, not being appointed to the highest command, as he desired, had retired into Egypt and engaged in the service of its king. Him Aristomenes sent back to Ætolia, with a large sum of money, to raise an army, from whence he returned with six thousand brave soldiers. This was about the year 200 B. C. In the spring and summer, 199, Antiochus was employed in a war with Attalus, in Asia Minor. The administration of Egypt took advantage of that fact, and sent Scopas, with his army, into Asia, who soon recovered Palestine and Celosyria, with their most important cities. He established a garrison in the citadel of Jerusalem, and, after plundering the provinces of a large amount of spoil, on the approach of winter returned to Alexandria. For this successful guerrilla expedition against this peaceful, unoffending, non-resisting people, he gained great credit and renown. The real cause of his success, was the absence of Antiochus.

The next year, B. C. 198, the king of Syria marched in

person to recover the lost provinces, and Scopas was again sent to resist him. The two armies met at Paneas, near the source of the river Jordan. Here a great battle was fought, and a great number of Egyptian soldiers slaughtered. Scopas retreated with ten thousand soldiers, and shut himself closely up in Sidon. Antiochus surrounded him, both by sea and land, and cut off all his supplies. The government at Alexandria sent out three generals and an army to relieve him, and to break up the siege, which they were not able to accomplish. Being upon the point of starvation, Scopas finally, upon promise of having his life spared, surrendered, but with the loss of every thing else, and Rollin says he returned naked.

After the siege of Sidon had closed, he marched along the coast and besieged Gaza. The inhabitants defended themselves obstinately and bravely for a time, which greatly exasperated him; but ultimately having taken the city, he devoted the inhabitants to butchery and their treasury to plunder. Then securing all the passes, through which he supposed an Egyptian army might follow him, and, turning backward, he recovered all Palestine and Celosyria.

Rollin, upon the authority of Josephus, gives us the two following accounts:

"The instant the Jews, who at that time had reason to be displeased with the Egyptians, knew that Antiochus was advancing toward their country, they came very zealously to meet him, and deliver up the keys of their cities; and when he came to Jerusalem, the priests and elders came out to meet him, paid him all kinds of honor, and assisted him in driving out of the castle the soldiers which Scopas had left in it. In return for these services, Antiochus granted them a great many privileges, and enacted, by a particular decree, that no stranger should be allowed access to the inner part of the temple — a provision which seemed visibly to have been made on account of Philopater's attempt, who would have forced his way thither. Antiochus, in his Eastern expedition, had received so many services from the Jews of Babylon and Mesopotamia, and depended so much on their fidelity, that when a sedition broke out in Phrygia and Lydia, he sent two thousand Jewish families to quell it, and keep the country in peace, and granted them a variety of extraordinary favors."

This account of the partiality of Antiochus for the Jews may be true; but I doubt it much, as it rests entirely upon the authority of a Jewish writer exceedingly partial toward that people, very much given to writing long and incredible stories about them. The Jews, so far from being quiet peace-makers, have, in every age, been famous for turbulence and rebellion.

"And he shall give him the daughter of women, corrupting her, but she shall not stand on his side, neither shall she be for him."—Daniel. And Antiochus shall give his daughter to the king of Egypt, that she might treacherously betray Egypt into his hands; but she shall not stand on her father's side, neither be for him; for she, as a true and faithful wife, shall adhere to the interest of her husband. Antiochus had not yet closed his wars in Asia Minor; he decided, therefore, not to be again annoyed by Egypt. To quiet all apprehensions in that quarter, he proposed to the council in Egypt to give his own daughter, Cleopatra, in marriage to the youthful king, with Palestine and Celosyria for her dowry, with the condition that the parties should not come together for a number of years, on account of their ages, Epiphanes then being but eleven years old. This was a measure of policy. He hoped, in this manner, to keep Egypt quiet until he could extend his empire, and become sufficiently powerful to do as he pleased. He could then either break off the engagement, or, if too late, through his daughter, Egypt might be betrayed and delivered into his hands. The administration at Alexandria did not discern his policy, but readily accepted the offer, and Cleopatra became the affianced bride of the youthful king of Egypt, and Antiochus was permitted to push forward his ambitious scheme undisturbed. He however never realized the advantage he expected to derive from the marriage of his daughter, for Cleopatra faithfully adhered to the interests of Egypt — administered the government, for a time, after her husband's decease, and transmitted the crown to her sons: thus fulfilling the words of the prophet.

After the retreat from Sidon, Scopas was again placed at the head of the army of foreigners in Alexandria. Contemplating the distracted state of affairs in Egypt and the youthfulness of the monarch, he conceived the idea of raising himself to the throne. He, with his Ætolian guards, conspired to assassinate the king, and usurp the reigns of government; but before their plans could be matured, they came to the knowledge of their prime minister, by whom Scopas was arrested, and he with all his associates were publicly executed. A rumor had gone out that Epiphanes was actually slain. Antiochus, who was then near Byzantium, wheeled suddenly and marched to invade Egypt; but, on arriving at Lydia, he learned his mistake. From this time Egypt ceased to confide in Ætolian soldiers, who had previously been celebrated for their fidelity.

In 187, Antiochus died, and was succeeded by his son, Philopater. On the same year, a son was born to Ptolemy Epiphanes by his wife, Cleopatra, who afterward ascended the throne of his father with the name of Philometor. Egypt celebrated this birth with great splendor and rejoicings. In 184, which was the year after this event, Ptolemy Epiphanes assumed the reigns of government, and commenced his course by pursuing most discreet and prudent measures, guided by the counsels of Aristomenes, who still held the office of prime minister; he renewed the alliance with the Achæans and other nations, and gave promise of an able and efficient reign.

The smiling tokens of future good were like the bright rays of the rising sun, soon, alas! to pass behind a cloud and be succeeded by a day of storms. The wise and just counsels of the prime minister, which foreshadowded so much good, at length became irksome to the young ardent king, who now relapsed into the footsteps of his father, and devoted himself to sensuality. The flatteries of corrupt courtiers caused him to err in the injudicious appointments of officers of trust, and the disposal of the recesses of government. Aristomenes faithfully counseled, warned and urged, until good counsel became so obnoxious that the king delivered himself from its annoyance, by causing his faithful monitor to be poisoned, about the year 184.

"Justice has fallen in the streets, and truth can not enter. He that departeth from evil, maketh himself a prey."

From that time Epiphanes treated his subjects with the greatest cruelty, and abandoned himself to every excess. The nobility and people, worn out by his tyranny and indiscreet conduct, began to plot for his removal, and had well nigh matured their measures when their intentions came to the knowledge of the king. He immediately appointed, for prime minister, Polycrates, a man of firmness and decision, by whose counsel he was enabled to quiet the rebellion. He persuaded the chief movers in the affair, under solemn promises of personal safety, to submit to him; then breaking his engagement, after treating them with every imaginable cruelty, caused them to be put to death. This breach of faith and barbarity stirred up the second rebellion; but by the skill and discretion of Polycrates, this was in like manner quelled.

Some time after this difficulty, Epiphanes conceived the idea of invading Seleucus, of Syria. His officers inquired of him, by what means he expected to raise the money for the expedition. He replied that his friends were his treasury. They well remembered his past cruelty, treachery and entire disregard for the rights of the people, and presumed that he intended rapaciously to rob and destroy them; they therefore determined on a third rebellion, to save themselves and deliver Egypt. This time the king was poisoned, and they were successful. Thus perished Ptolemy Epiphanes at twenty-nine years of age, having been nominally king twenty-four years.

He died 108 B. C., leaving two sons and a daughter, Philo Metor, Phsycon and Cleopatra.

GREAT EXPEDITION OF ANTIOCHUS IN THE EAST.

The ancient Persian empire had been constituted by the union of several different States, among which were Media, Elam and Parthia. After the death of Alexander, Persia was again resolved into its original divisions, each separate State being subject to a governor, appointed by the kings of Syria.

Parthia had revolted from the Syrians, and established an independent kingdon. Arsaces was their first king, and his son, of the same name, had succeeded to the throne. Taking advantage of the wars in the west, the Parthians soon after the suppression of Molo's revolt, had invaded Media, and annexed it to their own kingdom.

Antiochus having regulated the affairs of his kingdom, and subdued Achæus, in Asia Minor, commenced a grand expedition to the east, B. C. 212, not only to recover Media, but to invade other countries in that vicinity. Of the wealth and splendor of ancient Media, authors speak in extravagant terms.

"This country," says Polybius, "is the most powerful kingdom in all Asia, as well for its extent as for the number and strength of its armies, and the great quantity of horses it produces. Media furnished all Asia with these beasts, and its pastures are so good that the neighboring monarchs send their studs there. Ecbatana is its capital. The edifices of this city surpass in richness and magnificence all others in the world. The king's palace is seven hundred fathoms around. Though all the wood-work was of cedar and cypress, yet no joining, even in the least piece of timber was visible. The beams, the ceilings and columns, which sustain the porticoes and piazzas, were covered with silver or gold plate, and all the tiles were of silver. The greatest part of these materials had been carried off by the Macedonians, under Alexander the Great, and the balance plundered by Antigonus and Seleucus Nicator. Nevertheless when Antiochus entered this kingdom, the temple of Ænea was still surrounded with gilted columns, and the soldiers found in it a great number of silver tiles, a few golden brick, and a great many of silver. All this was converted into specie, and stamped with the image of Antiochus, the whole amounting to four thousand talents, equal to three millions of dollars.

Between Syria and the interior of Media, lies a barren, sandy desert. Antiochus having devoted the first year to the recovery of Media, and spent the winter at the temple of Ænea, marched with his army across this desert, to attack the Persians in their capital. Arsaces was not surprised that Antiochus advanced as far as the temple, but had not supposed that he would advance with his army across a barren, sandy desert, where no water could be found upon the surface. It is related that the ancient Persians had constructed acqueducts from Mount Taurus to a fountain in the midst of this desert underground, and that from this fountain other acqueducts conducted it all through the desert; and that there were secret wells communicating with these acqueducts. Arsaces had sent men to stop the fountains of water, and cause the army of Antiochus to perish in the desert, but in vain; for Antiochus anticipating this movement, sent a detachment of his soldiers, who succeeded in beating back the Parthians and taking possession of the fountains. He soon after entered and subdued all Media, driving Arsaces entirely out of it. The remainder of the year was devoted to regulating the provinces, and preparing for future campaigns.

The next year was occupied in the successful subjugation of all Parthia. Arsaces was forced to retire into Hyrcania, on the east of the Caspian sea, where he thought he should be undisturbed. But the following year, 209, Antiochus invaded Hyrcania, marched through the country and besieged Seringis, the capital. After making a breach in the walls he took the city by storm, when the inhabitants surrendered at discretion. Arsaces retired from Seringis in good order, re-collected his army, consisting of one hundred and twenty thousand foot and twenty thousand horsemen, and so successfully resisted and harrassed Antiochus, that at length terms of peace were considered, and finally, in 208 agreed upon. By these terms Arsaces was to retain possession of Parthia and Hyrcania, and was to assist Antiochus in the recovery of the other revolted provinces. East of Hyrcania was another small kingdom called Bactra. This country had been invaded and subdued by Alexander the Great, and had generally been considered a dependency of Syria, since that time. Some time previous to these events, Theodotus, who had been appointed governor of Bactria, had revolted from Syria, and set up his own independent throne, which he had transmitted to his son, who was subsequently invaded and dethroned, by one Euthydemus, who was now king in his place. Against Euthydemus Antiochus next turned his arms, in 207 B. C. After a long and fruitless effort to subdue Bactriana, negotiations were opened. The agents of Euthydemus represented to Antiochus, that Bactra had revolted a long time ago; that Syria had made no effort to recover possession; that the original rebels were not now in possession of it; that the present occupant of the throne had acquired it by conquest, not from Syria, but from the rebels, and that the present king had never been subject to Antiochus, but was the rightful sovereign of the country, and that, for these reasons, the present invasion was entirely unjust. It is scarcely possible that the justice of the plea had any effect on Antiochus, at a time when all claims of dominion rested upon a successful conquest. But the embassadors of Euthydemus presented a still more powerful argument. The Scythians, a war-like people, on the north, inhabiting the hills and the wild plains of Tartary, were watching the progress of this war, and rejoiced to see the parties weakening themselves. So soon as they should be sufficiently reduced this terrible people would fall upon Bactriana and possess it for themselves. Antiochus saw the force of this argument, and a peace was therefore concluded. All the elephants of Euthydemus were to be given to Antiochus, and a future marriage agreed upon for the son of the king of Bactriana, and the daughter of the king of Syria. Antiochus was at this time about thirty-one years of age, and had been married about fifteen years.

He next crossed Mount Caucassus and entered India, with whose king he concluded a treaty, established his authority in Arachosia, Drangiana and Carmania, and spent the winter in that mild climate.

In 205 he returned through Persia, Babylonia and Mesopotamia, and arrived at Antioch in safety, having spent seven years in this expedition, which had been crowned with so great success. Success — that is, in destroying a great number of human beings, distracting and impoverishing the world, and depriving many small kingdoms of their right to govern themselves, that upon their ruins he might build one great empire and rule over many people, without regard to the happiness of society or the prosperity of the human race. Success in war signifies success in diminishing the happiness and increasing the sufferings of mankind, as if the world had not sorrow enough without such aid.

A little after this time, he received intelligence of the death of his old and familiar enemy, Philopater, the hero of Raphia.

The further history of Antiochus is so blended with those of Greece, Macedon and Rome, that it will be suspended until we can take a hasty survey of the state of affairs in those countries.

MACEDON.

Demetrius, king of Macedon, died B. C. 232, leaving a youthful son, Philip. Antigonus, a distant relation, was appointed guardian, and soon after married the widow, the mother of Philip. He immediately assumed the throne, which he held twelve years to the exclusion of the legitimate heir. He was often engaged in the affairs of the Greeks, which involved him in several wars. It is impossible to give any definite idea of these wars, without involving the general history of Greece, which would be foreign to our purpose; a few sketches only is all that I shall now give.

GREECE.

The larger and smaller peninsula south of Macedon, was the home of the once mighty people, the Greeks, whose valor in arms, whose wisdom in council, whose excellence in literature and philosophy, have been extolled by all succeeding generations. Greece, from the earliest times, had been composed of several States, holding at one period some relation to each other, and at others at war with each other, and still at others united in war for the common defense. Their former government was so variable, that, to describe it, would require the entire history of that people. Macedon, although in the immediate vicinity, and a colony originally planted by Greeks, was not considered any part of Greece. From the time of Philip, the father of Alexander the Great, if not earlier, the Macedonian monarchs had been desirous of bringing the States of Greece under their control, not only to gratify their ambition, but to subvert their republican forms of government; because every independent State and free city in their vicinity rebuked royal tyranny. Antigonus had been very much exposed to the fatigues of war, which had brought on a consumption. He gained a victory over the Illyrians, and his excess of joy on that occasion caused the rupture of a blood vessel, in consequence of which he soon after died, B. C. 220.

PHILIP, SON OF DEMETRIUS, B. C. 220

Achaia, one of the Grecian States, lying in the north part of Morea, had, by internal strifes, become reduced to the lowest possible condition. At length the Achæan league was formed, by which these difficulties were healed, and the State revived and prosperity again began to smile upon them. Ultimately several of the other States joined the league, while others refused to do so. Wars were frequent between the confederate and non-confederate States. The exact cause of these wars it is difficult to determine, except in so far as a predisposition to quarrel, made any little difficulty a sufficient pretext to gratify that disposition. The Achæans being somewhat in fear of their enemies, applied to the Macedonians for aid against the States that had not joined in the league. The Greeks ought to have understood that the invitation of a foreign king, though it might afford for the time some relief, would, in the end, entirely subvert all Greece, and place them under foreign masters. The first interference seems to have been by Antigonus, about the year 225 B. C. After his death, the same invitation was sent to Philip, which he accepted, and which resulted in the war of the league. The Ætolians were the instigators and chief promoters of this war. Of this people, Rollin thus speaks:

"The Ætolians, particularly in the time we are now speaking of, were becoming a very powerful people in Greece. Originally their territories extended from the river Achelous to the straits of the Gulf of Corinth, and the country of the Locrians, surnamed Ozolæ. But, in process of time, they had possessed themselves of several cities in Acamania, Thessaly, and other neighboring countries. They had much the same life upon land that pirates do at sea, that is, they were perpetually engaged in plunder and rapine. Wholly bent on lucre, they did not consider any gain as infamous, and were entire strangers to the laws of peace or war. They were thoroughly inured to toil, and intrepid in battle."

In this war, each party alternately invaded each country, burned their cities, robbed their treasures, murdered their inhabitants and desecrated their temples, took and lost many important posts, until wearied with their efforts they stopped to take breath, after having consumed five years in the war to no purpose, and aiming at the attainment of no definite object.

All this while, the inhabitants of Rhodes and Chios were using their kindest influences and their utmost endeavors to persuade these parties to sheath the sword, and be at peace. About this time was fought the famous battle of Raphia, between Ptolemy Philopater and Antiochus. Hannibal, the Carthagenian general, having crossed the Alps, descended upon Italy. At length Philip called a council, to deliberate upon terms of peace. The ambassadors of Rhodes and Chios were urging this measure, and the Ætolians sincerely desired peace. While Philip professed the same desire, he secretly inclined to continue the war until all Greece should have become so impoverished that he could entirely subject them to his own will. How much it is to be regretted that rulers and monarchs, in both ancient and modern times, are so slow to learn their true policy and their true interest. Instead of exhausting their treasury in bloody campaigns to extend their dominion over fallen territory, after first ruining it so as to render it scarcely worth possessing, if they should direct their attention and their ambition to developing the resources already possessed, to secure the peace, prosperity, happiness and intelligence of the people, they would receive greater revenue and greater honor, and rule over more subjects and more wealth, though upon less acres of ground. He who, within a State, by peaceful means causes two bushels of corn to grow, instead of one — two spears of grass to spring, instead of one — two families to find employment and gain subsistence, instead of one — two yards of cloth to be manufactured, instead of one — has done more for the wealth, honor and defense of his State, than if, by foreign conquest, he had thribbled its territory. Had this sound political maxim been received and followed, seas of blood that have been shed might have been saved.

While the council above referred to was in session, a courier from Macedonia arrived and placed a letter in the hands of Philip, informing him that the Romans had lost a great battle in Tuscany, and that Hannibal was master of all the open country of Italy. Philip handed the letter to his friend Demetrius, with a strict charge to communicate its contents to no one. The importance of this intelligence may not at first be apparent to the reader. Rome and Carthage were the two great powers of the West. They had been some time engaged in a war with each other; yet this fact seems to have attracted no great attention in the East until this time. It now became apparent that one or the other of these great nations must be overcome, and the fall of one and the triumph of the other, whichever it might be, would materially affect the balance of power throughout the world. Demetrius saw, at a glance, the importance of the recent intelligence, although he knew not how to make a proper use of it.

The narrow Adriatic sea above, separated the territory of Rome from Greece, Epirus and Macedon. Demetrius believed that Rome was fitted to fall and become a prey to foreigners. Should it be given to Carthage, or should Macedon possess a share of it? He immediately drew Philip aside from the council, inflamed his youthful ambition with schemes of conquest, and urged him to strike for glory and universal fame. He urged the king immediately to settle all difficulties with Greece, unite his forces with those of Hannibal, and invade Rome. He represented to him that Greece might be easily overcome, if any of the States did not voluntarily submit after he should have extended his empire in the West and gained invincible power.

Demetrius had personal ends to gain in this advice. He had formerly been king in the little island called Pharos, in the north-east part of the Adriatic sea. For some of his piratical doings, the Romans had invaded and taken from him his island and city, from which he had fled a fugitive, and entered the service of Philip. A desire for revenge, though often buried in the rubbish of other cares, seldom dies; and will often break forth again when a fitting opportunity presents, with increased intensity, though with more cool, deliberate purpose. Nothing could be more gratifying to the feelings of Demetrius, than to see the Macedonian arms invading and devastating territories of Rome. He might even hope to be again king of Pharos.

Philip was still young, yet he had acquired some experience. He had been deceived and betrayed by counsellors, whom he punished according to the merit of their treason; but he had not yet learned to suspect the motive of his present counsellor. He saw nothing in the advice of Demetrius, but devotedness to his own personal aggrandizement. He eagerly caught at the bait, and determined on war with Rome. That was an unfortunate decision; from that time his fortunes paled, and a dark cloud cast its shadow over the Macedonian empire, portentous of the coming storm that should ultimately sweep away the last remains of the Kingdom of Brass.

A council of negotiation was appointed at Naupatum, composed of delegates from the different States of Greece and Macedon, which resulted in a treaty of peace, which was to be perpetual; but which, nevertheless, continued but a few years.

Philip next sent ambassadors to Hannibal to propose a treaty of mutual coöperation against Rome. These ambassadors, by accident, fell into the hands of the Romans. With great adroitness and deceit, they represented that they had been sent by Philip to conclude a treaty of peace with the Romans. Their statement was believed, and an escort was given to conduct them safely to Rome. They, however, made their escape and fled to the camp of Hannibal. A treaty was concluded and reduced to writing, in which it was stipulated that the Roman possessions should be divided between them. The ambassadors, with others from Hannibal, now attempted their return to Philip, but were again intercepted and carried to Rome, where the lie would not a second time answer their purpose. The Carthaginians were recognized by their personal appearance, dress and language; and upon the ambassadors were found the written treaty, and the letters of Hannibal to the king of Macedon. Philip, not discouraged by this event, sent a second embassy, which succeeded in arriving at the camp of Hannibal, and returning in safety with the treaty to Macedon. Thus ended the year 216 B. C.

The winter was devoted to thoughts, plans, and dreams of future conquest. The Illyrians built one hundred vessels for Philip. With these, after spending some time in able discipline, he put to sea and first seized upon the city Oricum, situated upon the western coast of Epirus. Valerius, a commander with a fleet, lay off at no great distance, reached anchor and put his ships in readiness for sailing. Philip having left a small garrison at Oricum, proceeded to Apollonia, and laid siege to that city. The next day, Valerius arrived and retook Oricum, and captured the garrison left by Philip. He then sent Nevius, an able and experienced officer, with a large reinforcement, to the relief of Apollonia. Nevius landed at the mouth of the river Taus, marched through a by-way, and unperceived by the enemy, in the night entered the city of Apollonia. The Macedonians supposing themselves perfectly secure, because an arm of the sea lay between them and the enemy, had neglected the usual precautions, and established no guards. Nevius learning this fact, marched again out of Apollonia, and entered the camp of the Macedonians, where he found the soldiers asleep. The work of death began; the cries of the wounded and dying fell upon the ear of their sleeping comrades, and aroused them from their dreams of conquest and glory to the stern reality — the enemy is in their tents. Arising in wild consternation, they seek safety by flight. Philip himself but half awake, and almost naked, with difficulty escaped to his ships, his soldiers pressing hard after him. Three thousand of them were either killed or taken prisoners.

Valerius soon received intelligence of this affair, and sent forward his navy to block up the mouth of the river, and thus prevent the escape of the enemy. Philip found it impossible to proceed further, or to regain the sea. He therefore set fire to his vessels, and with the shattered remains of his army returned by land to Macedon. Thus ended the great scheme of universal conquest.

The castle in the air has fallen. The beautiful cloud whose majestic cap towered high to heaven, has vanished, and has left nothing but an oppressive sense of vacancy. Philip's grand schemes of the conquest of Rome and of immortal fame, have disappeared forever; yet he has commenced a war which must result in the destruction of the third and the ascendancy of the fourth beast.

Previous to the battle of Apollonia, Philip had exhibited talent superior to his years. He had sustained a reputation for energy, discretion, and sound judgment. Subsequent to that event, having altogether abandoned the idea of winning a great name, he became insensible to all moral worth and committed the basest of crimes.

The treacherous, deceitful character of the leopard which had destroyed its feeder, was fully developed; yet, at times, he displayed some courage and won a few battles. He cast his eyes upon the rich fields of Messenia, and desired to possess them. This was one of the States of the Achæan league, which had assisted him in all the Grecian war, and was a party to the treaty of peace concluded just before engaging in the war with the Romans. Philip landed an army in Messenia, and by pretensions of friends, endeavored to persuade them to deliver up to him their fortresses, that he might protect them against the Romans. Suspecting his purpose, and being themselves at peace with Rome, they declined receiving his protection. He then threw off his mask, declared himself their enemy, and ravaged their country, committing acts of rapine and cruelty. He then retired with his booty into Macedon. Aratus, the chief ruler of Achaia, and head and originator of the league, had long been the friend of Philip, and by his counsels and aid, had secured that monarch most of his success. Owing to the indiscretion and injustice of Philip, he had withdrawn from his court. Aratus was as far a just and upright prince as in those tempestuous times a man could safely be. He remonstrated with Philip against this cruelty and injustice, and breach of faith with the people of Messenia.

The court of Philip was filled with corrupt advisers, who persuaded him that the glory of a king consisted in causing his subjects to yield a blind obedience to his will, whatever that will might be. He listened to their bad counsel, and sought by every possible means to distress his subjects, and crush them beneath his feet. One of the growing signs of despotism in a government, and the corruption of statesmen, is the desire to transfer appointing power from the people to the executive, whereby he may reward his partisans for favoring his infamous and oppressive measures, courtiers who advocate his policy with the desire of obtaining by favor posts of honor, profit and trust, to which they could never expect to rise by merit. Such counselors should ever be frowned down by upright rulers, and distrusted by an upright people.

Philip was not insensible to shame, and as he possessed no virtue in himself, he could endure none in others. He therefore employed one of his creatures, who, under the disguise of great friendship, found means to give slow poison to Aratus the senior. Of this, after some time, he died, a lingering and distressing death, greatly beloved by his people. With the wife of his son, Aratus junior, who was one of his best generals, Philip had been criminally intimate. He administered to the unsuspecting husband a poison which destroyed his senses, and after a time of raving madness, terminated his life.

Illyricum, lying north of Epirus, was a distinct State of itself, and not a part of the Macedonian kingdom. At this time it was in friendly alliance with Rome. It does not appear that either the Romans or the Illyrians had actually and formally declared war, but as Philip had previously commenced upon Rome, she had defended herself and repulsed him. In 213 B. C., Philip suddenly invaded Illyria, and captured the city of Lissus.

Rome now felt it her duty to interfere in the affairs of Greece, to defend her allies, and to check the barbarity of Philip. M. Valerius Levinus, a Roman prætor, was sent out in 211, to look after these interests. He succeeded in detaching the restless war-like Ætolians from their alliance with Philip, and attaching them to the Roman cause. Some other States were induced to follow their example, and the old war of the league was revived, with very nearly the same division of parties as on the former occasion.

Ætolia had always been the leading State on one side and Achaia on the other, in these wars. Philip was at Pella, his capital, where Achaia and Acarnania sent embassadors to inform him that a treaty had been formed by Ætolia and others with the Romans. A ludicrous little affair occurred about this time. The Ætolians prepared to invade the Acarnanians, their near neighbors, who had closely adhered to the interests of Philip, and were therefore fit subjects for the spoils of the Ætolians.

The Acarnanians being at a distance from Philip, despaired of receiving aid in time to save themselves; they did not suppose they could alone resist the war-like Ætolians, and therefore prepared for death. They sent their wives, children and old men, with their treasures, to Epirus for safety, and resolved to die sword in hand; they made arrangements for their funeral: the Epirots were to come and bury them after the battle. A monument was to be erected over their bodies, all of which were to be laid in one grave. The inscription upon the monument was prepared in these words:

"Here lie the Acarnanians, who died fighting for their country, against the violence and injustice of the Ætolians."

They then set out to meet the enemy upon the border of their country. Despair lent them courage and gave them a terrific appearance. The Ætolians became alarmed and retired, and no battle whatever was fought. The Acarnanians therefore returned home to attend their own funeral.

B. C. 210, Levinus besieged and captured Antagras of Phocis, in Achaia, and gave the city to the Ætolians, keeping the plunder for himself. The reader will perhaps inquire why, and on what account this city should be plundered and made subject to a foreign State, and what was the war itself about. Similar questions have often arisen in relation to the events of this period. We can sometimes discover the real or pretended cause of these wars, but more frequently that cause is so obscure, so indefinite, that it is not capable of being made manifest. The general fact was, that nations engaged in war, as school-boys play ball, just to see which can beat, and to plunder and destroy each other.

Let it be remembered that this is a part of the kingdom of the leopard. Why should the leopard treacherously and from his ambush, spring upon and devour the kid? Simply because he is hungry and is fond of blood. The different

States of Greece often took sides from mere caprice or fancy, sometimes for the convenience of easy plunder, and sometimes through fear of a superior power. It was rarely that the sides were chosen with any reference to equity or justice. Although war was not formally declared, Achaia was friendly to Philip, and Ætolia was not. This, in that day, was a sufficient reason for invading each others' territory, plundering cities, and butchering their inhabitants. Had these calamities fallen upon Philip, instead of his peaceful allies, there would have been a greater semblance of justice. About this time Levinus being elected to the office of consul, was re-called to Rome, and Sulpitius was sent a prætor in his place. Attalus, king of Pergamos, Pleuratus, king of Byzantium, and Scerdiledes, king of Illyria, joined the confederacy of the Romans and the Ætolians, and aided in the war. Both parties now sought to induce the Spartans to join their side.[*] Sparta was at this time divided into two factions, the one decidedly in favor of the interests of king Philip, and the other equally partial to those of the Ætolians.

In the midst of these divisions, and favored by their animosity, one Machanides had subverted their government, and made himself tyrant over them. The result of negotiations was, that Sparta once more cast her lot with Ætolia. This was just what Machanides wanted. He would thus have the opportunity of plundering other Grecian States, under the protection of the Ætolians and the Romans; and what was to him still more desirable, it would furnish him a pretext to plunder and exterminate, by cruel excesses and

---

[*] Lacedæmonia, sometimes called Laconia, was the most south-eastern part of Greece, lying in the Morea, anciently called the Pelleponesus; Sparta was its most important and capital city. The entire people are sometimes called Spartans, sometimes Laconians, and sometimes Lacedæmonians. In the preceding war of the league, Lacedæmonia had united with the Ætolians against the Achaians and Philip.

banishment, that portion of the citizens who were opposed to his tyranny, and who were generally opposed to renewing the war with Philip. Attalus and Pleuratus had joined the confederacy with other and more worthy motives. By looking at the map it will be seen that these territories were contiguous to those of Philip. They ruled over commercial nations, whose interests were peace. But Philip was not a man of peace. If he was not involved in war with Greece or Rome, or both, they feared he would be annoying them, as he often had done. It was natural, therefore, that they should desire to keep so ambitious and treacherous a prince occupied. It must be recollected that Pergamos, and indeed nearly all the States of Asia Minor, were originally Greek colonies, spoke the Greek language, and sympathized with the interests of Greece.

Rome was at this time a republic; she sympathized with her republican neighbors, and desired them to be secure from the grasping ambition of the king of Macedon. She also desired to check the pride of Philip, who, without cause, had dared to make war upon her. It does not appear that Rome had, at that time, any idea whatever, of conquering or subjecting either Macedon or Greece, or any other part of the east, to her authority. She only desired her own safety, and the peace and independence of Greece. Rome was likewise still engaged in her war with the Carthaginians, and Hannibal was yet in the field. For these reasons, although engaged in the affairs of Greece, she only gave a limited and indirect attention to them for a number of years. B. C. 208, Sulpitius and Attalus operated chiefly by their fleets, while the Spartans and the Ætolians were more efficient on land.

Scopas had retired to Egypt, and Pyrrhus commanded the Ætolians. Philip hastened to the relief of his allies. His enemies met him at Lamia, where he defeated them in two battles, and shut them up closely in the city. He then retired with his army to Phalaria. Shall the sword devour forever — shall all mankind be interrupted in their regular and useful pursuits, by the folly of a few quarrelsome neighbors? Ptolemy, king of Egypt, the inhabitants of Athens, of Rhodes and of Chios, sent embassadors to urge Philip and the States of Greece to be at peace. Ptolemy was so steeped in debauchery that he could have had but little policy whatever in this movement; yet sober statesmen and nobles there were in Egypt, whose far-reaching political sagacity discerned that if Greece should become subject to Philip, he would become a powerful monarch, and too near a neighbor. Egypt possessed Crete, Cyprus and Cilicia; they might be the next prize for the ruthless king of Macedon. Egypt therefore desired the independence of Greece. Rhodes and Chios were isles of the sea, and independent States. Their commerce extended over all waters; this commerce could not but be interrupted and suffer, during the war in their immediate vicinity.

After various negotiations without success, and a number of battles with no definite result except a wanton destruction of life, in 104 B. C., a peace was concluded between Philip, the Romans, and the several Grecian States. It was, however, of short continuance.

INVASION OF SIOS, RHODES, PERGAMOS AND ABYDOS, BY PHILIP, B. C. 203 TO 201.

Bythynia was a small kingdom, situated directly south of the Black Sea, and east of Constantinople. It was a part of the once kingdom of Thrace, which had long before been dismembered. At the time of which we are speaking, Prusias was governor of Bythynia. He was the son-in-law of Philip of Macedon. Philip, like any other pirate, sought to rob somebody, and Prusias was disposed to point out the game. Sios was a small city in Bythynia, with which the Rhodians and others had some trade. Prusias, pretending to have received some insult from the people of Sios, delivered it up to the destroyer. Philip captured the town by force of arms, plundered its treasures, and laid it in the dust. He put part of the inhabitants to death by the most cruel torture, and sold the others, men, women and children, into slavery worse than death. This uncalled for cruelty, as well it might, provoked the displeasure of the Rhodians, as well as the Ætolians. There seems to be no apology or extenuating circumstance on record for this wanton barbarity, or even for invading this little city. Philip next turned his piratical navy against Rhodes. He fought one battle upon the water, in which he was somewhat successful, but did not take the city. He next invaded Pergamos, whose king was Attalus. He besieged the city, but was unable to capture it. Enraged at his failure, he attacked the temples of the country, demolished them and their idols, and carried off all their valuable contents. In 202, Attalus joined his forces with those of Rhodes, against their common invader, and a battle was fought off Chios, (now Scio), in which Philip was terribly beaten. He lost in killed three thousand Macedonians, and six thousand allies; and two thousand Macedonians and seven hundred Egyptian allies were taken prisoners. Although he had sustained great loss, and was forced to abandon the war upon these two powers, he still pushed on for conquest and plunder. He invaded Thrace and the Chersonesus, where, although he met with some energetic resistance, several cities submitted to him.

THE FALL OF ABYDOS.

Directly across the Strait from Sestus, and near where the Dardanelles empties into the Archipelago, on the Asiatic side, stood the city of Abydos. Its site was a rising ground with a gradual descent in every direction. Crowning such an eminence, and overlooking the narrow straits that connect the sea, with the outlet of all the upper waters, Abydos must have presented an imposing appearance. It was a city of some military, as well as commercial importance.

The rapacious Philip could not endure its prosperity, nor abstain from coveting its treasures. He therefore invaded its territory, and commenced a regular siege upon the city. He was greatly exasperated at the obstinate resistance with which the Abydenians met and often repulsed him from their walls. No art of war then known, was omitted either in the attack or defense. The conflict often rose into a fury resembling the death-struggle of savage beasts. Philip, landing great machines, brought them against the walls of the city, on the side toward the water. The Abydenians by their ballistæ, hurled masses of rock against them, and dashed them to pieces, or succeeded in setting them on fire. Even the ships were exposed to be burned, and the besiegers were often in danger of perishing. On the land side, though also terribly resisted, the invaders carried mines under the outer walls, and were sapping their foundations; they even extended their trench under the second wall. Perceiving the progress that the enemy had made, and the prospect of being speedily assaulted, the Abydenians sent to Philip, and proposed to surrender upon terms one would think quite reasonable enough to have been accepted: they only asked that the soldiers of Rhodes and Ephesus, who had come to their assistance, should be permitted to return to their homes unmolested, and that the citizens of Abydos should be permitted to retire into other countries, wherever they pleased, with the clothing they then had on, leaving for the Macedonians all the rich treasures which their commerce had accumulated.

Philip replied that they had only to surrender at discretion or continue to fight. The citizens in transports of depair, assembled to consider what was to be done, inferring that as these humiliating terms were rejected, some worse fate was in reserve for them, such as befel the unfortunate people of Sios, who were all massacred or sold into slavery. In this council, the frantic people came to one very wise and just, and several very rash, foolish and wicked resolutions. They first gave freedom to all their slaves, the better to animate them to defend the city. They then shut up all the women and children in the temple; brought all their gold and silver into the public square, and sent their other valuable effects into the vessels of their allies. Next the wise old men, too feeble to fight, yet possessed of sufficient energy to do the work assigned them, were called in and required to take an oath, that the instant the enemy should enter the inner wall, they would kill the women and children, set fire to the galleys, burn the goods and throw the gold and silver into the sea. The priests were then called in, before whom the soldiers took a solemn oath either to conquer or die sword in hand. They required priests and priestesses to pronounce the most solemn curses upon any one of them who should not keep this most unwise and rash obligation.

Soon the undermining of the invaders caused the inner wall to tumble to the earth, and exposed the city to the assault of the enemy. The Abydenians were shortly in the trench, where, with the ferocity of despair, they fought, and for a time held their ground, dealing out death on every hand, although fresh supplies of Macedonians were brought to stand upon their dead comrades. Night put an end to the bloody conflict, leaving it quite doubtful who had gained the victory. The breach was covered with the dead bodies of the Abydenians, and of those not slain, so overcome with fatigue and covered with wounds, that they could scarcely stand. Now the dreadful oath to kill the women and children, began to stare in the face those who were to do the deed. Four of the principal citizens, who could not endure to have their wives slain, determined to send to the camp of Philip, the priests in their sacred robes of office, to implore mercy, which was accordingly done next morning at day-break, and the gates of the city were opened to the enemy. The surviving soldiers vented their curses against the men who surrendered the city and saved the lives of those who had been devoted to death, alleging that it was awful injustice to those who had perished believing that the oath would be kept.

Philip, without further opposition, marched into Abydos, and seized all the treasures, collected as they were, in one place. Now a new and fearful tragedy was being enacted before the eyes of the Macedonians. Wounds, rage and disappointment had rendered the Abydenians frantic, if not insane. Some were smothering their wives and children, others were stabbing them with their own hands. Some were trying to strangle them, and still others were precipitating them from the tops of houses. Thus death presented itself in all variety of violent forms.

Philip, old blood-thirsty warrior as he was, became terrified at these sights. He ordered his soldiers to stop plundering and try to save the people from suicide. He published that three days of safety should be granted to them if they would not kill themselves. But the appeal was in vain. Their fellows and the husbands of these women had died in their defense, and they thought it dishonorable to survive them. Not a life was saved, except those whose hands were tied to prevent them from committing suicide.

Rome heard of the piratical war with Philip, and sent embassadors to protest against his course. These embassadors arrived at the camp of Philip, while the siege of Abydos was in progress. They protested, and threatened in the name of Rome, but to no purpose.

Philip answered them roughly, and in effect bade Rome attend to her own affairs and let him alone. The Romans soon declared war against him, defeated him in many an engagement, stripped him of all his territories acquired by conquest, brought him to his senses, and made him a dependant upon their will for the rest of his life. But how could his humiliation bring any compensation to the butchered citizens of Abydos. Alas! this world's justice comes too late to be of any value. Violence triumphs and her victims perish. Little more of interest is known of Philip, except his domestic calamities, by which he was induced to slay his innocent son, Demetrius, and was succeeded upon the throne, by Persius, an illegitimate son, who was subsequently captured by the Romàns, and all Macedonia absorbed into their empire.

ANTIOCHUS AND THE ROMANS.

THE war of Rome with Carthage had been concluded, and Hannibal had retired for a time from the field of Mars. The Romans had overcome Philip and subdued Macedon, and thus, as they supposed, secured freedom to the Greeks of Europe. Antiochus having returned from his great eastern expedition, in which he was crowned with unparalleled success, against the feeble, effeminate Asiatics, now supposed himself invincible against any foe. Like many others, even in our time, he entertained a contempt for western people. The East seldom learns to appreciate the West. The East is the land of luxury, of pompous ceremony and display; the West is the land of strength, of action and of successful enterprise. Antiochus now entertained an idea of subjugating all Asia Minor to his control; after which he contemplated an advance into Europe, there to contend with Rome for the empire of the world. These lofty schemes he intended to conceal in his own breast until he found means to execute them. But the keen sagacity of the Romans detected his plans; they were prepared to meet him. Rome wisely determined, as they had freed the cities of the Greeks from foreign masters, they would not permit those of Asia Minor to be subdued.

In 196 B. C., the movements of Antiochus indicated an intention to invade Asia Minor. Smyrna, Lampsacus, and other cities along the sea coast, becoming alarmed, applied to the Romans for protection. It was manifestly detrimental to the interests of Rome, that Antiochus should establish himself along that coast, where he might annoy her allies, and at his pleasure, suddenly invade Europe. Rome therefore lent a willing ear to the call, and sent embassadors to Antiochus, who, before their arrival, had commenced the siege of those cities, and had crossed the straits into Europe, and made himself master of the Chersonesus of Thrace. Here he commenced building the city of Lysimachia, intending to construct a new kingdom in Thrace, for his son Seleucus, with this city for the capital. While thus occupied, the Roman embassadors arrived (one of them was L. Cornelius), at the camp. After the ceremonies of civility, they proceeded to business. The interest of the Romans was at that time to diminish as far as possible the power of Antiochus, who might otherwise be dangerous to Rome. Let it be remembered that some of the cities and territories of southern Asia Minor had belonged to the Ptolemies, but had been taken from that crown by Antiochus, of which an account is given in the history of Ptolemy Epiphanes. The cities which, at this time, were being besieged, had been subdued by Philip, and again restored to liberty by the

Romans, in their recent war with Macedon. Cornelius now in the name of Rome spoke — not as a suppliant entreating favor, not as an equal soliciting a treaty—but with authority as a master, he commanded that the cities belonging to Ptolemy should be immediately restored to him, and those against which Antiochus was now waging war should be instantly left to their liberty. He next reproved Antiochus for daring to cross into Europe, and bade him return to Asia. Antiochus, the conqueror of the East, ever surrounded with flatterers, was unused to listen to the language of authority. He answered with a haughty insolence, for which in a few years he paid most dearly, as we shall see in the sequel. As to the cities which belonged to Egypt he replied, that matter would be settled when Ptolemy should marry his daughter. As to the other cities of Asia Minor, they should receive their liberty from him, not from the Romans. In regard to his invasion of Europe, he was only taking possession of his rightful territory, conquered from Lysimachus, by his predecessor, Seleucus I., four generations previous, and that he had a perfect right there to establish his son on the throne of European Thrace. He indignantly demanded what right Rome could have to dictate to him which cities he might conquer, and which not. The embassadors from the invaded cities were now admitted, and complained of the invasion. The Romans heard, and judged that the acts of Antiochus were unjustifiable. Antiochus, offended at the bold plainness of the embassadors, declared in effect that Rome had no right to judge in these matters, and ought to attend to her own affairs, and allow him to do the same. The council broke up in confusion, with no other result than the manifestation of the fact that Rome, the greatest power of the West, and Antiochus, the greatest monarch of the East, must settle their difficulties on the field of battle.

Just at this time occurred the rebellion of Scopas, in

Egypt, which was however soon quelled, but out of which grew the rumor that Ptolemy was dead. Antiochus now manifested how little regard he had for Egypt, and how strong his determination to rule supreme. He started immediately for the conquest of all Egypt. But learning his mistake he sailed to attack the island of Cyprus, which belonged to Ptolemy. A storm arose, shattered his fleet, and frustrated all his purposes, and he retired to Antioch, with the fragments of his army and navy, and rested through the winter, devising new campaigns. The Roman embassadors having settled affairs in relation to Philip of Macedon, and held their fruitless interview with Antiochus, were witnesses to these ambitious projects of Antiochus, and understood them.

They returned to Rome, reported all, and apprised the Senate that although they had closed the war with Macedon, they must now prepare for a greater and more extensive one. They assured the Senate that whatever might be the promises of Antiochus, he certainly intended to invade Europe, and undo all that Rome had done for the freedom of the Greeks; even if he did not invade Rome itself. All perceived that these accusations were founded on truth, and immediately prepared for the forthcoming event. Greece was not yet entirely free from evil. Nabis, the tyrant, exceeded his authority in Sparta, and resisted the Romans. The Ætolians, ever restless and impatient of restraint, anxious for an opportunity to engage in war for the sake of plunder, were ready to throw off the yoke of obedience to Rome. These were elements that Antiochus might use to further his schemes. Embassadors were again sent out to watch closely the designs of Nabis, and to observe all the momements of Antiochus; but other steps were taken by Rome beside sending embassadors. They prepared to enforce their orders with an army.

Meanwhile a council was held in Rome. The Romans occupied the year 195, in partially subduing Nabis and regulating affairs in Greece. In the spring Antiochus left Antioch and repaired to Ephesus, to concert measures for future wars. He was now pondering in his mind whether it would be safest to declare war against Rome, and then make war upon the cities and States that had put themselves under Roman protection, or to invest and capture these cities singly without any formal declaration. Just at this time an event occurred that determined his purpose. Since the conclusion of the war between Rome and Carthage, the great Hannibal had been trying to remain in quiet. But he found it impossible to do so. The fires of ambition, the restless spirit of enterprise, and the deadly hate of Rome, kept the elements of his soul agitated. He kept an eye on all the affairs of the world. He well understood the relations between Rome and Syria, and was suspected of holding secret correspondence with Antiochus. Whether true or not, the charge reached Rome, and commissioners were appointed to visit Carthage and ascertain the facts. Hannibal did not wait for their arrivals, but having a vessel at his command, he immediately left Carthage, and soon presented himself at Antioch. But Antiochus had gone to Ephesus.

Hannibal followed him, and while the king of Syria was deliberating what to do, Hannibal arrived. Hannibal, the enemy of Rome, the great hero of many generations, was now in the council of Antiochus. The king no longer doubted his ability to cope with Rome. Very little was done in the year 194, except to regulate the affairs of Nabis in Greece, and to augment the armies of Rome and Syria.

The year 193 B. C., was marked by vigorous preparations for war on the part of the two great powers of the world. At Rome the embassadors of the cities of Asia Minor, and those of Antiochus and of other portions of the world, were pleading their cause with the Senate. The affairs of Syria were so extensive and complex, that a more private council was appointed, in which Quintus and his colleague, on the part of Rome, heard the complaints of the representatives of Asia Minor and the embassadors of Antiochus.

The cities claimed their freedom; the Syrians were not authorized to yield up any of the lofty pretentions of Antiochus. The council concluded without settlement, but convinced the Romans of the necessity of war with Antiochus. His agents solicited Rome not to let loose the dogs of war, but were unwilling to relinquish one jot of those claims that provoked the war. The various embassadors on the Eastern question had scarcely departed, before others arrived from Carthage, informing the Romans that Hannibal was with Antiochus, and from his movements it was certain that they were preparing to invade Europe.

Hannibal was indeed advising Antiochus to declare war against Rome, and counselling how that war ought to be conducted. Had the Carthaginian counsel been pursued, the fate of the war might have been materially changed, but the effeminate Syrian could easier approve than execute his plan. Hannibal told him that war was certain, whether he chose it or not, and that it were better to choose than be compelled. He also advised that Roman and not Syrian ground be made the theater of action. Attack and eat up the food of the enemy's country, and not be invaded and eaten up. He desired Antiochus to march immediately into Greece, take advantage of the discordant element there, to make himself master, and after rest and preparation, hold out the appearances of invading Italy itself. Seeming always on the point of moving forth with this intention, he would thus cause Rome to exhaust herself in the defense of home, while he, (Hannibal), would retire to Carthage, where he had many friends who would rally to his call. With these he would invade Rome on the opposite side. In this mauner they could keep Rome in trouble, consume her resources, and devour her substance; and while this was passing, Antiochus could not only establish his authority in the free cities of Asia Minor, but gain a sure footing in Greece, and ultimately overcome Rome itself. Hannibal assured Antiochus that if he did not pursue this policy, Rome would certainly enter Asia, and treat him in this manner. The result confirmed the worth of this sagacious counsel. Antiochus approved but did not profit by the advice. Hannibal sent a Tyrian into Carthage to sound the people, and prepare adherents against his arrival, but the agent was discovered, and escaped with difficulty. The whole affair being thus made known, was communicated to the Romans, who now feared a war with both Carthage and Syria at the same time. But Carthage had made already a terrible experience of the effects of war with Rome, and remained quiet.

The Ætolians of Greece, full of hatred against the Romans, now attempted to induce Philip of Macedon, once again to rebel and engage in a war with Rome, assuring him that all Greece was tired of these new masters, and that all the Greeks and also Antiochus would unite with him in such a war. They also sent word to Nabis to rise against Rome with such of the Greeks as were under his control, assuring him that Antiochus and Philip were already engaged to sustain him in the effort. A third embassador repaired to the court of Antiochus, with just the same assurances in regard to the others. But neither Philip nor Antiochus dared place implicit confidence in the Ætolians, who within a few years had been on all sides of every question, fought for and against all parties, and changed sides with every fleeting change of success or defeat. Antiochus, although he heartily entered into all their schemes, had the caution not to declare himself openly, but proceeded in his work secretly. He proceeded to consummate the marriage of his daughter with Ptolemy Epiphanes, so as to secure peace on the part of Egypt. Another daughter, Antiochia, he offered in marriage to Eumenes, king of Pergamos, but that sagacious prince saw less advantage in being the son-in-law of Antiochus, and involved all his wars, than in his independence and the friendship of Rome. He, therefore, declined the proposed alliance, and Antiochus drove a different bargain, giving his daughter to Arianthes, king of Cappadocia. Eumenes clearly saw what we all would see from the result, that this marriage was consummated without any reference to the happiness of his daghter, or designed to confer favor upon his son-in-law, but simply to subject the latter to his control, and make him contribute to the advancement of his schemes of ambition. When the war was completed, he would be just as ready to rob his own children as any other. The marriage was consummated in 229, after which, in the depth of winter, Antiochus repaired to Ephesus; from whence he sent his son back to Syria, to take care of the home cabals. But he found it necessary to march back to the East, to subdue the Pissidians who had revolted from him.

War having not yet been formally declared, Rome sent three embassadors to Antiochus. They repaired first to Pergamos, where they were assured of the regard of Eumenes, who, possessing but a small country, feared that he should be devoured by Antiochus, for which reason he earnestly desired Rome to declare war against him.

Antiochus having quelled the revolt of Pissidia, had retired to Appama. Sulpitius, one of the embassadors, being sick, was left at Pergamos, while Villus proceeded to Ephesus, where he met Hannibal. He here displayed great diplomatic tact, by consulting often with Hannibal, assuring him he had nothing to fear from the Romans. Although these consultations were of no value in themselves, they produced a desirable result, for Antiochus learning the intimacy of Villus and Hannibal, suspected the latter to be an enemy in disguise, attempting to reconcile himself with Rome by betraying the king of Syria into their hands. This, though false, caused Antiochus to avoid the counsel of Hannibal and distrust his friendship.

From Ephesus, Villus repaired to Appama, where he met with Antiochus. Each party criminated the other, and the interview closed with no definite result, except an increased hatred of each against the other. The conference was broken off by the sudden death of the son of Antiochus. The king repaired to Ephesus to mourn his loss, while Villus retired to Pergamos, where he found his colleague entirely recovered. Soon after, the embassadors, at the request of Antiochus, appeared at Ephesus, where another interview was had, but still with no more harmony of counsel. Negotiations were broken off, and the embassadors returned to Rome.

Left to himself, Antiochus summoned a great council of his own friends, none of whom would dare give advice different from the king's own choice. They flattered him as the greatest of Monarchs, and urged him immediately to declare war against Rome, and pass over into Europe. One Alexander of Acarnania, especially exhorted him not to delay, and gave substantially the same advice that Hannibal had previously given. All united in condemning the insolent demand of the Romans. Ah! they who roll in oriental luxury, little understand the inflexible energy of the hardy western soldier. Hannibal was not called to the council, on account of the suspicion excited against him; but subsequently he, by his public acts of hostility against Rome, regained the confidence of Antiochus. Thus ended the year 192 B. C.

Nabis, the tyrant of Greece, although brought to terms, and a treaty with Rome, had violated that treaty, and she was again compelled to declare war against him. An army was sent to Greece to aid the Achæans against the tyrant. The great Philopœmen was at the head of the Grecian army. While these things were transpiring, the Ætolians sent an earnest invitation to Antiochus, to invade Greece. A messenger was sent in return from Antiochus to the Ætolians, who described in glowing colors and pompous language, the power, glory, and riches of Antiochus, who would soon come into Greece and deliver the people from the yoke of the Romans. Antiochus heartily accepted the invitation to enter Greece; he did not wait for the arrival of his army from Syria, and the forces which were marching to join him. He had invaded but not yet subdued Smyrna, Lampsacus, and Troas.

These powerful enemies he left in the rear, and indiscreetly, at an unsuitable time, and not in the manner recommended by Hannibal, entered Greece with some ten thousand foot and five hundred horse, altogether too small a force to hold even a defenceless country, much less sustain himself on foreign soil against powerful enemies. Arriving in Greece, he called a council at Lamia, made a speech, apologizing for coming with so few forces, and assured them he would soon fill all Greece with his invincible army, and navy, engines of war, etc., and instead of talking about arbitrating between them and the Romans, spoke of himself as the head of their army, and proposed to lead them against their enemies.

The wise and grave members of the Ætolian council, saw that they had only promises instead of aid, and a master instead of an auxiliary; yet the faction succeeded in passing a vote declaring Antiochus the commander in chief of the Ætolian forces. Then came the deliberation upon the question, how shall we begin? whom shall we attack? where and upon what shall we commence the war? Very important questions indeed, at that late hour, after having entered the foreign country.

They proposed to attack the Island of Chalcis, but fearing to do so, after some demonstrations, retired to the city of Demetrius. They next tried, but in vain, to win the Achæans to their cause. Failing in this, they retired again to Chalcis, where the gates were opened from within, by a faction who chose to favor the cause of the Ætolians and Antiochus. The Romans now declared war against him and his adherents, and the hostile forces were soon put in motion. With all the diplomacy of Antiochus, he was able to form but few alliances, for just at this juncture, Egypt, Carthage, Syracuse, and Philip of Macedon, with others, sent embassadors with men, and ships, corn, wine, oil, and money, to aid the Roman cause against the Syrian monarch. Antiochus now found it necessary to hold council with his eyes open to the facts, instead of his ears open to the voice of flattery. Hannibal was now in his council, and advised the most strenuous efforts to win Philip to his cause; but should that fail, to send Seleucus with an army to invade Macedon from the north-east, and thus prevent Philip from aiding the Romans. He also urged Antiochus to hasten his troops from Asia, and march to the west of Greece, and from thence sail immediately to attack Rome at home, asserting constantly, as he had often done before, that the only place to conquer Rome was in Italy. Antiochus was still surrounded by courtiers who loved the luxury of the camp, but not the struggle and danger of the field of battle. They therefore advised him against invading Italy; first, because if successful, Hannibal, who had advised it, would receive the glory of that success, and second, because he

14

could not fail of overcoming the Romans with his numerous hosts. His indolence, not his judgment, caused him to reject the only counsel at that time of any value to him. He hesitated; sent for his army and navy in Asia, and squandered away his time in a fruitless expedition against Megara, then retired into Chalcis, where the foolish old monarch, instead of soliciting the favors of Mars, fell asleep in the lap of Cupid.

He fell desperately in love with the daughter of a man at whose house he chanced to lodge; he a man of more than fifty years, and she a maid of less than twenty. Forgetting the great object of the expedition—the deliverance of Greece, and the conquest of Rome—he married the maid, and, spent the winter in celebrating the nuptials in riotous debauchery. The army caught more fully than before the spirit of revelry, and the winter passed away while they were being enervated and unfitted to cope with the more temperate Romans. The spring was approaching, and Antiochus was aroused from his revery by receiving information that the Roman consul was in Thessaly, not far distant—that the storm had prevented the army and navy from Asia from landing, and that the forces of Greek allies, on which he so much depended, had been greatly over-estimated, and that of those who could once have been relied upon, many, during his carousal, had forsaken his standard.

He had less than ten thousand men. By a desperate effort, he now gained the straits of Thermopylæ, and there attempted to defend himself, but was attacked by the Romans, defeated, and most of his army cut to pieces, while he, with the very small number of five hundred men, retired, first to Chalcis, and then to Ephesus.

In the action at Thermopylæ, a stone struck Antiochus,

and broke a number of his teeth, giving him such pain that he was compelled to retire, leaving his soldiers to perish by the hands of his enemies.

The remainder of the year was occupied by the Romans in subduing and punishing the Ætolians, and other disaffected Greeks.

The King of Syria, abandoning all thought of the conquest of Rome, supposed the war at an end, and resigned himself to pleasure, and the pernicious counsel of his flatterers. But Hannibal, at length, once more roused him to a sense of his danger, assuring him that soon he would not have to fight Europe for Rome, but for his own crown and kingdom, and that Asia would be the field of conflict; that he must immediately prepare either to defend himself, sword in hand, or resign all thoughts of retaining the empire. Aroused by these judicious counsels, he again sent orders to hasten the march of his eastern army. To prevent the Romans from crossing into Asia, he sent a fleet into Chersonesus, fortified Lysimachia, Sestus and Abydos, and then again relapsed into quiet at Ephesus. It was, however, resolved that the navies of the two powers should try their strength. Polyxendius, the commander, was ordered to advance with the fleet against Livius, at the head of the Roman navy. Near the coast of Ionia, the belligerents met, and after a desperate strife, in which both parties displayed great courage, the Syrians were defeated, with a fearful slaughter. Ten of the ships of Polyxendius were sunk, thirteen were captured, and the remnant, in a disabled state, returned to Ephesus. Antiochus was at Magnesia, inspecting his land forces, when he received intelligence of the naval defeat. He instantly hastened to the sea-coast, where he repaired the disabled vessels, and added others to them. He then committed them to the care of Hannibal, with orders to sail and bring the army, whose movements overland were too slow.

Hannibal, though a good general on land, was unfitted to command at sea, and in this new capacity accomplished almost nothing. Seleucus marched westward with part of the army, to watch the movement of the enemy. Thus closed the campaigns of the year 190 B. C.—opened with such important events in the field of war.

ANTIOCHUS THE GREAT.

Defeated in Europe—defeated on the water—compelled to evacuate and destroy his fortress in Thrace, Antiochus concentrated his forces at Magnesia, where the Roman army surrounded and attacked him, and, after a spirited battle, the Syrian hosts were overcome, and Antiochus was compelled to fly. It was then in the power of Rome to have taken possession of all Syria; but their dominions were sufficiently expanded for the time, and prudence required them to grow more gradually. It was the policy, not to destroy, but to diminish the power of rival nations. For this reason, the Romans had not completely destroyed Philip, when in their power, but were content with reducing him to a state of dependency, and then granting him liberal terms.

This was their policy in their war with Syria. One object of the war was to free the cities of Asia Minor from foreign Asiatic masters. Another object was to so reduce the power of Syria as to be under no future apprehension from that quarter. These ends being attained, they could annex Syria to the Roman Empire at some subsequent period, if that event became desirable. Instead, therefore, of pushing Antiochus to extremities, a negotiation was opened, resulting in a treaty of peace. The conditions of that treaty were exceedingly humiliating to Antiochus, whose ambition, but a little time previous, had extended beyond the bounds of his kingdom, even to the conquest of Rome itself.

Instead of establishing himself in Europe, he was compelled to abandon all that he claimed as his own in Asia Minor, west of the mountains of Taurus. He was also required to pay all the expenses of the war, amounting to the vast sum of fifteen thousand talents—equal in value to four hundred and fifteen million dollars—part at the time of concluding the treaty, and the remainder in annual payments. As a guaranty of his fidelity, he was required to deliver to the Romans a number of hostages of rank, one of whom was the second son of Antiochus, then living, who subsequently became king of Syria, with the title Antiochus Epiphanes.

By the treaty of Antiochus with the Roman consul, Hannibal, the friend and ally, was to be delivered to the enemy. Hannibal had long been the invincible foe of Rome, and he well knew his fate if he fell into such hands. After the defeat of Antiochus, and the opening of negotiations, Hannibal, with the sagacity of a crafty politician as well as warrior, suspected at once that he should be made the prize and be bargained away to his enemies. Waiting for no intelligence of this kind, the moment that he heard negotiations were in progress, he, without ceremony, fled to Egypt.

By all these events Rome had gained such advantages that although Syria still existed as a State, it was peculiarly under the shadow of the Roman wing. No subsequent Syrian monarch could attempt any great enterprise without the consent of Rome. A position had been obtained in Asia, which in due time resulted in bringing completely the third head of the third beast under the control of the Roman kingdom—the fourth beast, "dreadful and terrible, and strong exceedingly."

LAST EVENTS IN THE LIFE OF ANTIOCHUS THE GREAT.

Rome must be paid. The money must be raised. But from whence is it to come? The coffers of the King of Syria are empty—his country is desolated by war, and his revenues all dried up by foreign conquest. He takes a journey through his provinces. In the province of Elymas, a part of Media, stood the famous temple of Jupiter Belus. Within the temple were large sums of money, which the priests had been collecting for a long series of years. The necessities of Antiochus pressed heavily upon him. His adversities had hardened his heart, naturally generous and kind, and like Hermias, the counselor of his youth, he had become insensible to the claims of justice or religion. Covering his evil deed under the pretense that the province had rebelled against him, in the silence of the night, he entered the temple, and carried off all its treasures.

The inhabitants, exasperated by this sacrilege, rose and, aided by some of his officers whom he had abused, fell upon Antiochus, and slew him and all his attendants. Thus fell a great man and a great monarch.

Betrayed and deceived in his youth, crafty, energetic and successful in his manhood, in old age he declined to a second childhood. With his cup almost full, he was tantalized with desire to see it overflow, when vaulting ambition, overleaping itself, reduced him to poverty. Then, adding crime to misfortune, he terminates the play, and the curtain ignominiously drops, leaving the throne to his son, Seleucus, the *raiser of taxes*.

SYRIA—SELEUCUS PHILOPATER, B. C. 187.

"Then shall stand up, in his estate, a raiser of taxes in the glory of the kingdom, but within a few days he shall be destroyed, neither in anger nor in battle."

Antiochus the Great left several children. His daughter Cleopatra had previously married Ptolemy Epiphanes. She was the mother of Philometor and Physcon. His second son, Antiochus Epiphanes had been left a hostage in Rome. Seleucus being the older son, ascended the throne of his father. His reign continued about eleven years, and was distinguished by no very remarkable event. Owing to the treaty of peace of his father with the Romans, in which he engaged to pay them large sums of money, it became necessary for Seleucus to raise heavy taxes, and to seize upon the treasures of his people wherever he had opportunity. It is highly probable that he sent ȧn officer, Heliodorus, to seize upon what treasure he might find in the temple of Jerusalem. To prevent this plunder, the Jews may have got up a riot, and the priest may hàve played some tricks upon the officer, but it is hardly probable that the following story in the Maccabees, quoted approvingly by Rollin, can be true. It must be an exaggeration adorned with fictions:

"Under him happened the famous incident concerning Heliodorus, related in the second book of Maccabees. The holy city of Jerusalem enjoyed at that time perfect tranquility. The piety and resolution of Onias, the high priest, caused the laws of God to be strictly observed there, and prompted kings and idolatrous princes to hold the holy place in highest veneration. They honored it with rich gifts, and king Seleucus furnished it from his own private revenues, all that was necessary for the solemnization of the sacrifices. Nevertheless the perfidy of a Jew called Simon, governor of the temple, raised on a sudden great disorder in the city.

This man, to avenge himself of the opposition which Onias, the high priest, made to his unjust enterprises, informed the king that there were immense treasures in the temple, which were designed for the expenses of the sacrifice, and that he might seize upon them all. The king, upon this information, sent Heliodorus, his first minister, to Jerusalem, with orders to carry off all those treasures. Heliodorus, after having been received by the high priest, with honors of every kind, told him the motive of his journey, and asked him whether the information that had been given the king in regard to the treasures was true. The high priest told him that the treasures that were deposited there were a trust, and were allotted to the maintenance of widows and orphans; that he could not absolutely dispose of them to the prejudice of those to whom they belonged, and who imagined they could not secure them better than by depositing them in the temple, the holiness of which was revered throughout the whole universe. The treasures consisted of four hundred talents of silver, about fifty thousand pounds sterling, and two hundred talents of gold, about three hundred thousand pounds sterling. However, the minister sent from the prince, demanded the treasures, and told him plainly that this money, whatever might be the consequences, must be carried to the king. The day appointed for carrying it off being come, Heliodorus came to the temple, designing to execute his commission. Immediately the whole city was seized with terror. The priests dressed in their sacerdotal robes, fell prostrate at the foot of the altar, beseeching the God of heaven, who enacted the law with regard to deposits, to preserve those laid up in his temple. Great numbers flocked together, and jointly besought their Creator upon their knees not to suffer so holy a place to be profaned. The women and maidens were seen covered with sackcloth, and lifting up their hands to heaven. It was a spectacle truly worthy of compassion, to see such multitudes, and especially the high priest, pierced with the deepest afflictions, under the apprehension of so horrible a sacrilege. By this time Heliodorus, with his guards, was come to open the gates of the treasury. But the spirit of the Almighty now revealed himself by the most sensible marks, insomuch that all those who had dared to obey Heliodorus, were struck down by a divine power, and seized with a terror which bereft them of all their faculties. For there appeared to them a horse, richly caparisoned, which, rushing at once upon Heliodorus, struck him several times with his fore feet. The man who sat on the horse had a terrible aspect, and his arms seemed of gold. At the same time there were seen two young men whose beauty dazzled the eye, and who, standing on each side of Heliodorus, scourged him incessantly, and in a most most violent manner. Heliodorus fell to the ground, and was taken up and put upon his litter, and thus this man, who a moment before had come into the temple with his guards, was forced away from this holy place, and no one to succor him, and that because the power of God had displayed itself in its strongest manner. By the same power he was cast to the ground, speechless and without the least sign of life, while the temple, which before resounded with nothing but lamentations, now echoed with the shouts of all the people, returning thanks to the Almighty for having raised the glory of his power. But now some of Heliodorus' friends besought the high priest to invoke God in his favor. Immediately Onias offered a sacrifice for his health. While he was praying, the two young men above mentioned appeared to Heliodorus and said to him, 'return thanks to Onias, the high priest, for it is for his sake the Lord has granted your life. After having been chastened of God, declare to the whole world his miraculous power.' Having spoken these words, they vanished. Heliodorus offered up sacrifice, and made solemn vows to him who had restored his life. He returned thanks to Onias, and went his way, declaring the wonderful works of the Almighty to which he had himself been an eye-witness. The king asking him whether he believed that another person might be sent with safety to Jerusalem, he answered: "In case you have an enemy, or traitorous wretch, who has a design upon your crown, send him thither, and you will see him sent back flayed with scourging, if he come at all, for he who inhabiteth the heaven is himself in that place; he is the guardian and protector of it, and he strikes those mortally who go thither to injure it."

After a reign of about ten years, Philopater, for some reason, desired the counsel and aid of his brother, who was still in Rome. He therefore sent his own son, Demetrius, afterward called Soter, as a substitute to Rome, that Antiochus might return to Syria. While this change was being effected, Demetrius having gone to Rome and Antiochus not having yet arrived, Heliodorus, the officer who had such trouble in Jerusalem, conceived the idea of gaining the throne of Syria for himself. He therefore poisoned Seleucus, in the year 175 B. C. Seleucus seems to have been a mild, inefficient prince, possessing none of the energy and perseverance of his father. His only faults arose from the necessity imposed upon him of raising heavy taxes. By the treachery of his officers, he came to his end, "not in anger, nor in battle."

PTOLEMY PHILOMETOR, B. C. 180.

This young prince was about six years of age when his father died. He immediately received the kingdom, but his coronation was deferred to a subsequent day, and the care of the government was committed to his mother, Cleopatra, the daughter of Antiochus the Great. Accordingly, she for nearly seven years administered affairs with ability and fidelity. At her death, the government devolved upon the prime minister, Leneas. Egyptian statesmen, in the name of the young king, demanded of Antiochus the restoration of the provinces of Phœnicia and Palestine. These provinces had ever been deemed tributary to Egypt, but had been taken from that kingdom by Antiochus the Great, and transmitted to his son Seleucus, from whom they had passed to the present Antiochus. During the life of the queen mother, these difficulties had been prevented, she being the sister of the king of Syria; but after her death, the ministers were determined upon the recovery of their rights. This revived the war between Syria and Egypt—the uncle against the nephew. The Egyptians, in addition to the early right by the partition in the days of the first Ptolemy, claimed that these provinces were given as the marriage dower, by Antiochus the Great to Cleopatra, the mother of the king of Egypt. Antiochus Epiphanes denied both these claims: the parties, therefore, determined to decide them on the field of battle. Philometor being now fifteen years of age, assumed the reigns of government, B. C. 172.

This coronation was attended with great pomp and ceremony, and was witnessed by many foreign princes. Antiochus sent an embassador to offer presents, and affected to rejoice in the coronation; but the real object of the messenger was to discover the strength of Egypt, and her plans in regard to the disputed provinces. Ptolemy had sought the aid of Rome; but Antiochus believed that power had but little time to aid Egypt, as it was now engaged in the conquest of Macedon. He therefore determined to begin the war, not by defending the provinces, but by invading Egypt. The army of Ptolemy met that of Antiochus, in the year 171, near Mt. Cassius, in Pelusium. A battle was fought, in which not justice, but victory, crowned the standard of the king of Syria. Thus the very entrance of Philometor upon public life, was marked by a defeat—the harbinger of an unfortunate reign. His enemy fortified Pelusium, so as to secure it for all future purposes, giving him not only the means of preventing the Egyptians from marching into Palestine, but also opening for himself a door of access into Egypt whenever he might please to invade them. Antiochus then retired into his own country, and placed his army in winter quarters at Tyre. The succeeding spring brought no peace to Philometor. Antiochus had devoted the winter to the work of collecting materials of war and maturing schemes of future aggrandizement. Early in the spring, he again invaded Egypt, both by sea and land. Ptolemy sent out an army to meet and check the enemy, but the Egyptians were defeated in several engagements. Pelusium was re-taken by Antiochus, after which he pushed on to the capital. All Egypt, except Alexandria, submitted to him. Rollin informs us, that after the people had submitted, Antiochus commanded his officers to cease from slaying the inhabitants, although they were completely in his power; for which reason, the Egyptians became greatly attached to him. It is not very apparent that a great amount of gratitude is due to an invader, after having killed many people, simply for not having killed everybody.

It is generally admitted, that in this invasion and the one of the preceding year, Philometor exhibited a lack of talent and courage. These defects were accredited to the prime minister, who, having the care of the youthful king, had labored to render him effeminate by luxury and indolence, the better to control him and his government. In subsequent years, we find Philometor a man of energy and decision, not afraid to meet his foe in the field of Mars.

In this last campaign, Philometor either surrendered himself, or was captured by Antiochus, but was set at liberty. He however spent much of the time with his captor, ate at his table, and entered into his counsels. The plans of Antiochus, though not acknowledged, were evidently now formed to subvert the entire government of Egypt, and annex that kingdom to his own. He fortified Pelusium, left a garrison there to keep it in his own name, and retired into Syria, where his presence was needed. Alexandria had not submitted to the conqueror. Supposing that Philometor was entirely in the interest of Antiochus, the citizens called in and raised to the throne his younger brother, afterward called Physcon, B. C. 169.

Antiochus having subdued a rebellion at home, as soon as he heard of the crowning of Physcon, invaded Egypt the third time—ostensibly for the purpose of restoring the government to the elder brother. After one battle by land, and another by sea, he marched directly upon Alexandria, which he besieged. Physcon, finding himself greatly embarrassed, was advised by his ministers to negotiate for peace with the invader. The foreign ministers, especially those of Greece, who were at his court, conducted the mediation, and for this purpose, repaired to the camp of Antiochus, presented their mission, and urged him, by the ties of near relationship, not to oppress his nephews.

He gave them but indifferent answers, and renewed the seige of Alexandria. The two brother kings had a sister, Cleopatra, who, about this time, attracted much attention, and who, some years afterward, became conspicuous in Egyptian history. Subsequent to these events, she was the wife of Philometor, and after his death married Physcon; then was divorced by him, and fled to Syria, where she died. At this time, however, she was unmarried, and associated with her brother in managing the desperate affairs of

Egypt. Physcon and Cleopatra sent messengers to Rome, who represented to the Senate, that the monarchs of Egypt had long been in alliance with Rome ; that they were now greatly distressed, that it would be dishonorable for Rome to permit one of her allies to be rudely subjugated, and closed by requesting that Rome would use her kind offices in persuading Antiochus to retire from Egypt. A greater argument than the honor of Rome or the love of Egypt influenced the Senate. They were jealous of the power of Antiochus, and would rather diminish than increase his authority. The cause of Egypt was heard and her request granted. Three noble Romans were commissioned to repair to Egypt, with authority to settle difficulties and expel Antiochus. These events required some months of time. Antiochus met with a spirited resistance at Alexandria ; he therefore changed his plans. He arrayed one brother against the other, that they might exhaust their resources in civil war, until they should become so weak that he could conquer them both and take the kingdom.

Concealing his purpose for a time, he incited wicked Philometor against his brother, gave him the control of Egypt, except Pelusium, which Antiochus kept in his own hands, and again retired to Syria.

While the embassadors of Physcon and Cleopatra were in Rome, and before Antiochus had retired from Egypt, the Rhodians sent messengers to him urging him to be at peace with Egypt. But the embassy produced no good effect upon the ambitious king of Syria ; he protested to them that his only object in invading Egypt was to place the elder brother on his rightful throne.

Philometor was now becoming a man. His judgment had ripened, and he had acquired some experience. After Antiochus had retired, he reflected thoroughly upon the state of affairs. He penetrated the policy of his uncle ; he saw that if Antiochus intended him any good he would not have retained Pelusium. He therefore, like a noble, generous man, communicated this suspicion of his uncle's policy to Physcon. The brothers met, their differences were adjusted, they were reconciled, and agreed to reign together in brotherly love. Believing that Antiochus would renew the invasion in the spring, the two brothers immediately fortified Egypt against Syria, and sent to foreign states, especially Greece, for soldiers to aid in their defense.

Agreeably to this suspicion, Antiochus hearing that the two brothers were reconciled, invaded Egypt for the fifth time, and sent his fleet into Cyprus, to take possession of that Island. This was in 168 B. C. He entered Egypt with a large army, and renewed the war openly and without any pretext of coming to aid his nephew, but as the declared enemy of both the kings. The embassadors of Egypt met him, and demanded why he came, what were his intentions and desires. He answered, "that he would have Cyprus, Phœnicia, Palestine, Pelusium, and all of Egypt lying east of the Nile, abandoned to him forever, and that he would have peace on no other terms;" and fixed a day for the kings to give him their final answer.

Antiochus had not much regarded the determination of the Romans to aid Egypt, for he believed they were sufficiently employed in the war with Macedon. But just about this time the war was closed by the defeat of Perseus, the last Macedonian king. The commissioners sent from Rome to settle the Egyptian difficulties, now arrived at Alexandria. The time for the answers to the unreasonable demands of Antiochus had expired, and he had already commenced his attack upon the city when the Roman embassy arrived. At the head of this embassy, was Pompilius, whom Antiochus had known in Rome many years before. The Romans met Antiochus at a little distance from Alexandria, and delivered to him the decree of the Senate, that he should depart from Egypt. He received and read the order, but desiring to gain time for new intrigues, said that he would consider it among his friends at leisure, and then give his answer.

On the one side stood three Romans, unarmed and defenseless; on the other, a triumphant king, surrounded by his army. What could the Romans do? What did they do? Pompilius, with a wand, drew a circle round the king, and bade him in the name of Rome not to depart out of that circle until he answered whether he would or would not obey the decree. Antiochus, struck with fear at the bold manner of the Romans, replied that he would obey, and very soon after departed from Egypt, with all his army. Thus ended his great scheme of unrighteous aggrandizement, by the ruin of his sister's children. Pompilius returned with his colleagues to Alexandria, where he brought to a conclusion the treaty of peace between the two brothers, which had hitherto been but slightly sketched. He then crossed into Cyprus, sent home Antiochus' fleet, which had gained a victory over that of the Egyptians, restored the whole island to the kings of Egypt, who had a just claim to it, and returned to Rome, in order to acquaint the Senate with the success of his embassy. We must now leave the two brothers in Egypt, and for a time observe passing events in the other divisions of Alexander's empire.

ANTIOCHUS EPIPHANES, 175 B. C.

"And out of one of them came forth a little horn, which waxed exceeding great toward the south, (Egypt), and toward the east, (Persia), and toward the pleasant land, (Judea).

EVERY student of the Bible, and every person who would have an intelligent opinion upon the questions of prophesy, ought to be familiar with the history and doings of this king of Syria. He was the special subject of the visions of Daniel, as recorded in the Book of Daniel, eighth chapter, from the ninth to the fourteenth verses, and in the eleventh chapter, from the twenty-first verse to the close.

Antiochus Epiphanes was born about 210 B. C. He was the second son of Antiochus the Great, and the fourth king of Syria who had borne that title. On the death of his father, his brother, Seleucus Philopator, succeeded to the throne, and, after reigning eleven years, died, leaving an infant son. Epiphanes had been sent to Rome, as a hostage, according to an agreement made with that people, by his father, of which an account has been given in the life of that monarch. He was returning home from Rome by the way of Greece, and stopped at Athens, to view the works of art in that classic city. While there, he received intelligence that his royal brother had been murdered by one of his officers, Heliodorus, who had assumed the reigns of government; that he was sustained by a powerful party of adherents, but that there were other political parties in the field. The then Cleopatra of Egypt was the daughter of Antiochus, the sister of our hero, the widow of Ptolemy Epiphanes, and the mother of Philometor and Physcon. One party were desirous to bestow the crown of Syria upon Philometor of Egypt, by virtue of his mother; another party sought the interest of the child of the late king. Eumenes, king of Pergamos, and his brother, Attalus, were the ardent friends of Epiphanes. To them he applied for aid, which was promptly afforded him; and by this, in opposition to all claimants, he was established on the throne of his father, after having subdued and slain the usurper. Daniel thus foretells of him: "And in his estate, shall stand up a vile person, to whom they shall not give the honor of the king, but he shall come in peaceably, and obtain the kingdom by flatteries." The new incumbent received the title of Epiphanes, which signifies the illustrious, although no action of his ever merited so exalted a name. Daniel calls him the vile person, which was by far the more appropriate title. It must, however, be confessed that in this world of strife, and turmoil and violence, they usually receive honor and illustrious titles, who, in harmony with the spirit of the world, that lieth in wickedness, do the most evil and cause the largest amount of human suffering.

The prophesy of Daniel is thus explained: The people of Syria did not give him the honor of the kingdom, but he was forced upon them by the king and prince of Pergamos; yet he obtained it without fighting with any except the usuper. He obtained the kingdom by flatteries, by persuading these princes that he would be of advantage to them, by flattering the Romans that, as he had lived with them and become familiar with their manners and customs, which he approved, they ought to favor his claims. Thus the usurper gained the honors, while the brother's child and the sister's children gave place to him.

It matters little to us who had the best claim to the throne, so that he who gained used it to promote the happiness of the people and the honor of himself. Epiphanes made himself vile by mingling freely and with an indecent familiarity with the common people. Sometimes he would throw handsfull of corn among the crowd, and laugh to see the scramble to obtain it. Liberality on the part of a monarch toward the worthy, the humble and the poor, is not vile, but a commendable virtue. But the indiscreet bestowment of treasures, without regard to merit or necessity, when the rude and not the deserving are the most successful in securing the gifts—treasures gathered by the strong arm of the government from the virtuous, and distributed among favorites, or without any specific object, is robbery vile, and only vile. Epiphanes would often dress in disguise, or in some lowly habit, and, rushing into the street among the rabble, play all manner of antic tricks. Sometimes he would hold a sham court, plead law, or take the judge's bench, and decide imaginary suits. Sometimes, with a foreign dress, he would hold a sham election, after the style of Rome, and, with cap in hand, go among the crowd and solicit their votes, to elect him to some petty Roman office.

In all these ways he made himself a vile person. Let not the reader suppose it unbecoming the dignity of a ruler, be he king or president, to commingle freely with the masses of the poor, and learn their joys and sorrows, trials and necessities, that he may the better appreciate their wants and protect their rights. All this may be done without detriment. A ruler may, and ought to be easily approachable by the humblest citizen; but familiarity and sociability need not compromise dignity. There may be affability and kindness, coupled with all that self-respect which becomes the representative of authority.

A ruler is contemptible who has no other dignity than a haughty distance, which holds no common sympathy with his fellow-beings. He is equally contemptible who permits his familiarity to degenerate into buffoonery and frivolity. Antiochus Epiphanes to the vileness above described, added habits of excess in eating and drinking, and rude and immodest behavior, such as visiting vulgar gatherings, and there using obscene and corrupt language, and dancing in a state of semi-nudity. Knowing these matters of a private and personal nature, let us study his more public relations to the world. These for the sake of convenience, we will divide into three sections: first, his wars with Egypt; second, his persecution of the Jews, and third, his administration of the government of Syria.

SEC. I.—TOWARD THE SOUTH.

"And after the league made with him he shall work deceitfully, for he shall come up and shall become strong with a small people.

Soon after the coronation of Antiochus, the old and hereditary question was revived, in regard to the possession of Palestine, Cyprus and Phœnicia. As usual, the Jews frequently changed masters, and every change was accompanied with the sacrifice of a vast amount of human life. In the history of Philometor and Physcon, these wars have been related, so far as they have respect to Egypt; but in giving the history of Syria, they must necessarily be again spoken of, by which means some repetition can not well be avoided.

While Cleopatra, the queen-mother, lived, her influence was sufficient to restrain the two nations from war. These provinces, having previously been taken by Antiochus the Great, remained under the control of Epiphanes. But that queen died in the year 173, leaving her throne to her son, still quite young, and under the care of the prime ministers. The regent sent a deputation to Antiochus, to urge their claim, and demand of him the restoration of the provinces in dispute, not only on account of the original partition, but also because they had been given to Ptolemy Epiphanes as the dower of his wife, who, being now dead, her claims descended to her son, the young king. But Antiochus denied both these claims, declaring, first, that the original partition, if ever made, had been annulled by the successful conquest of his father, and that the dowry was a pure fiction, which he would not acknowledge. Soon after this, the coronation of Ptolemy Philometor took place, though he was but fifteen years of age. On that occasion,

Antiochus was represented by his minister Appolonius, who made a league with Egypt to remain at peace. Yet he proceeded immediately to fortify the coast of Palestine as far as Joppa, and made all preparation for a war of invasion. In the year 171, he invaded Egypt with a small army.

The Romans had warned him against any encroachment upon the rights of Ptolemy, but Antiochus believed that the Romans were sufficiently occupied with the war in which they were engaged in Macedon. He therefore disregarded this admonition, and marched upon Pelusium. Here he met the army of the young Ptolemy. He engaged it in battle near Mount Cassius, defeated the Egyptians, and put a garrison into the fortress at this place, by which he was enabled to keep a check upon the Egyptians, and prevent them from invading him. This was his first expedition into Egypt, which fulfilled the words of the prophet: "And after the league made with him," [with Ptolemy Philometor, at the time of the coronation], "he shall work deceitfully."

While he pretended friendship, and a desire for peace, he was making great preparation for a war of invasion. "For he shall come up and shall become strong with a small people." His army was small compared with the one brought afterward on his subsequent invasion of Egypt. He became strong, successful, triumphant over his opponent. After this, he returned to winter quarters in Syria.

In the spring of the year 170, Antiochus invaded Egypt both by sea and land, and marched into the heart of the country, capturing Memphis and almost all the principal cities except Alexandria. It was in this campaign that he captured Philometor, and the people, supposing he had attached himself to Antiochus, placed upon the throne his brother, afterwards called Physcon. Philometor was soon set at liberty, but remained with Antiochus, and they both ate at the same table. Many of the cities, seeing the feebleness of the government at Alexandria, and the power of Antiochus, submitted peacefully to him, and gave him the fattest of the land, without resistance. The treasures he took in this campaign were very freely distributed among the officers and soldiers of his army. Thus, "he shall enter peaceably even upon the fattest places of the province, and he shall do that which his fathers have not done, or his fathers' fathers—he shall scatter among them the prey and the spoils, and the riches; and he shall forecast devices against the strongholds even, for a time; and he shall stir up his power and his courage against the king of the south, with a great army; and the king of the south shall be stirred up to battle, with a very great and mighty army, but he shall not stand. For they shall forecast devices against him—yea, they that feed upon the portion of his meat shall destroy him, and his army shall overflow, and many shall fall down slain. And both these kings' hearts shall be to do mischief, and they shall speak lies at one table, but it shall not prosper, for yet the end shall be the time appointed. They that ate of the portion of the meat of the king of Egypt shall destroy him and his government, and the army (of Antiochus) shall overflow Egypt, and slay many people."

Just at this time a revolt in Palestine caused Antiochus to depart from Egypt in order to see to matters in his own country. He therefore established a strong garrison at Pelusium, and returned into Asia.

Having accomplished there his purposes, and learning that Egypt had placed upon the throne the younger brother of Philometor, he again marched into that country, under the pretext that he was going to place Philometor on the throne, instead of his brother. The third expedition of

Antiochus into Egypt was about B. C. 168. Between the second and third expeditions, Philometor remained at Memphis, while his brother resided at Alexandria. To Memphis Antiochus again repaired with a large army. He also sent a navy to block up the mouths of the rivers, and aid, if possible, in capturing Alexandria. It was at this time that the embassadors interposed their efforts to negotiate for peace, which proved unsuccessful. After this failure, Physcon and his sister fled to Rome for aid, which was speedily granted them.

Antiochus, having attacked Alexandria without success, retired to Memphis, placing the government nominally in the hands of Philometor, but in reality retaining it in his own. He kept the garrison of Pelusium, and retired himself to Antioch. Thus ended the third expedition.

Immediately after the close of this expedition, the brothers came to a reconciliation, and agreed to reign jointly, and unite their strength to defend Egypt against the ambitious schemes of their uncle.

"And both these kings' hearts (Antiochus and Philometor) shall be to do mischief." Antiochus professed to be only desirious to establish Philometor on the throne; whereas, he intended to destroy him, and take the kingdom to himself—while Philometor professed to have all confidence in the good intentions of his uncle, yet was desirous to get rid of him, and assert his independence. "But it shall not prosper." Antiochus shall not get Egypt. Neither will Philometor, at present, have undisputed possession of the throne, for "The end shall be at the appointed time." Both of these kings belong to the Kingdom of Brass, as the third beast, whose end must come, and the fourth take their place. Therefore Rome will not have to interfere, thus preparing the way at the end of the time appointed.

"Then shall he (Antiochus) return to his own land with great riches."

"At the time appointed, he (Antiochus) shall return, and come toward the south (toward Egypt), but it shall not be as the former or the latter expedition, for the ships of Chittim (Rome) shall come against him, therefore he shall be grieved in return." Dan. xi, 29, 30.

"And ships shall come from the coast of Chittim, and shall afflict Asher, and shall afflict Eber, and he (Eber, or the Israelites) shall perish forever." Numb. xxiv, 24.

The quarrel between Egypt and Syria was the same long mooted question of the possession of Palestine and Phœnicia, to decide which Antiochus had gone beyond the bounds of those countries, and invaded Egypt. Being successful, his ambition aspired to govern all that country. He, however, pretended that his only purpose was to aid his nephew against his brother. But his real object was to dethrone both. Instead, therefore, of being pleased that they were united peaceably upon the throne, he threw off all disguise and declared himself their enemy, and invaded Egypt the fourth time. It was then that the Roman deputies, three in number, defying all his power, bade him, in the name of the senate, to depart immediately from Egypt, which command he dared not disobey. And it was not this time as in the former expedition.

The relation of Antiochus to the Jews next demands our attention.

SECTION II.—ANTIOCHUS AND THE JEWS.

"And out of one of them came forth a little horn, which waxed exceeding great toward the south, and toward the east, and toward the pleasant land."

When Antiochus Epiphanes ascended the throne of Syria, Palestine was subject to him. Since the return of the Jews from the great captivity they had been governed by their high priests, who were usually tributary to some of the surrounding nations, who constantly quarreled for the possession of that province. The office of the high priest, which had been the prize of ambition among themselves, became the cause of many of their calamities.

At this time one Onias was high priest, and his brother desired his place. Jason immediately repaired to Antioch, and marking the vile character of Antiochus, concluded to strike a bargain with him. He offered the king, for the revenues of Palestine, three hundred and sixty talents, equal in value to about four hundred and fifty thousand dollars, with eighty talents more, (or about sixty thousand dollars), on condition that he should be made high priest. The offer was accepted. Onias was deposed, and Jason placed in the highest religious seat, by the authority of a pagan king. This was about 174 B. C. Onias was what the Jews of that day would have called a very godly man; that is, he was zealous for the customs of his fathers, and the ritual of the Jews' religion. Jason was of a very different spirit; he cared little for any religion, but sought the office for the emoluments thereof. By extortion and avarice he accumulated great wealth, but being desirous to maintain his popularity with the king of Syria, he corrupted the faith and practice of his fathers, and introduced many heathen notions into the service of the temple.

Two years only did Jason enjoy the office he obtained by bribery. In 172, he sent his younger brother, Menelaus, to Antioch to pay the tribute, and the latter succeeded in supplanting him, just as he had done Onias, by offering a bribe. This second change in the high priesthood caused a tumult in Jerusalem, in which some lives were lost, and among others Onias was murdered. But Menelaus firmly

16

established himself in the office, where he committed many acts of sacrilege and profanity.

During the residence of Antiochus at Tyre, between his first and second expedition into Egypt, the Sanhedrin sent a deputation of three men to him to complain of the impiety of the high priest. We should in our day think it a strange proceeding, to accuse and try a priest or bishop of a Christian church before a pagan king, especially for the crime of heterodoxy or informality in religious ceremonies. But so degenerated had become the Jewish church, that the highest offices of the priesthood were bought and sold in pagan markets, and pagans decided church quarrels; thus preparing the way to set up the abomination that maketh desolate and pollutes all that remains of virtue in the church. Antiochus heard the case, gave judgment against the accused, and was about to pass sentence of death upon him, but another actor in this trial appeared upon the stage.

When Ptolemy Epiphanes died he left one Ptolemy Macron, governor of Cyprus. During the minority of Philometor, Macron withheld from the treasury all the revenues of Cyprus. For this he was accused of fraud, but the ministry tried in vain to get possession of those funds. The truth was that Macron was a faithful officer and worthy of all praise. He understood the profligate character of the ministry, and knew that if the treasures were given to them they would be imprudently squandered. He therefore retained the funds in his own hands; but when Philometor took the control of the government for himself, Macron repaired to Egypt, and delivered up the money which he had preserved for the young king. Here was a man of noble soul and faithful purpose, traduced and abused by the ministry, who were far less worthy than himself. Had he been duly appreciated, and treated according to his merit, Egypt might have found in him a valuable friend in her subsequent times of need. The ministry could not endure the presence of a man whose virtue was a constant rebuke to their dishonesty. Macron was ill-treated and abus d by the ministry, and the young king had not firmness and honesty enough to defend his faithful servant. The affection of Macron was wounded, and turned into hate. Alas! how often are the best friends of a cause driven to forsake it by the abuse of unworthy men, who control it? Macron concluded that he served an unworthy master; that there was no merit in being faithful to one who did not himself possess the virtue of faithfulness. He therefore delivered the possession of the island to Antiochus, which was at that time a great favor, for which Macron was rewarded by being made governor over all Celo-Syria and Palestine. Macron was at Tyre, at the trial of Menelaus. The offender was from a province over which Macron was Governor. It was therefore natural that he should have something to say. Macron and Menelaus seemed to have been friends. The governor interceded for the prisoner. Antiochus, more intent on pleasing his favorite, than protecting goodness or punishing offenses, pardoned the culprit, and caused the three deputies who had accused him, to be put to death as false witnesses. The Tyrians seemed to have more respect for justice, for they buried the bodies of the deputies in an honorable manner. Let all men learn the fate of those who upon religious questions appeal to civil power, and govern themselves accordingly.

PERSECUTION OF THE JEWS.

While Antiochus was besieging Alexandria, in his second expedition to that country, a rumor reached Jerusalem that he had been slain. Since the death of the three deputies at Tyre, the Jews had not esteemed Antiochus very highly.

When therefore they received this false intelligence, they made great rejoicings, which were accompanied with some acts of violence. Jason thought this a good occasion to recover the office from which he had been suspended. He accordingly marched upon Jerusalem with a small army of but little more than one thousand men, made himself master of the city, drove out Menelaus, who retired to the citadel, and established himself in power. He practiced all manner of cruelty, and put to death many innocent persons, whom he suspected of opposition to his violent measures.

It does not appear that the Jews contemplated any rebellion against Antiochus. They only desired to regulate the office of high-priest. When Antiochus heard of these transactions, he concluded that all Palestine had rebelled against him, and to quell this rebellion, he at that time left Egypt.

Exasperated at this rejoicing for his supposed death, he marched to Jerusalem, besieged the city, captured it, and gave up the innocent inhabitants to slaughter. Eighty thousand men were slain, and forty thousand captured and sold into slavery. Menelaus, who was with him, led Antiochus into the temple, even to the holy of holies, where he polluted the sanctuary. He carried off the altar of incense, the table of shew-bread, and the seven golden candlesticks, with other sacred vessels. He also plundered the whole city and country, and then returned to Antioch, laden with the spoils of Egypt and Judea.

He reäppointed Menelaus high-priest, Philip of Phrygia, governor of Judea, and Andronicus, governor of Samaria—three as wicked men as could well have been selected. This robbery and pollution of the temple was the event foretold by Daniel: "And it, the little horn (Antiochus), waxed great even to the hosts of heaven, and it cast down some of the host and the stars to the ground, and stamped upon them. Yea, he magnified himself even to the prince of the host, and by him the daily sacrifice was taken away, and the place of the sanctuary cast down, and a host was given him against the daily sacrifice, by reason of transgression, and it cast down the truth to the ground, and it practiced and prospered [how long?] unto two thousand three hundred days, then shall the sanctuary be cleansed." Dan. viii, 9–14.

This occured in the year 120 B. C. The cleansing of the sanctuary has been supposed to refer to some great event to take place about this time. Rev. William Miller computed the time to expire in 1843. Modern adventists supposed the event would occur in 1855, while millenarians say the time will run out in 1866. All these computations are based upon the inference that a day signifies a year. This is sometimes the correct use of the term *day*, but manifestly not always. When should the time expire by that calculation? Will it be two thousand three hundred years from the time the vision was seen by Daniel? This vision occurred in the third year of the reign of Belshazar, which was five hundred and fifty-five years before the birth of Christ. Then the event should have transpired long ago. Let us state it thus:

2300 the length of the vision.
555 the vision given.
———
1745

So that the event should have transpired one hundred and eleven years ago. But no remarkable event occured at that time.

Did the time begin with the event of taking away the

sacrifice, and polluting the temple? Then the figures should stand thus:

2300
170
———
2130

Then the time will not elapse until about two thousand one hundred and thirty, about two hundred and seventy-five years yet in the future. Is it not probable that all these are false calculations, and that in this instance, a day does not mean a year? In the tenth chapter of Daniel, we are told that the Prince of Persia resisted the angel one and twenty days, and until the Prince of Grecia came. In this instance a day signifies a decade of years, and the one and twenty days refers to the two hundred and ten years of the power of the Persian Empire, beginning five hundred and forty years before the birth of Christ, or the defeat of all the great armies of Babylon, ten years before the taking of the city, and ending in three hundred and thirty, when Alexander took the capital of the Persian Empire, and burned it to the ground.

The two thousand three hundred days may, and probably does, mean literal days. This would occupy about seven years, and end exactly with the death of Antiochus, who, in his last agonies, revoked his decree against the Jews, and although his successor did not much respect that decree, the Jews then commenced again the services in the temple, 164 B. C., under the government of Antiochus Eupator.

A former chapter closed with the return of Antiochus from Egypt, the fourth time, at the bidding of the Roman deputies. Exasperated at the failure of all his great schemes of aggrandizement, he was in no very good frame of mind toward any of his subjects, but his especial indignation was against the Jews. It does not appear what new provocation they had given him, if any. As his army marched along near the sea-coast, on his direct route to Antioch, he detached Appolonius, with his two thousand men to destroy Jerusalem. The year previously he had razed the temple; now he prepared to exterminate the city. The commander arrived in the midst of the night, and exhibited no disposition to do harm. He thus quieted the fears of the inhabitants. The Sabbath approached—that day for the sanctity of which the Jews, ever since the great captivity, had great reverence—but they repaired not to the temple that had been polluted two years before. No morning and evening sacrifices ascended thence to the God of Israel. The golden altar had been removed. No light from the seven golden candlesticks was there. But the abomination which maketh desolate had been set up. The high-priest was the corrupt creature of a pagan king. Synagogues had been reared in many parts of the city and vicinage, where multitudes, leaving the temple, convened to hear the law read and expounded to them, to sing hymns of praise, and offer humble prayers to the God of Israel. On that day the solemn chant of heavenly song was disturbed by other sounds — the groans of the dying, the screams of the wounded, the clash of arms, and the shouts of combatants, rent the air. Appolonius, obedient to his orders, fell upon the unsuspecting people, in the midst of their devotion, and put them to death. The army fell upon them and cut them to pieces, and the women and children were sold as slaves. Not a man that fell in their way was spared. The streets flowed with human blood, while the soldiers plundered the houses of the butchered inhabitants. After this, several parts of the city were set on fire. Of the ruined houses, they took materials and built fortresses on the hill of Zion, which would command and overlook the temple. There they stored the plunder, with all the implements of war, and from this garrison they went out, and attacked and slew such of the people from the country as came up to the city to worship.

Many were slain in and around the temple, and their carcases thrown among the ruins, the more completely to pollute the holy place. Some writers suppose that this is the time from which we ought to date the abomination, and that from this time (instead of ten years before), the morning and evening sacrifices had been discontinued. But this is hardly possible, since the golden altar, on which alone the daily sacrifices was offered, was carried off on the previous occasion. "Then shall he be grieved, and return and have indignation against the holy covenant" (with Menelaus and his associates, who corrupted the religion of their fathers).

Having returned to his regal city, Antiochus conceived the idea of establishing uniformity of religion. He published a decree, that all the different people in his kingdom should lay aside the ancient faith, and worship the same gods and in the same manner as did the king. His kingdom then embraced Parthia, Media, Elam, and many other nations, whose religions were as diversified as their languages. Some of the Eastern tribes were worshipers of the sun and of the sacred fire. The king's religion was that of the ancient pagan Greeks. This decree, although general in its terms, was intended specially to annoy the Jews. Commissioners were sent into all the provinces to put this decree into execution; but we do not hear of its enforcement throwing any place in commotion, except Judea. It may not have been enforced or even attempted elsewhere, and was probably only proposed to cover up the tyranny which was used against the Jews. The Jewish historians say that no people were more ready to comply with this request than were the Samaritans, who, from a deep-seated hatred to the Jews, their neighbors, (of a common stock of Israel), were anxious to see them exterminated. They had built a temple upon Mount Gerizim, but had not dedicated it to any particular deity. They presented a petition to Antiochus, in which, after denying that they were Jews, they asked permission to dedicate their temple to the Grecian god, Jupiter, and call it after the king's name, Antiochia. Their petition was received and the request granted, and the deputy governor instructed not to disturb them in any manner. The Samaritans and many of the apostate Jews joined with Antiochus, and became the most cruel persecutors of their brethren. It must be recollected that the hatred between the Jews and Samaritans was mutual, and that the Jewish writers being prejudiced have probably colored the offenses of the Samaritans, higher than the truth would bear.

We have here the Samaritans living in Samaria three hundred and seventy years after the return of the Jews from captivity, and only one hundred and sixty-eight years before the birth of Christ. May we not safely infer, that the ten last tribes returned from this captivity at the same time with the Jews, and that those who adhered to the faith became commingled with that people, losing their identity, and thus fulfilling the prophecy of Ezekiel, that the two sticks should become one stick, having thus lost their national identity, and that the apostate Samaritans became merged in the Syrian nation. Hence, is it more than an illusion to seek for the lost ten tribes among the Anglo-Saxons or the American Indians, or anywhere else?

Of the operation of this decree upon the Jews, Rollin thus speaks: The commissioner who was sent into Judea and Samaria to see the king's decree punctually obeyed, was called Athenæus, a man advanced in years, and extremely well-versed in the ceremonies of the Grecian idolatry. He had been, for that reason, judged a most fit person to invite a strange nation to join in it. Immediately upon his arrival at Jerusalem, he began his operations, by putting a stop to the sacrifices which were offered up to the God of Israel, and suppressing all the observances of the Jewish law. They polluted the temple in such a manner that it was no longer fit for the worship of God; profaned the Sabbath and other festivals; forbade the circumcision of children, and carried off and burned all the copies of the law upon which they could lay hands. They abolished all the ordinances of God in every part of the country, and put to death whoever was found to have acted contrary to the decree of the king. The Syrian soldiers and the commissioners who commanded over them, were the chief instruments by which the Jews were converted to the religion professed by the sovereign. To establish it the sooner in every part of the nation, altars and chapels filled with idols were erected in every city, and sacred groves were planted. Officers were appointed to these, who caused all the people in general to offer sacrifices in them every month, on the day of the month on which the king was born. They forced them to eat the flesh of swine, and other unclean animals sacrificed there. The officers of the king, in their effort to compel the Jews to abandon their religion, met with a spirited resistance. Many lives were lost on both sides; among others, Matthias, the father of Judas Maccabæus, was slain, after a manful and heroic resistance.

In 167, tidings of this resistance reached the king at Antioch. He marched into Judea, determined to subdue his rebellious subjects. In this he was, however, entirely unsuccessful, although he committed many acts of cruelty too horrible to relate. It was in this expedition that he executed Eleazar, a man of ninety years, venerable for his piety and his deference for the faith of his fathers. At the same time was put to death, by cruel torments, a mother and her seven sons, spoken of in the Maccabees. Many of the heroic deeds of the Jews, at this and subsequent times, are recorded by those authors who are very far from being accurate as impartial historians. Their statements, though marvelous and exceedingly interesting, and perhaps, in general, founded on fact, must be taken by the inquirer after truth, with liberal allowance for national and religious partiality. There is, however, no doubt that the Jews, ever tenacious of their religion and obstinate toward their foes, resisted most nobly the unreasonable demands of the pagan monarch, and, favored by the Supreme Being, were victorious against vastly superior numbers. The reader will find a more full history of these deeds in the authors just referred to, and can attach as much importance to them as he may think they merit. I shall here only give the most authentic and prominent events in these campaigns.

The history of the past should teach modern church and statesmen and religious persecutors, and all politicians, that it is impossible to CRUSH OUT a conscientious resistance to an odious and unjust law.

When Antiochus had drenched all Judea with the blood of its martyred inhabitants, without producing the desired effect, he returned to Antioch to attend to matters in relation to the Romans and other nations. An account of this is reserved for the third section of his life. Thus ended the persecution, B. C. 167.

While Antiochus was thus occupied, Judas Maccabee was fast recovering all the important posts and fortresses held by the Syrians. Appolonias, governor of Samaria, and Seron, another officer, each with a strong army, attempted to check his progress, but were both defeated with a great destruction of their men and the loss of their own lives. Antiochus hearing of the defeat of the two armies, and the death of his two officers, was exceedingly enraged, and determined to re-visit Judea and exterminate the whole race. He was, however, prevented from going there in person, for his treasures were well nigh exhausted, and disturbances had broken out in Armenia and Persia, which required his presence in those countries.

"But tidings out of the east, (Persia), and out of the north, (Armenia), shall trouble him; therefore, he shall go forth with great fury to destroy and utterly make away many." He therefore, in 160 B. C., divided his forces, taking one army with him into the north and into the east. The other he committed to Lysias, a prince of royal blood, whom he appointed his deputy at Antioch, with specific instruction to exterminate the Jews, so that their lands might be given to other people, among whom they were to be divided by lot. He was anxious to fulfill this mission, but hearing of the army of Judas he became alarmed. Philip the Phrygian was at this time governor of Judea, and Ptolemy Macron of Celo-Syria. Lysias sent an army to the aid of Philip, and appointed Macron commander-in-chief, and Nicanor, a particular friend, Lieutenant. They, with Gorbias, a distinguished officer, marched into Judea with forty thousand foot and seven thousand horse, and encamped at Emaus. Another and a very singular group were also collected there. More than a thousand merchants of great wealth, from different nations, had assembled here to buy the captives who they expected would be taken and sold. Nicanor had advertised extensively that these captives should be sold into slavery at the rate of ninety for a talent, by which he intended to raise the sum of two thousand talents which the king owed to the Romans.

This would require the sale of one hundred and eighty thousand slaves. As it was the intention to cut to pieces all the able-bodied men, and only spare and sell the women and children, we may form some idea of the extent of their anticipated conquest. But the game was not yet caught. Oh, what a gathering was this. How unlike this the scenes enacted in Emaus when, two hundred years later, two lowly disciples, in the evening shade, walked with disconsolate spirit from Jerusalem to Emaus, their hearts burning by the way, as the Master spake unto them. Judas, aware of the eminent danger to which he was exposed, gathered up his small army of about six thousand soldiers and repaired to *Neshap*, the *Nispa* where Samuel of olden time worshiped, before the temple of Solomon was built. Here they performed divine worship, and implored the aid of the Supreme Being. After dismissing one-half of his soldiers, who were either afraid or had some legal excuse for not engaging in war, he marched with the remaining three thousand and encamped in the vicinity of his enemies. In the night season, Gorbias, guided by an apostate Jew, led out several thousand of the best of the soldiers, and attempted by a secret pass in the mountains to fall by surprise on this handful of men. Judas was apprised of this, and after the detachment had left the camp, he fell suddenly upon the body of the enemy, who, taken by surprise, and deceived by the darkness of the night, were thrown into utter confusion. A vast number of them were slain and the rest dispersed. Gorbias not finding Judas as he expected, returned and found his own camp in flames, the body of his army dispersed, and Judas triumphant. His men threw down their arms and fled. Judas pursued them, and slew in the flight, of these and the main army, about nine thousand men. Then returning to the camp, he collected a large amount of plunder, and also captured the slave merchants, who, instead of buying slaves, were themselves sold into slavery. Their money was confiscated to the treasury of Judas. The next day being sabbath, was celebrated with solemn joy and thanksgiving. This victory encouraged many others to join the army of Judas, so that with his increased force he was able to pursue the different branches of the retreating enemy, and in other battles won several victories, and slew twenty thousand men. Thus ended the campaign of 166 B. C., to be revived again the next year.

WAR CONTINUED.—B. C. 165.

The campaign of the preceding year against Judea, had closed with the defeat and almost annihilation of the Syrian army. Dismay filled the court of Antiochus. The king was still in the east. The viceroy had not been able to obey the royal instructions regarding the extermination of the Jews. Lysias felt the necessity of doing something to sustain his own position, and retrieve the honor of the army under his charge; but he had not yet learned that he was fighting against the Most High. He was beginning to experience that it was hard to kick against the pricks. He again raised a large army for the conquest of Judea. This army consisted of sixty thousand foot, and five thousand horse; the very last troops that Syria could produce. At the head of this army he proceeded southward, pregnant with the resolution to exterminate the Jews. Passing around Jerusalem, he encamped about ten miles south of that city, at Bethima, in the borders of Idumea. Judas still lived to defend the lives, liberty, property, and religion of his countrymen.

Elated with the victory of the preceding year, and animated by the enthusiasm of a religious belief, that Deity had special respect for him, and would aid him, he marched upon the invader with about ten thousand men. The contending parties were soon engaged in battle. The frantic enthusiasm of the Jews made them desperate. They rushed upon the foe with impetuosity, slew five thousand of their enemies, threw the whole army into confusion, and caused a precipitate flight of the whole Syrian band. Lysias in dismay at the valor of the Jews, and the defeat of his army, retreated with such of the remnant of his forces as he could collect, to Antioch, threatening to revisit Judea the next year. But the next year brought a new master to Syria. And thus closed so much of the public life of Antiochus Epiphanes, as relates to the Jews.

SEC. III.—SYRIA DURING THE REIGN OF EPIPHANES.

The city of Antioch had now been the royal residence of the kings of Syria, from the time of Seleucus Nicator, about one hundred and twenty-five years. Nearly every monarch of Syria had contended with Egypt, about the possession of the intermediate countries, and in these contests spent a vast amount of human life and treasure, but ever leaving the quarrel just as they found it, to be settled by some future appeal to arms. Antiochus the Great had used every care to possess himself of it, but without success. Epiphanes now determined to accomplish the desired task, and would probably have succeeded, but for foreign interference. Rome had now risen, not only to take her place among the nations, but be the umpire between them, to decide their quarrel, sometimes indeed, according to equity and the interests of human liberty, but more frequently according to the dictates of her own selfish interests. Greece was already under the Roman protection. Macedon and Rome were engaged in war during the entire year of the reign of Epiphanes, but before the close of his life, Macedon yielded up the ghost, and became also a Roman province. Rome did not desire to see any other nation extend its empire and increase its power, lest it should become too strong and endanger the independence, or perhaps become the rival of herself. For this reason she had checked these ambitious schemes, and finally subdued Antiochus the Great, when he labored for the conquest of the provinces in Egypt, and four times invaded that country for the purpose of annexing it to Syria.

At this time Physcon and Cleopatra fled to Rome and presented their petition. The Roman Senate, not so much out of pity to Egypt, as jealousy of the great power of Syria, espoused the cause of Ptolemy. The result is already recorded. Rome persuaded the Syrians to remain in Egypt, and Antiochus obeyed. His schemes of ambition were all blown away, just as those of his fathers had ever been; yet he learned no lesson of wisdom by the experience of generations. Then commenced his campaign against the Jews. The Greeks had their temples, their imaginary gods, and their religious festivals, which consisted in games of athletic exercise, and hand and foot races, or what we might in these days call gambling, in honor of the gods. Other peculiarities of the services were much like the modern performance in theaters. The Persian mythology differed but little from that of the Greeks.

Paulus Æmilius, the Roman officer at the head of the Macedonian affairs, after the conquest of that country, celebrated the games as they were called, at Amphipolis, on the Strymon, with great pomp and solemnity—if ostentatious show can be called solemnity. Epiphanes was desirous to do the same thing at Daphne, the locality of the temple of Apollo and Diana. He sent abroad invitations for multitudes to collect for the celebration. Immense numbers congregated. Many days were devoted to carousals in honor of the gods. If in this celebration Epiphanes had any object whatever, it must have been, first, to rival Rome, as a matter of pride, and secondly, for the mere gratification of his sensuality, for he regarded no religion nor god except his own will. It was while contemplating this great festival, that he determined upon the wild and unparalleled project of creating, by law, uniformity of religion throughout his kingdom. In the celebation of this festival, Epiphanes behaved so shamelessly, and associated with such obscene women and men, that multitudes of virtuous citizen, as well as strangers from all parts of the world, left in disgust at his abominable vileness. This was the man whom Daniel calls vile. The debauch, for such it properly ought to be called, cost immense sums of money, exhausting his treasury, and embarrassing him in raising an army to invade the Jews.

Rome did not lose sight of Syria; she observed all the movements there with Argus eyes. For this purpose Tiberius Gradias was sent to Antioch, to keep an eye upon passing events. He arrived just at the close of the great religious festival. Syria owed Rome a large amount of money; this was demanded, but the treasury was empty; its contents had been squandered in rioting. The war against the Jews was at hand. Just at this time arose a new trouble — for misfortunes usually combine and unite their forces against man, when he abandons himself to intemperance and carousing.

Bad tidings from the East and from the North. Armenia, lying nearly north and east of Syria, had long been subject to this country, and paid an annual tribute into its treasury. Antaxias was the local governor of Armenia. He, with his people, rebelled against Epiphanes, and set up his independence. Persia lying east of Syria, also at that time refused to pay tribute, and sought to throw off the yoke of dependence. Both these rebellions were probably the consequence of the mal-administration of Epiphanes, whose time was wasted between a fruitless attempt to conquer Egypt, and idle dissipation at home, entirely neglecting such careful and judicious regulation of his provinces as was necessary. He had not learned the true political economy, that to take care of what one has, and develop its resources, will fill a treasury faster than the attainment of foreign power, difficult and costly to hold. It was to reclaim these rebellious provinces in the north and east that Epiphanes marched in this direction, leaving Lysias to administer affairs in his place at home.

Let us follow this vile hero in his expedition. Soon after the close of the festival, which, it will be recollected, was in the year 166, Epiphanes invaded Armenia, conquered the whole country, and took Antaxias prisoner. Armenia is a cold, mountainous country, not very productive nor abounding in wealth. Epiphanes, although he was triumphant in arms, did not enrich his exhausted treasury by his success; but he hoped for the same success in Persia.

Early in 165, Epiphanes marched into Persia. He met with some success in reclaiming his revolted subjects, and was occupied in arranging the taxes of that country, when he heard of the defeat of his armies in Judea. This filled him with exceeding wrath. Finding it impossible to collect any revenue from his best but oppressed subjects in Persia, he determined to try pillage. Elymæs, a city of Media, was the site of a famous temple, dedicated to Diana, and, as some say, to Venus—that is, the goddesses of hunting and of lust. This temple was known to abound in treasures consecrated to religious worship.

To Elymæs, Epiphanes repaired, and besieged the city, intending to pollute the temple. The inhabitants, both of city and country, rendered desperate at the prospect of so great a sacrilege, came together in vast multitudes, and fell impetuously upon the army of the king, defeating and dispersing the entire host. Without obtaining the prize, he retired with his army. In addition to the mortification of this repulse, it will be remembered, he had heard of the defeat and slaughter of his army in Palestine, by Judas Maccabæus. Full of wrath, and determined to make the Jews feel the weight of his displeasure, he led his forces to the west. He arrived at Babylonia, where the particulars of the fall and terrible defeat of Lysias were told him, which, already excited as he was, brought him almost to insanity. Threatening to make Jerusalem the burying place of the whole Jewish nation, he ordered his coachman to drive with all possible speed. In the very moment of uttering his threats, he was seized with most severe colic, which the Jewish rulers thought was the direct judgment of God upon him, for his cruelty to their nation. Still he ordered all possible speed to be made, on the journey homeward, that he might not die before he could wreak his vengeance upon the Jews. Driving furiously along, he was thrown from his carriage, and dreadfully bruised by the fall, which, in connection with his previous malady, greatly disabled him, and filled his body with excrutiating pain. He was placed upon a litter, and borne upon the shoulders of his servants. But his bruises mortified, and his body became full of sores—his intestines, as well as externally. Hovering between the living and the dead, he was thus carried along for some days. The stench of his body became almost unendurable to his attendants and the whole army. In his unutterable anguish, he called one of his officers, and acknowledged that there was a God in Israel mightier than man, that his sufferings were the penalty of his cruelties, and that he could not contend with the Almighty. He now made solemn vows that if the God of heaven would restore him to health, he would revoke all the edicts against the Jews, and even become a Jew, and worship the true God. How vain are all resolutions and promises made upon a bed of sickness and death, and extorted by pain or fear, not by love of truth and goodness! Perceiving his end approaching, the king called to him Philip, a favorite, and bestowed upon him the regency of the government during the minority of his son, then but nine years of age, and afterwards known as Antiochus Eupator. He gave some directions for the education of the child, laid down some general rules for the future government of the kingdom—rules which he had not enforced by his example—and then yielded up the ghost. "And he shall come to his end, and none shall help him."

Thus, in the year 164 B. C., ended the reign and the life of the greatest persecutor, the vilest and must cruel king, that ever sat on the throne of Syria. Let all tyrants learn of him a lesson, and tremble.

"But O, this end, this dreadful end. Thy sanctuary taught me so. Yet a little while, and the wicked shall not be."

ANTIOCHUS EUPATOR, B. C. 164.

PHILIP, the favorite of Epiphanes, who was with that monarch at the time of his death, and when he received the authority of prime minister and regent of the young prince, repaired to Antioch to fulfil the duties of his mission. But he found another already in his place. Lysias had for some time had the care of the government, and hearing of the death of his master, placed the youthful son and heir on the throne, retaining, however, all the power and authority in his own hands. Eupator was then but nine years of age.

Lysias was not disposed to surrender his authority to Philip, considering that the possessor had better title than he. In vain did Philip endeavor to obtain possession of the authority conferred upon him by the late king. The wishes of a dead king, expressed in his expiring moments, in a foreign land, had far less influence with the nobles than the authority of one already in power, who had become accustomed to command. Philip repaired to Egypt, hoping to receive aid from the Ptolemys.

But while all these events were transpiring in Syria, the two brothers in Egypt were not reigning in the most brotherly harmony. They were, therefore, indisposed to afford aid to Philip.

The next year, Philip retired into the east, assembled an army of Medes and Persians, and marched suddenly upon Antioch, while Lysias and the youthful king were absent on an invasion of Judea. He attempted to establish himself in power, but the sudden return of his opponent to the capital drove the usurper out of the city, and he came to Tyre, where, very soon after this, he was slain. Lysias was thus rid of one rival, but was soon to meet another and more powerful one.

A change of masters is not always a change of burdens. Lysias, although terribly defeated in his former wars with the Jews, gained now the mastery. Yet the first year of his reign with Eupator was spent in another fruitless campaign against that people—a full account of which is reserved for a section relating to the Jews.

At the battle of Silus, many years before, Antiochus the Great was defeated, and compelled to negotiate for peace, with Rome, on most humiliating terms. Among others, he agreed that Syria should keep but a certain number of ships, and a certain number of elephants and munitions of war. Rome, ever jealous of the growing prosperity of that nation, had heard with displeasure that Syria had increased her military department beyond the stipulated terms. Three deputies, who had been instructed to visit Egypt, and try to terminate the quarrels between the two brothers, were also directed to visit Syria, and see the treaties fulfilled. On arriving at Antioch, they found the charges to be true. They caused the excess of ships to be burned, and of the elephants to be slain. It is not surprising that such selfish policy, and such needless waste of property, should exasperate the people of Syria. We can not find, at this day, any excuse for such ignoble conduct on the part of the Roman government, except in the barbarism of the age.

But in Syria, as well as elsewhere, the Kingdom of Brass was destined to yield to that of Iron. Septimus, a citizen of Antioch, was so enraged at the destruction of property, and the humiliation of his nation by foreigners, that he could not restrain his wrath. While Octavius, one of the Roman deputies, was bathing, Septimus fell upon him and killed him. Lysias, the prime minister, was suspected of having instigated this deed, although he denied it, and there was never any proof of his guilt. Octavius had been consul in Rome, and was highly esteemed. His murder caused great indignation, and a statue was erected to his memory. He was the founder of one branch of the family of Augustus Cesar. Eupator sent embassadors to Rome to protest that he had no part in the death of Octavius; but the Senate sent them back, without giving them any answer, and reserved to themselves future action in the matter. Other important events transpired in the same year.

One condition of the peace concluded between Antiochus the Great and the Romans was, that a number of hostages should be sent to Rome as security for the faithfulness of Syria to the engagements into which they were then entering. Antiochus Epiphanes, the second son of Antiochus the Great, was one of these hostages. He resided in Rome until the death of his brother, Seleucus Philometor, when he returned to take the throne of Syria, by the aid of the king and prince of Pergamos, of which an account has already been given in this history.

Demetrius Soter, son of Philometor, a lad of about eleven years, took his place and remained there until he was about twenty-three years of age.

It will be seen that Demetrius Soter was a cousin of Eupator, by an older branch of the royal family, and had therefore as good a title to the throne as the incumbent. Desiring to secure his rights, he petitioned the Roman Senate for permission to return and take the throne. But the Romans thought it better for their interest that Syria should be ruled by a young king, under the direction of ministers, than by a man of the age and talents of Demetrius. They therefore refused his petition, and directed their deputies, among other things, to look after this question. Sometime subsequently, Demetrius, against the advice of his friends, (among whom was Polybius, the historian), once more solicited the Senate for leave to return, and was again denied. His friends had advised him not to petition, but to escape without leave. After the second denial, he took that advice, and so effectually concealed his departure, that it was not known to the Senate until he was far on the way. Having taken passage on a Carthaginian vessel laden with fruits and other cargo, bound to Phœnecia, he, with a small retinue, landed at Tripoli. Although he came a fugitive, the report spread that Rome had sent him to take possession of the crown and throne of Syria, and was determined to support him. This was very credible, in view of the late difficulties about the murder of the deputy, Octavius, and the silence of the Roman Senate on that subject. Confidence is often stronger than physical power, and a rumor, however unfounded, destroying confidence, is often a more potent enemy than a mighty army. The fear of Rome was all-powerful in Syria. All looked upon Lysias and Eupator as already destroyed, and that anticipation caused the event. Princes, nobles, army and people forsook their sovereign, and joined the standard of the new claimant. The soldiers seized Lysias and Eupator, and delivered them to Demetrius, who immediately caused them to be put to death, and thus, without opposition, mounted the throne, by the murder of his cousin, against whom there was no charge, nor even suspicion of crime. In the close of his own life, we shall see the measure meted out to him which he has given to others.

JEWISH HISTORY UNDER THE THIRD BEAST.

At the death of Alexander, Judea, in common with a vast number of other provinces, was subject to the Macedonians, and in the conflicts and jealousies that arose between the great generals of that time, Palestine was often the theater of their bloody strife. In these wars, the nation of the Jews, which at that time probably embraced a remnant of all the original tribes, suffered severely. Hostile armies traversed Palestine no less than ten times previous to the reign of Antiochus Epiphanes, of Syria. That monarch invaded Judea, either in person or by his lieutenants, nine times, and his successors and others invaded the same country eleven times previous to the birth of Christ, and the full establishment of the fourth beast, making at least thirty invasions by hostile armies, in the space of about three hundred years, equal to a war once in ten years. This, it must be admitted, was far from being a state of peace or prosperity.

Death, by Poison, of the Elder Cleopatra, of Syria.—See page 203.

1st, In the year 321, and immediately after the burial of Alexander, we find his generals dispersed into various provinces, as governors. Perdiccas, who was regent of the kingdom, was in the South of Asia Minor, at the head of a Macedonian army. Having a dislike to Ptolemy, he determined to invade Egypt. He marched with a devastating army around the sea coast, through Palestine, producing confusion and suffering through all Judea, as he traversed their country toward the possessions of Ptolemy. Entering Egypt, he soon perished by the hands of assassins. Two years of peace only to Judea was the result of his death.

2d. In 319 B. C., Antigonus, having assumed the office of governor over Syria and its dependent provinces, appointed one Leomadon his lieutenant-governor in Palestine. Ptolemy claimed that Palestine belonged to Egypt; he therefore marched into Judea, and defeated Leomadon, who was slain in battle, and recovered possession of all that province. The Jews, who had been accused of inconstancy and rebellion, now passed to the opposite extreme. They resolved tenaciously to adhere to the interests of Syria, and refused to acknowledge Ptolemy for their master. He therefore marched against Jerusalem; but owing to its impregnable position among the mountains, and fortified by works of art, it could not have been easily conquered, but by taking advantage of the religious observance of the Sabbath by the people. On that day, knowing that the Jews would not resist, he commenced the attack, captured the city, and treated the Jews with great severity. He carried captive into Egypt one hundred thousand of them; but afterward finding them peaceable and valuable citizens, he made their conditions more comfortable, taking thirty thousand of them into the army, and stationing them at military forts. Here was the beginning of the introduction of the Jews into Egypt, where afterward some of the apocryphal books were written, and where subsequently a temple was erected, and five cities of Egypt spoke the language of Canaan, as spoken by the prophet Isaiah. Nearly six years passed before Antiochus was prepared to reclaim these countries.

3d. But in the year 313 he marched against the generals of Ptolemy, and besieged Tyre, which, after a spirited resistance, submitted to him; and thus all Palestine and Phœnicia again changed masters.

4th. The next year (312,) Ptolemy again invaded Palestine and Phœnicia, fought a great battle, and defeated Demetrius, the son of Antigonus, at Gaza, and recovered to Egypt the control of those countries. In this siege and capture of Gaza, Demetrius lost five thousand men slain, and eight thousand taken prisoners. The citizens of Gaza, chiefly Jews, suffered most severely, and great numbers of them were slain.

5th. In 305, Antigonus again sent his son Demetrius to invade Egypt, by sailing along the coast, while he marched an army through Palestine, along the coast of Gaza, with the intention of entering Egypt by land. They succeeded in invading the borders of Egypt by sea and land, but the fleet was shattered by a storm, and the army greatly diminished by sickness and desertion, and checked by the judicious arrangements of Ptolemy. Antigonus was therefore compelled to retire with the shattered fragments of an army, leaving Palestine still under the control of Ptolemy.

6th. In 264, the war between Magus and Ptolemy Philadelphus broke out, and Antiochus Soter sympathizing with Magus prepared to invade Egypt.

Ptolemy marched an army into Palestine, while his fleet invaded the seacoast, where conflicts between the Egyptians and Syrians again distracted all Palestine.

7th. In 246, occurred the war of Ptolemy Evergetes against Syria, on account of the divorce and murder of Berenice, and the death of Theos by the hands of his wife Laodicea. In this campaign, the hostile forces of Ptolemy again ravaged Judea; but, on his return home, he stopped at Jerusalem, offered sacrifices to the God of Israel, and conferred some privileges on the Jews. After this, Judea enjoyed a tolerable state of quiet for about forty-three years.

8th. In 203, B. C., Ptolemy Philopater having died and left an infant heir to the throne, Antiochus the Great, of Syria, and Philip of Macedon entered into a league to conquer and divide the territory subject to the crown of Egypt. In pursuance of this league, Antiochus took Palestine, conquering the whole country and capturing many cities, and the Jews became once more subject to Syria.

9th. In 199, Scopas, an Ætolian general in Egypt, serving under Ptolemy, defeated the officers of Antiochus and reclaimed the whole country to the crown of Egypt.

10th. In 198, Antiochus again invaded Celosyria, Phœnicia and Palestine, and defeated Scopas, when all these countries were reverted to Syria. During the short reign of Seleucus Philopater, of Syria, we hear of no invasion of Palestine. He was succeeded by Antiochus Epiphanes, of whose nine invasions an account is given in the second section of the history of that monarch. He was succeeded by his son Antiochus Eupator, whose administration is fully given in a preceding part of this work, where it will be seen that, in his short reign of but two years, he, although but a child, by his minister Lysias, made war upon the Jews three times.

It would seem that the Jews, by their bigotry and obstinacy, and their deadly hatred to other nations, drew upon themselves many of the calamities to which they were in those times exposed. When it was known in Jerusalem that Antiochus Epiphanes was dead, and that in his last moments he was favorably inclined toward the Jews, instead of taking advantage of these facts and seeking for peace, Judas Maccabæus, encouraged by the successful defense of his country and people, took the aggressive, and began an invasion of the Iturians, near Damascus, who were subject to Syria. There seems to have been no provocation for this course, except retaliation, where, too, retaliation could secure no benefit. The only pretext for this course was, that these people were Gentiles, and, like Joshua of old, he had a right, for that reason, to destroy them. As might have been expected, the very success of Judas against his neighbors involved him and his country in trouble which he might have avoided.

Epiphanes was dead, Lysias was still prime minister, and had the care of the young king; but Philip had attempted to gain possession of his office. Lysias having now a rival, could not safely loose credit by neglecting his duty to defend the provinces of his kingdom. He was terrified at the progress of Judas, in his war upon those provinces. It is difficult to say what less he could do than maintain the dignity of the government, by invading and chastising the Jews for thus disturbing their neighbors. Hence, whatever was the cause of the preceding wars against the Jews, this one seemed to be of their own inviting.

Accordingly, Lysias formed an army of eighty thousand foot and a large body of cavalry, with eighty elephants, and marched to Judea. Avoiding Jerusalem, he proceeded to the south of Palestine and besieged a fortress called Beth Suva: this was on the borders of Idumea. Judas, among other operations, had invaded the Idumeans, and slain multitudes of the unoffending people, and placed a strong garrison in Beth Suva. Lysias besieged the fortress. Judas devoutly besought the Lord for aid, and marched from Jerusalem toward the enemy. Jewish writers assert that as the little army proceeded toward the enemy, there appeared before them an angel, or some mysterious being, riding upon a horse, clothed in white, with arms of gold and a lance in his hand. It is incredible that the Supreme Being condescended to give such a display, or optical illusion, for the benefit of a people who, whatever the case might once have been, were, at that time, of all people least worthy of Divine favor. Besides, such a sight was a mere phantom, and could be of no practical value, except as far as it affected their courage. It is by far more probable, that Judas perceiving the declining and desponding spirit of his little army, played off the illusion to encourage them. The result was as he might have anticipated. The Jews, with frantic enthusiasm, threw themselves upon the enemy. The suddenness and desperation of their assault struck their opponents with a panic, and rendered them powerless. Twelve thousand six hundred of the Syrian army were slain, and the rest fled, many of them wounded and without weapons.

After this defeat, Lysias, tired of war with a people of such desperate valor, made a treaty of peace with Judas, in which it was stipulated that the decree requiring the Jews to conform to the Syrian religion, should be revoked, and the Jews might live according to their own laws. The young king was required to ratify this treaty, which he accordingly did. But it brought no peace to Judea.

Whatever cause might have produced it, there existed a deadly hatred against the Jews among their neighbors. Timotheus, a general of the king of Syria, by whose authority we are not informed, raised another army of one hundred and twenty thousand foot and two thousand five hundred horse, and again invaded Judea. Judas, with a little handful of men, rushed upon the new foe, slew thirty thousand and defeated the entire forces of Timotheus, which greatly inspired his people with courage. The reader must bear in mind, that the tremendous victories of a little handful of Jews over great numbers of their enemies, are only authenticated by Jewish writers, to whose exaggerations each one may give as much credit as he pleases.

The king, still not ten years of age, with Lysias, raised another army with thirty-two elephants and thirty chariots of war, and again invaded Judea. The forces of Judas had been greatly diminished by so many wars, and this time he found himself unable to resist the invasion. He was defeated in an engagement, and retired to Jerusalem; the king pursued him and invested the city, pressed closely the siege, and would probably have caused the besieged to surrender, had not relief appeared from another quarter.

Philip, who had been appointed prime minister by Epiphanes, could not remove Lysias nor gain possession of his office. He had in vain sought aid from Egypt, and had retired into the east; once there, he had skill and talent sufficient to raise a large army of Medes and Persians, and with these he marched into Syria, intending to attack Antioch, and place himself in power during the absence of the king and Lysias. Information of this invasion reached the ears of Lysias, while he and the king were pressing the siege of Jerusalem. They were obliged to make peace with the Jews, in order to march against Philip. A treaty was entered into and sworn to by the king, who, within a few days, violated his oath by demolishing the fortifications of the temple, after which he retired to Syria. These three invasions, under Antiochus Eupator, all occurred in the same year. But less than two years more, saw Syria under new rulers, and another invasion occurred under Demetrius Soter.

Antiochus Eupator, at the time of the treaty of peace made with the Jews, appointed Alsimus high priest, as the successor of Menelaus who was dead. But the Jews refused to accept of him or permit him to handle the sacred vessels or administer in his office. He had joined with the enemy of the Jews under Epiphanes. He exerted himself to corrupt the religion of his fathers, and induce the Jews to accept the pagan religion according to the decree of the king of Syria. For this act, the Jews rightly decided him unfit for the office of high priest. Disappointed and exasperated at his rejection, Alsimus gathered together all the disaffected and apostate Jews and enemies of Judas, and presented a petition to Demetrius, alleging that the Jews of the Maccabæan party were his enemies, and had slain all who adhered to his party in the collision with Eupator, accusing them at the same time of many other abominable practices. Whether any of these accusations were founded upon truth or not, Demetrius listened to them and pursued the policy of his predecessors by beginning his reign with an invasion of Judea. In 162, Demetrius confirmed Alsimus in the office of high priest of the Jews, and directed Bachides, his general in Mesopotamia, to march with a large army into Judea, expel Judas, and place Alsimus in his office. Alsimus had also an army, and with it proceeded to the Jordan to accomplish this purpose. Another army was also raised, and Nicanor appointed to commanded it. Judas was successful in defeating all the measures of the Mesopotamian commander, and slew multitudes of his soldiers. Nicanor, exasperated to see a little handful of Jews thus successfully oppose the operations of all the forces, marched alone into Judea, where Judas defeated and entirely overwhelmed the whole army. Nicanor was found among the slain; his head and hands were carried off in triumph, and placed upon one of the towers of the temple. Judas now had a little respite, and fearing future invasions, he applied to Rome for protection, thus clearing the way for the final triumph of Rome over Judea, as well as all the other portions of the old kingdom of Macedonia. The Romans lent a willing ear to this application, declared the Jews their friends, and forbade any nation to invade them. But before this decree was kown in Asia, Demetrius had commenced his second war upon the Jews. Alsimus and Bachides, although defeated, still lived. Demetrius increased their army, and ordered them to invade and subdue Judea. As they entered that country, Judas met them with his little band of eight hundred men, and engaged them. As might be expected he was slain, and his little flock dispersed. It is believed that Alsimus was also slain at the time. Thus ended the war of 161, and the promulgation of the Roman decree, secured peace for a long time.

Jonathan, a brother of Judas, was placed in the office of high priest, and temporal ruler of the Jews. In the year 148, Alexander Bala, and Demetrius Nicanor, were contending for the throne of Syria. Jonathan having taken the oath of allegiance to Alexander, adhered to him with fidelity. Appolonius, governor of Celo-Syria and Phœnecia, deserted his master and advocated the cause of Demetrius. His first object was to reduce Jonathan to subjection to his cause. In an effort against him, in one day he lost eight thousand men. Bala now appealed to Ptolemy Philometor, his father-in-law, for aid, who immediately marched an army into Palestine. Jonathan met him at Gaza, and accompanied him to Ptolemais, where a conspiracy was discovered to exist against the life of Ptolemy. This discovery resulted in a quarrel between Ptolemy and Alexander. The wife of the latter was taken from him, and given to his rival, Demetrius. This woman was that Syrian Cleopatra, whose history is given in other places, and who was the wife of three kings. Her subsequent marriage preceded the death of her former husband. This left Jonathan in an unpleasant position, deserted, as he now was, by all his allies; for Bala was soon after slain in Arabia.

In the city of Jerusalem stood a citadel or strong military fort, of which we have given an account in speaking of the Macedonians and Jews. In this citadel were stored arms and munitions of war. It was held by a garrison of Greek soldiers, in the service of the Syrian government. Through all the changes and wars in India, this citadel seems to have remained in their hands. The respite which Jonathan had from 149 to 145 B. C., was spent in an effort to reduce this citadel, driving out the pagans, and restoring possession to the government of the Jews. He invested the fortress, brought large machines of war to bear upon it, and pressed the siege vigorously. Demetrius Nicanor, who had assumed the government upon the defeat of Bala, heard of these doings, repaired to Ptolemais and cited Jonathan to appear before him. The high priest directed his officers to press the siege vigorously during his absence, and taking a number of priests and principal men of his nation, with rich presents, obeyed the summons and presented himself before the king. His gifts gained the favor of Demetrius, and he obtained many favors for his nation, among which were a discharge from all service and taxes, except three hundred talents.

This must have occurred about 145 B. C. The next year Jonathan resumed and pushed the siege of the citadel vigorously, but still without success. He certainly exhibited no great sense of justice or military skill, in his prosecution of this undertaking. He met with no success in arms, and was at last compelled to resort to a means which was at his command from the first negotiation, to accomplish his purpose. He applied to Demetrius and requested him to withdraw the garrison, which he accordingly did. One condition of this withdrawal was, that Jonathan should assist Demetrius in his difficulties. We have seen one of the causes of the endless calamities of the Jews. It was the union of the two offices of priest and governor. The high priest was also the political ruler of the people. This fact involved the sacred office in the quarrels of the various pagan nations with whom the Jews were at various times connected, and consequently often called forth the direst hate of other nations, against the religion as well as the whole people of the Jews. This union of the secular with the priestly office was no Divine arrangement — was not according to Moses — but was a usurpation of temporal power by the high priest, which dates from the return from the Babylonian captivity. Demetrius, by his mal-administration, had alienated the people of his own city and country, to such a degree that signs of insubordination began to appear. Fearing to trust his native soldiers, he had surrounded himself with foreign guards. His late favor to Jonathan was on condition that he would furnish troops to aid in suppressing the rebellion of the inhabitants of Antioch. Jonathan accordingly sent his three thousand troops. When Demetrius found himself thus defended, he resolved to disarm all the native inhabitants and issued a decree accordingly. This so exasperated the people that they arose and attempted to kill the king. One hundred and twenty thousand men invested his palace with this determination. The Jews furnished by Jonathan fell upon this multitude, and slew one hundred thousand of the inhabitants, burned part of the city and saved the king.

They thus subdued the rebellion and restored peace, and as they boasted, had obtained a sweet revenge upon the innocent inhabitants, for the sufferings the Jews had previously endured at the hands of the Syrians, under Epiphanes.

It is manifest that the Jewish religion did not teach, at that time, much forgiveness or justice, but allowed of indiscriminate revenge. These sad results are not chargeable to the teaching of Divine revelation, but to the corruption engrafted upon it by the traditions of the Pharisees, then the reigning sect. What apology can be offered for a high priest of a holy religion, who not only defends his temple and subjects at home, but sends off his armies to other countries to butcher the people, burn cities and plunder houses, to sustain an idolatrous king upon the throne which he had disgraced by his tyrany? After this they retired to Jerusalem, laden with booty and what they called honor — such honor as belongs to pirates, thieves and quarrelsome dogs. What impression could such a representative of the only true religion make on the citizens of surrounding nations? Is it to be wondered at that they had bitter enemies? Surely there was need that a Messiah should come to teach the duty of man to his fellow man.

This service of Jonathan did not make Demetrius any the less a tyrant toward his native subjects, or any the less an enemy of the Jews. Although he received the three hundred talents, he still demanded all the usual duties and taxes, and threatened to make war upon Jonathan if he refused to pay them.

Another revolution now took place at Antioch. Demetrius Nicanor was expelled, and Tryphon, who had been minister under Bala, brought the youthful son of Bala and placed him upon the throne; retaining, however, the power in his own hands.

Jonathan, exasperated at the ingratitude of Demetrius,

had joined the standard of young Antiochus, and engaged in a war against Demetrius. But no sooner had that monarch been expelled, and the war ended, than he found himself in a new trouble; the usual consequence of being entangled in the affairs of other nations. Tryphon, the protector and prime minister of the king, had only used him as a tool, to accomplish his purpose. He now desired to rid himself of Antiochus, and assume the crown himself. He easily persuaded most of the officers to acquiesce in his scheme of ambition. But Jonathan, with his usual tenacity and obstinacy, refused to acknowledge this new master. This act can hardly be accredited to honest motives on the part of Jonathan, for at that period the Jewish rulers evidently had no conscience on any subject except the forms and rites of their religion.

In 144 B. C., Tryphon therefore invaded Judea with an army, and Jonathan met him with a force of forty thousand men. Tryphon fearing to engage so powerful a force, changed his mode of proceeding. He pretended to have come on an errand of friendship, and was desirous to consult him in some matters of state policy, having for their object the protection of the young king. He also proposed to put Jonathan in possession of Ptolemais, a city which, at that time, was attached to the province of Phœnicia, and not subject to Jerusalem. To Ptolemais accordingly Tryphon repaired. Jonathan, dismissing all his army except three thousand men, of whom he sent two thousand into Galilee, and having full confidence in the good intentions of Tryphon, proceeded to Ptolemais. He had no sooner entered that city than the gates were closed upon him, himself secured, and his attendants put to death.

Tryphon then dispatched soldiers to overtake and destroy the two thousand troops who were now on their way to Galilee; but these men having learned the fate of Jonathan and his men, were on their guard, and made so formidable a defense that the soldiers of Tryphon dared not attack them. They changed their course, and arrived safely at Jerusalem. Tryphon now marched toward Jerusalem. The people, alarmed at what had befallen Jonathan, appointed Simeon (his brother) to the command, who immediately repaired and completed the defenses about the city, and, raising an army, was shortly ready to resist the invader. In all this time, Tryphon had not declared war, and had committed no overt act which could not be explained. He was, as yet, only prime minister; but the king was but a child, and his will is not known in any of these movements. The prime minister feared to attack Simeon, but again resorted to deception and treachery. And strange as it may seem, with his recent conduct before their eyes, the Jews were again completely deceived by false promises. Tryphon sent word to Simeon that he had not come to do him harm; that he had only arrested Jonathan, because he owed to the treasury of Syria a thousand talents. He therefore requested Simeon to send him that sum, and, as security for the future fidelity of Jonathan, he wished him to give up the two young sons of Jonathan as hostages. Simeon seems to have had some suspicion of treachery. Yet he feared that his brother, now a prisoner, might be murdered, if he refused to comply with these demands. He was so imprudent as to send the children and the money. The traitor received the treasure, but, instead of retiring, gathered his army and advanced upon Jerusalem. Simeon followed him so closely and annoyed him so continually, that he was unable to accomplish much, and finally retired into Gilead, on the east of Jordan, into winter quarters, where he put Jonathan to death. Simeon afterward obtained his bones, and brought them to Jerusalem for burial. The fate of the two children is unknown.

Tryphon having disposed of Jonathan, now compassed the death of the young king, and ascended the throne of Syria. But Demetrius Nicanor still lived, and had his party and friends. After the cruelties and treachery of Tryphon, the Jews sympathized with Demetrius. Simeon formed a kind of league with him, by which on him was conferred the office of the high priesthood, and the old treaty was renewed, by which the revenues were remitted and all offenses forgiven. This was in the year 143 B. C.

Until this time, the exercise of political and military authority by the high priest had been rather a matter of assumption than of any regularly acknowledged right. It grew out of the existing state of things and the necessities of the times. Judea had indeed had no distinct form of government for many hundred years, but had been floating between a state of dependence upon Egypt and Syria and one of anarchy and military dictatorship.

In 141 B. C., Demetrius being in Parthia contending with Tryphon for the possession of this dependency of Syria, and affairs in general being in a state of confusion, the Jews essayed to build up a government of their own. Taking advantage of the troubled state of affairs, they began to assert a greater degree of independence.

Egypt had, for a long time, neglected to enforce her claim to the province of Palestine. Her princes were either sufficiently engaged in family quarrels, or steeped in abject debauchery. The Jews had been pleased with the administrations of Judas, Jonathan and Simeon. Demetrius had declared Simeon governor over Judea, but that honor was confined to his own person. In an assembly of priests, officers and people, it was formally declared that the office of high priest should be legally united to that of the temporal power, at the head of civil and military affairs, and that Simeon should fill that office, and that it should be hereditary in his family. This was only acknowledging and making legal a state of affairs which had obtained for some centuries.

In 139 B. C., Simeon being acknowledged a temporal prince, sent an embassy to Rome and renewed the friendship with that people, which had been begun by Judas some years before. The Roman senate received the embassadors, heard them, and renewed the alliance. They advised the nations surrounding Judea, who were also in alliance with Rome, of these facts, and commanded them not to invade Judea, or disturb the government of Simeon.

Antiochus Sidetes, before he had expelled the usurper, Tryphon, had formed a very favorable alliance with Simeon, in order to obtain his aid. But having reaped the benefit of his services, and obtained the throne, he no longer needed his friendship. In order to recover his revenues, which had been restored, he therefore, contrary to his solemn promises made in time of need and in disregard of the Roman mandate, undertook to conquer Judea and depose Simeon; but Judas and Jakin, the sons of Simeon, met and overthrew his army. The invasion of the army of Sidetes, in 139 B. C., is the twenty-seventh from the death of Alexander.

In 135 B. C., Antiochus Sidetes, having no enemies at home, and his brother Demetrius being in Parthia, found time to invade Judea. Simeon and his two sons being dead, John Hyrcanus, his third son, was proclaimed high priest and prince of the Jews. Sidetes marched against Jerusalem and besieged the city. Hyrcanus was closely shut in, yet he resisted the enemy for a long time. But being driven to extremities, and in danger of starvation, he sent to Sidetes proposals for capitulation. The enemies of the Jews, retracing all their past history, the wars and rebellions, their obstinate valor, and the turbulence of their nature, urged upon Sidetes to exterminate the whole race, now that he had them in his power. Historians declare that it was purely the good disposition of Sidetes that prevented him from yielding to their solicitation; but I much more think that his clemency proceeded from a selfish policy. He had just exterminated the faction of Tryphon, the usurper.

He might have to contend with other usurpers. His elder brother, though a prisoner in a foreign land, still lived, and in some emergency that yet might occur, Sidetes might be in want of the aid of the Jews, to hold the balance of power in his own hands. He might also have some fear of offending Rome, whose influence would benefit him in some future emergency. These are the most probable reasons why he inclined to clemency.

A treaty was the result, in which it was stipulated that the siege should be abandoned, and the besieged should surrender their arms to Sidetes; that the fortifications of Jerusalem should be demolished, and tribute paid for Judea and the sea coast. Sidetes demanded also that the old citadel should be rebuilt, and a garrison of Syrian soldiers stationed there; but to this Hyrcanus refused to consent, and instead thereof paid the conqueror an additional five hundred talents, about half a million of dollars.

This treaty was a severe humiliation to the Jews, more so than any which had occurred in the preceding invasions, for many years. In 131 B. C., Antiochus commenced his great campaign against the Parthians, in the first part of which he was entirely successful, and in the latter of which he lost his life. John Hyrcanus, with an army of Jews, accompanied him in this expedition, and contributed largely to his first success. At the close of the year Hyrcanus retired to Jerusalem, laden with honor. Sidetes, being left without his aid, lost his life the next year.

In 122 B. C., after the death of Sidetes, and before his brother, Nicanor, could take possession of the throne and kingdom, Hyrcanus availed himself of the confusion incident to these changes at Antioch, to deliver his country from the odious conditions imposed upon her by Sidetes. He not only restored his national bounds, but conquered and subjected to his control many places on the side of Syria, in Arabia, and declared anew his entire independence of any foreign master. Syria never again attempted a conquest of Judea, although that independence was not acknowledged till some time subsequent to this.

Hyrcanus in 128 B. C. again sent ambassadors to Rome, who were kindly received, and the Senate declared that all the invasions of Judea by Sidetes were contrary to their decrees, and unjust, and that all the conditions he had imposed upon the Jews were by Roman authority void. All the privileges of the Jews, which Hyrcanus had obtained for them two years before, were confirmed to them. The kings and rulers of Syria were forbidden to invade Judea.

This was forever afterward observed; and the next troubles of the Jews will be found to have arisen among themselves, or with the Romans, excepting only the siege of Samaria.

In 127 B. C., while Cleopatra and Zebirna were rivals for the government of Syria, Hyrcanus obtained from Zebirna a confirmation of their independence, and many other considerable advantages.

JUDEA UNDER KINGLY GOVERNMENT, B. C. 106.

When the Israelites first cast off the democratic form of government and elected Saul, son of Kish, for their king, they introduced with royalty the elements of strife and civil war, which resulted in their division into two nations, and received none of the advantages they proposed to themselves by this change in their form of government. In like manner, in later times, a transition from the government of a high priest to that of a king, brought no relief from their enemies, and no peace to themselves, but introduced confusion and distraction, ending in the entire subversion of their nationality, and the transfer of all rule to a foreign power. If we think the scenes transpiring about this time in the courts of pagan nations were of revolting cruelty, we shall find that the Jews, who once claimed to possess the only true religion, were not behind in any of the crimes which distinguished their neighbors.

The religion of that time had become so corrupted, and was so destitute of all that commends itself to the moral sense of mankind, that the nation which professed it was, by a decree of God, dispersed to the earth's remotest bounds, as unfit to be recognized among the nationalities. The principal actors in these ignoble scenes were:

Aristobulus, Antigonus, Alexander Jonas, and Absalom, sons of Hyrcanus; Salome, wife of Aristobulus; Alexandria, wife of Jonas; Hyrcanus II.; Aristobulus II., son of Alexander; Antipater, an Idumean proselyte; Pompey, Crassus, Cæsar, Marc Antony, Roman Consuls; Alexander and Antigonus, sons of Aristobulus; Herod and Phocas, sons of Antipater.

The death of Hyrcanus, high priest and governor of Judea, had been before mentioned. He left five sons; the name of the fourth, who was slain by the third, is not transmitted to us. Aristobulus, the eldest, assumed the office and duties of his father as high priest. But not contented with the civil power, he desired a higher title than any Jew had assumed for a long time. He claimed the dignity of a king.

This might be offensive to the neighboring nations, but we must remember that the remnants of the once powerful kingdom of Macedon were now in a weak and shattered condition, and Rome was fast rising to be the dictator of the world. The power of the world was passing from the third to the fourth beast of the prophet's vision. Thrace had ceased to be of importance, and Macedon had become a Roman province nearly a century previous to these events, and Syria had now become, to some degree, dependent upon Rome for its existence. Neither Egypt nor Syria had power to dispute the claims of Judea to take rank as a kingdom. It was the policy of Rome to encourage their pretensions, the better to check the surrounding nations and aid Rome in subduing them. Aristobulus therefore assumed the crown and title of king without opposition, and reigned about one year. He adopted all the vices of kingly government, and far from acting the part of a father of his country, or bearing in mind the holiness of his religion, his first public act was to shut up his own mother in close confinement and starve her to death. What crime she had committed, or how she had offended his majesty, we are not informed. He next imprisoned his three younger brothers, keeping them in that state until his death. The next movement was a war against the Iturians. This was a tribe of Syrians living on the north-east of Galilee, in the direction of Damascus. What they had done, or for what cause they were invaded, is unknown, except that as one of his ancestors had conquered Idumea, and compelled the inhabitants to embrace the Jewish religion, he thought he must do the same in Ituria. In 105 B. C., Aristobulus crossed the Jordan with an army, and compelled the Iturians to embrace the Jewish faith and become circumcised, or leave their country, their homes and the graves of their fathers, and emigrate to distant lands. Most of the people having no redress, or means of escape, complied with the conditions, and were ever after identified with the Jews. How very dark and unintelligible must be the idea of religion and duty to God, when men embrace a religious faith, not from choice or approbation, but from inability to resist a superior force! The act of Aristobulus was tyrannical, yet the principle which prompted it was the same that, alas! still prompts many persons in our day in their religious efforts. Before the year closed, the king of the Jews became afflicted with a malady which compelled him to return to Jerusalem. He committed the further prosecution of the war to his brother Antigonus, who completed the work of conquest, and returned in triumph to Jerusalem. These two brothers were greatly attached to each other. They had fought side by side in the wars of their father, and especially at the siege of Samaria. Aristobulus had a wife, Salome, of whom we know but little, except that, like too many women, she abused her lord's confidence, by stirring up strife in public matters. She did not partake of the king's partiality for Antigonus, but sought the destruction of that worthy officer. She and her favorites accused him, before the king, of an intention to rebel and usurp the government, and asserted that he had returned in arms and triumph for that purpose. It so happened that Antigonus had returned just at the time of the feast of the Tabernacles, and, without changing his apparel, had repaired to the temple to thank the Lord for his success. Aristobulus, disquieted by these rumors, sent orders for Antigonus to appear before him in his citizen's dress, without arms, presuming that if his brother were innocent, he would obey the command; but if guilty, he would come with his military dress and weapons of war. The guards were therefore ordered to await his arrival, and treat him accordingly.

The queen, perfectly apprised of the state of things, bribed this messenger to vary the order, and, in the name of the king, command Antigonus to appear before him immediately, in his military dress, just as he was. The unsuspecting victim left the solemn festival, and repaired to the royal presence without ceremony, supposing, from the haste of the order, that the king wished to inquire about some business of state that would not admit of delay. As Antigonus approached his brother, the guards observing that he was armed, obeyed their secret orders, fell upon him and slew him. Here we have a specimen of the indiscretion and injustice which always attends absolute monarchy; and all monarchs are just as far absolute as they can find means to be. After the cruel deed was done, the silly king discovered the cheat; yet he could not undo the evil. Within the year, disease caused the king to follow his mother and brother into the shades of death. Salome, as if to ease her troubled conscience for the murder of Antigonus, caused his three brothers to be immediately released from prison. The eldest of these brothers, Alexander Jonas, assumed the crown and high priesthood. His next younger brother desired to divide these offices with him, and he, in consequence, caused the young aspirant to be put to death, thus baptizing his administration in the blood of his brother.

Across the Jordan and south of Ituria, dwelt the Gadarenes, a mixed multitude, famous in the time of the Saviour for the number of swine they kept—some of whom were possessed of devils, and drowned in the sea.

For some reason, not distinctly known, it entered into the mind of Jonas to besiege Gadara. He therefore crossed the Jordan, as his brother had done the year before, and commenced the war. After a struggle of about ten months, he captured Gadara and several other important stations, and commenced his return, flushed with victory. At this time Grypus and Cyzicus were engaged in their civil war, and Lathyrus of Egypt rather favored the interests of Grypus, who resided at Damascus. This invasion of Gadara was deemed an invasion of the territory of that part of Syria. On his return, Jonas found the tide of war against him, for in crossing the Jordan he was intercepted by the enemy, and lost ten thousand men.

He therefore returned to Jerusalem in mortification and disgrace. It now appears that he had not the confidence or affection of the dominant party at home. The Pharisees had long entertained a dislike to his family, and as we have abundantly seen, that a religious class, when in the ascendant, generally bring their power to bear so as to annoy whomever they dislike, they rejoiced at his defeat, derided him, and increased his mortification.

A few years after this event, in 100 B. C., Jonas commenced another campaign. The sea coast along the borders of Palestine and Arabia, had been under the control of Syria, but as that kingdom was engaged in civil wars between Grypus and Cyzicus, these places had been somewhat neglected. Jonas, with the usual ardor and injustice of the Jews, invaded Raphia and Anthadon, two places near Gaza, took them, and by this means blocked up Gaza. Jonas seems to have been actuated in this war, in no small degree, by a desire for revenge. The people of Gaza had united Lathyrus to invade Asia, and aid Grypus. This, it was supposed, contributed to the former misfortune of Jonas at the Jordan.

In 98 B. C., Jonas having possession of the two places before mentioned, brought a large army and besieged Gaza. Apollodorus was then its governor. He defended the place with skill, bravery and success. For this fidelity he was gaining a reputation, when he experienced the fate so common to those, who, in any good cause do more than their indolent associates, and are therefore traduced and belied, in order to afford a place for the indolent and incompetent. Lysimachus, a brother, envying his good name, assassinated Apollodorus, and took the command of the city, but very soon after surrendered it to Jonas, who immediately entered Gaza, and at first exercised so much lenity as to encourage the inhabitants to hope for kindness. But after a few days having well secured his position, he satiated his revenge, by letting his soldiers loose upon the unoffending people, to butcher, plunder, and ravish to their hearts' content. The inhabitants, driven to despair, resisted heroically, and great numbers on both sides were slain. The city was reduced to a heap of ruins. Thus closed the year 97 B. C., and Jonas retired from his holy war to Jerusalem. Such was the character of the kingly high priest of the Jews. Need we then wonder at any of the religious barbarities practiced in the time of Christ, by the same people?

Whatever may have been the depravity of the most vile person in Judea, it appears that there were those among the people, who did not approve of this sanctified wickedness; for two years after the fall of Gaza, in 95 B. C., while the king or high priest was officiating at the altar, he was severely pelted with lemons thrown at his head, in token of contempt; and at the same time called by every opprobrious epithet. Exasperated by these insults, he ordered his guards to fall upon the people, by which act six thousand of them were killed. From that time he no longer ventured to trust himself among the Jews, but surrounded himself with six thousand foreign soldiers, brought from Cilicia.

After this terrible revenge upon his own people, he thought himself safe from other insults, and according to the uniform customs of the restless, turbulent Jews, he began a war upon the neighboring provinces of Syria. In this he was at first successful, but ultimately fell into an ambush, and lost a great number of his men, and returned to Jerusalem in disgrace. Not having the confidence or good will of his own people, instead of sympathy or kind regard, he was met with the spirit of censure and turbulence, which increased into a formidable rebellion and civil war. Jonas was not the man however to be discouraged under difficulties. He was cruel, implacable and treacherous, but he did not lack courage and inventive talent. He planned a terrible revenge, and having, by the sagacity of his arrangements, secured the victory over his rebellious subjects, concluded a six years' internal war with a great slaughter. During this civil war, on one occasion, he captured a city, took eight hundred men captives, and carried them and their families to Jerusalem. Here he made a feast for himself, his wives and concubines, where, from the banquet hall, they had a fair view of the spectacle he was going to present for their entertainment, and then caused the eight hundred men to be crucified. While they were being nailed to the cross, their wives and children were brought before them and had their throats cut. Such was the royal high priesthood, in 86 B. C. In this war not less than fifty thousand Jews were slain; by far more than in any one of the invasions of Nebuchadnezzar.

Subsequent to this rebellion, Jonas was successful in several wars of little note. Finally he became diseased of an ague, of which , after three years' illness, having meantime become very intemperate, he died, in 79, having reigned twenty-seven years.

ALEXANDER, 79 B. C.

Alexander Jonas left a wife, Alexandria, and two sons, Hyrcanus and Aristobulus between whom the family quarrels were perpetuated. The two prominent sects, the Pharisees and Sadducees, had already divided the Jewish nation into factions. Not contented with their religious treachery, they carried this animosity into deadly political strife. Some modern writers have endeavored to show that a third sect then existed, called Essenes—that Jesus of Nazareth was of that sect, and that the Essenes being before his advent, taught all the essential doctrines of Christ. Whatever may have been the fact in some other countries, there is not the least particle of evidence that any such a people existed in Judea until after the time of Christ. These warring parties are often spoken of. Hostile armies of different nations were frequently passing through Judea, and must have come in contact with such a people if any existed; yet all the writers of these times are silent about the Essenes. The strong presumption is, that no such people existed, at least in Judea, and that Jesus Christ borrowed none of his great truths of mortal men. Jonathan had some difficulty with the Pharisees, and on this account gave the whole weight of his influence to the Sadducees. The Pharisees laid great stress upon the traditions and formalities which had been appended to the sacred scriptures, and believed in a resurrection of the dead and a future existence, which it seems, was only defended by these traditions, while the Sadducees adhered only to the inspired word without appendage or tradition, and maintained that the Hebrew scripture alone revealed no future existence for man. Jonathan reflected the tradition of the Pharisees. This sect, ever pre-eminent for their bigotry, as men are always more apt to be, for the traditions, faiths, formalities and creeds, than for the original word upon which they base those human productions, were exceedingly vindictive toward the whole house of Jonathan, and endeavored to harass and perplex the royal high priest and all his adherents. They had been the cause of the recent civil war, in which, not only their opponents, but themselves suffered severely. They were exceedingly spiteful toward Jason during his life. But after his death, affairs took an entirely new turn. Alexandria found herself suddenly at the head of the government, a weak, defenseless woman, unable to cope with the crafty bigots, by whom she was surrounded. She immediately called the Pharisees around her, professed her attachment to their faith, and desired to put the affairs of the government into their hands. She intimated that this course was in compliance with the wishes of her late husband. Elated with this preferment, they made a pompous funeral for the late king, and extolled him as one of the best and most religious of men, although in his life-time, they had said and done all in their power to injure him.

The funeral over, these religious bigots began the work of vengeance for their past calamities. They persecuted even unto death, great numbers of those who adhered to the former monarch. Men, women, and children, were often slain without even the shadow of a crime being charged against them, except that in the preceding reign they had obeyed their lawful sovereign, and were friends of the Sadducees. In the mean time Hyrcanus, the elder son of the queen, was made high priest. But he was a stupid, inactive man, and took no conspicuous part in the events that were transpiring.

At length the distressed inhabitants, with Aristobulus, the younger son of the late monarch, applied to the queen for protection from the fury of their persecutors. They represented that these calamities were brought upon them purely from having been faithful to her husband, and that she ought either to protect them in their homes or permit them peaceably to depart into other countries where quiet might be enjoyed. The artful Pharisees had so adroitly planned their measures, and surrounded the queen with their creatures, that she had no power to help herself or aid her people. She had completely yielded her person and kingdom into the hands of their infamous council. Whatever of remorse she might suffer, aid she had none. She however, granted part of their requests, and sent many of the sufferers to fill her remote fortresses and garrisons, thinking that in any emergency that might arise, she could rely upon them for aid. Nearly six years had transpired under the cruel persecutions of the Pharisees when Alexandria fell sick, and was evidently near the end of her life. In 73, Aristobulus, who had long meditated this step, took measures to secure the crown to himself. Stealthily, and in the night, he glided out of Jerusalem with one servant, visited the garrison of the country, where his friends were prepared to receive him, and in fifteen days was at the head of a formidable army of those, who, by persecution, had been brought to detest the dominant party. Twenty-two towns, and many castles, with multitudes of all the people, weary of the tyranny of the Pharisees, joined Aristobulus.

When the dominant party saw him approach Jerusalem with an army, they immediately crowned Hyrcanus king; not however, until they had visited the chamber of the dying queen, and informed her of the state of affairs. But she was too far gone to meddle longer with temporal matters. The Pharisees pretended that she bequeathed the care of the kingdom to them, appointing Hyrcanus her successor; but of this there is doubt. It is probable that she expired amid their importunities.

Aristobulus had a wife and child in Jerusalem. These the Pharisees seized and shut up in the castle of Bares, hoping thereby to intimidate him. But not succeeding in their purpose, they raised an army to sustain Hyrcanus, and resist his brother. The two hostile forces met, and an engagement ensued on the banks of the Jordan, near Jericho. Hyrcanus, being of a feeble intellect and timid heart, fled early in the battle, and his friends were entirely defeated, while most of his effective forces went over and joined the standard of Aristobulus. Hyrcanus fled to the castle of Bares, and his adherents to the temple, where they were invested by the victorious army, and compelled to surrender. An accommodation was the result, in which it was stipulated that Hyrcanus should retire to private life, which seemed best suited to his nature and wishes, and that Aristobulus should fill the office of high priest and king.

ARISTOBULUS II., B. C. 69.

One Antipas, sometimes called Antipater, and subsequently distinguished as the father of Herod, a native of Idumea, in common with many of his countrymen, had been compelled by force to embrace the Jewish religion. He had become prime minister under Alexander Jonas, and continued in office under the queen. He had high hopes that, by sustaining Hyrcanus, he should still keep himself in power, and through the weakness of that prince control the government; but the defeat of Hyrcanus and the coronation of Aristobulus had frustrated all his ambitious hopes. He therefore sought to restore Hyrcanus. For the space of four years, without success, he importuned a king of Arabia, and other powers, for aid. About this time, 65 B. C., Pompey, the famous Roman, having returned from Parthia, halted in Syria, which had recently become a Roman province. Antipater repaired to Damascus, complained of Aristobulus, and besought Roman aid to restore Hyrcanus. Aristobulus, aware of these measures, also applied to Pompey to confirm him on his throne.

A much more reasonable application was made by the people, who represented that the kingly form of government was of recent origin, and a usurpation, and that they were accustomed to be governed by the high priest alone, according to the ancient usage of their fathers. They therefore desired to be delivered from both the brothers. The policy of Rome for a number of generations had been adverse to all kings, and in favor of some Republican form of government, but they had suffered the high priests of Judea to assume the title of king, in order to annoy Syria. Syria had now been subdued, and become subject to Rome, and it became desirable to reduce the kingdom of Judea also.

Aristobulus defended himself, and declared that he had practiced no injustice against his brother, who was removed simply on account of his incapacity. He stated that he had assumed no other title nor authority than those possessed by his father and grandfather before him. His claims were sustained by a body of nobles dressed in gay and princely apparel—whose manners were haughty and insolent, greatly disgusting the plain Roman Consul.

Pompey was not in haste, as he had other interests at heart. Flushed with the glory of having checked the Parthians and completed the subjugation of Syria, he desired also to add the conquest of Arabia to his laurels. Arabia had often been been invaded, but seldom if ever conquered, since the days of Nebuchadnezzar. In the impregnable rock of Petra, so often spoken of as the astonishment of modern travelers, dwelt Auretus, king of Northern Arabia.* The hostility of Aristobulus might obstruct his campaign in this direction. Pompey therefore gave

---

*This stronghold had once before been stormed by Antiochus the Great, but was still the capital of a mighty and free people.

evasive answers to the several petitions; but his future purposes were formed. He pursued his journey down the Jordan, around the Dead Sea, and among the defiles of Idumea. Unaccountable as it may appear, the Arabians were not aware of his approach.

He took Petræa by surprise, and captured the city of the rock with its king. Aristobulus, suspecting the policy of Pompey, immediately departed from Damascus, without the usual tokens of respect to the Roman Consul; and while Arabia was being overrun by Pompey, Judea was being fortified for a visit from him on his return. Having accomplished the expedition, and set Auretus free upon a promised submission to Rome, Pompey returned to Damascus, where he learned of the formidable preparations for war which had been made during his absence. He now marched his army toward Judea, and Aristobulus came out to dispute his progress.

The advancing host encamped near a mountain, on which stood a castle called the Alexandrus. In this castle Aristobulus with his guides lodged. It was a strong place built by his father, Alexander Jonas.* Aristobulus visited Pompey in his camp several times, and labored to persuade him to declare in his favor, against the claims of Hyrcanus. But the Consul had his own ends to accomplish. At length he seized Aristobulus, and compelled him to sign orders for the delivery of several fortresses to the Romans; after which the prisoner was released.

Incensed as well he might be at this treachery, Aristobulus hastened to Jerusalem, and prepared for a vigorous defense. Pompey pursued his way southward to Jericho,

---

*I have been unable to determine with certainty the exact locality of this hill and fortress, but believe it must have been on the east of Galilee, a little north of the east branch of the Jordan, and about twenty miles north of Gadar.

near which place he received intelligence of the death of the great Mithridates, with whom Rome had long been at war. Ascending the barren mountains, the Roman army approached Jerusalem. Aristobulus had not yet abandoned all hope of the favor of Pompey. He came out to meet him, and endeavored once more to persuade him to declare on his side. He offered him large sums of money and entire submission. Pompey was not insensible to the charms of money, although far less avaricious than many of the Roman officers. He accepted the offer, and sent Gelanor, his lieutenant, to Jerusalem, to receive the treasure, retaining Aristobulus in his power. The inhabitants of the city were unwilling to ratify the bargain, and shut the gates against the Roman officer. Exasperated at this refusal, Pompey put Aristobulus in chains, and marched against the city. But it being well fortified, a vigorous defense, lasting three months, abated somewhat his ardor. Civil dissensions within now began to weaken the defenses of the city. The adherents of Hyrcanus proposed to surrender to Pompey, well knowing that by so doing they should gain his favor for their chief. The adherents of Aristobulus, on the contrary, determined still to resist. The party of Hyrcanus prevailed, and opened the city to the Roman army; but not until the opposite side had fortified themselves in the temple, and the wall and towers in connection with it, broken up the bridges that crossed the defiles, and thus made themselves quite impregnable.

Three months they sustained themselves in this stronghold, and perhaps would have compelled the Romans to abandon the siege, had it not been for their superstitious regard of the Sabbath. As in the war of Antiochus Epiphanes, the Jews would neither guard, work, nor fight on the Sabbath day, unless directly attacked. Pompey, aware of this, did not attack them on those days, but employed his men in breaking down works of defense, and rearing his engines near those of his enemies, which the Jews could but would not prevent. At length a tower and portion of the wall were thrown down, and a breach made, through which the besieging army passed, sword in hand, and captured the place, slaying twelve thousand persons. This was the first invasion by the Romans, and opened the way for that Roman influence which we find prevailing over the Jewish nation, at the birth of Christ. This year, which was 65 before the birth of Christ, was thus marked by the subjection to Rome, of Mesopotamia, Armenia, Pergamos, Syria, Arabia and Judea, and the fourth beast was fully established over all the head of the third except Egypt, which continued independent thirty-five years longer.

While the temple and citadel were being taken, the citizens being slaughtered, their blood flowing upon the ground and floor of the sanctuary, and the cries of the wounded, and the groans of the dying were rending the air, the priests were engaged in their usual sacrifices, from which service they did not desist, but proceeded as leisurely as if naught was transpiring. While true and intelligent piety promotes benevolence, and in no small degree consists in utility, a false and corrupt religion stupifies and annihilates all the finer feelings of our nature, and causes a servile adherence to the mere forms of religion, without the principles of righteousness or utility. This is the case in every age, and under every dispensation. I speak thus of the religion of those times, as corrupt, false, and useless, not because the Bible was not the word of God and the only record of divine truth, but because the Jewish nation had so changed the sacred teaching that it was not indeed the same religion, but a system of their traditions engrafted upon the truth, and often perverting it.

Pompey and many of his officers entered not only into

the temple, but into the holy of holies, thus polluting the sacred retreat of the high priest. This event keenly afflicted the Jews. It had occurred but a very few times since the destruction of the original temple of Solomon. Pompey, with commendable modesty, did not touch the sacred treasures in the temple, which were deposited there for charitable purposes, and amounted to the enormous sum of one and a half million of dollars. What possible charitable use could demand so great a sum? Was it not collected by the avaricious priests for their own purposes, under pretext of charity? Of this moderation of Pompey, Rollin thus speaks:

"It was not out of respect for the majesty of the God adored in that temple, that Pompey behaved in this manner, for according to him, nothing was more contemptible than the Jewish religion; more unworthy the wisdom and grandure of the Romans, or more opposite to the institutions of their ancestors. Pompey had no other motive in this disinterestedness than to deprive malice and calumny of all means of attacking his reputation. Such were the thoughts of the most learned pagans with respect to the only religion of the only true God. They blasphemed what they knew not."

All this may sound well, but it is susceptible of criticism. For what did Pompey invade Jerusalem but for money, which Aristobulus promised, but the people refused to pay? For what but money did he attack and conquer the temple? Surely some other motive, whatever it might be, deterred him from enjoying what he had slain twelve thousand men to obtain. That motive is not apparent. Rollin speaks of the Romans despising the only religion of the true God, but what was there at that time in the conduct, morals, or habits of the high priests, priests, Levites, Pharisees, or people, that would lead one to suppose they, and they only, were the devoted servants of a Holy God?

All their religious conduct was abhorrent to every sense of justice and honesty. However holy and heavenly might have been, and evidently was the religion of Moses, of David, of Isaiah, and of Daniel, it would be difficult to find, save in a few obscure individuals, anything in the Jewish religion of the time we are describing, that is not revolting to contemplate, and calculated to fill a noble Roman's breast with disgust.

HYRCANUS II., B. C. 63.

Pompey having ended the present war by the capture of the temple, demolished much of the wall of Jerusalem, re-established Hyrcanus upon the throne of Judea, and sent Aristobulus and his sons Alexander and Antigonus in chains, prisoners to Rome. But Alexander effected his escape before arriving at the seven-hilled city, and returned to Judea, where he was not idle. Several cities were detached from the kingdom of Judea, and added to Syria. A heavy tribute was imposed upon Hyrcanus, and Antipator was appointed prime minister. In 57 B. C., young Alexander finding himself at the head of an army, laid claim to the throne of his fathers. The feeble and effeminate Hyrcanus was either unwilling or afraid to meet him in battle, he therefore sought Roman aid, and Gabinius, governor of Syria, marched to his assistance. He met and defeated the army of Alexander, and restored Hyrcanus the third time to the office of high priest, but not to the throne.

Gabinius, for a short time, abolished the monarchial form of government. In the year 54, Crassus, the Roman, was on his unfortunate expedition to Parthia, and passed through Jerusalem, where he, less scrupulous than Pompey, robbed the temple of all its treasures, amounting in value to ten thousand talents, or seven and a half millions of dollars. At this time Cæsar was becoming the great man of Rome. He had beaten the unfortunate Pompey in the great battle of

Pharsalus, in which Hyrcanus and Antipater had been of some service to him. These were also the days of trouble Ptolemy and Cleopatra, the last of the Lagidæ in Egypt. Cæsar visited Egypt to adjust these difficulties, where he had his remarkable adventure with that most remarkable of women. The object of this mission was greatly facilitated by the kindly aid of Hyrcanus and Antipater.

While Cæsar was in Syria, soon after his adventure in Egypt, Aristobulus and his son Antigonus effected their escape from Rome, and also repaired to Syria, where they besought Cæsar to restore them to their rights, and at the same time complained of the mal-administration of Hyrcanus and Antipater. But Cæsar, partial to Hyrcanus, by whom he had been aided, rejected their petition, and confirmed Hyrcanus, not only in the office of high priest, but also restored to him the title and authority of king of Judea, which had been annulled by Gabinius, about ten years before. Antipater was appointed pro-consul and collector of the revenues of Judea, under Hyrcanus. Antipater, it will be remembered, was an Idumean proselyte, and not a native Jew. He had two sons, the oldest of whom was called Phasæl and the second was Herod, in whose time Christ was born. To Phasæl was given the government of Jerusalem, while his brother was appointed governor of Galilee. By Cæsar's permission the walls of Jerusalem, which had been thrown down by Pompey, were rebuilt and strongly fortified, thus furnishing work for Titus many years afterward, in the final conquest of that city. The same year Cæsar returned to Rome, sought the imperial dignity, and was slain in the Senate Chamber, 44 B. C.

In 40 B. C., new actors appear in the field of strife. Crassus had lost his life in his rash enterprise against the Parthians, and that nation had followed the retreating Romans into Syria. Pacorus, their king, sent a detachment of his army into Judea, with orders to place Antigonus, son of Aristobulus, upon the throne. Antigonus had also raised an army to accompany this expedition. Hyrcanus and Phocas ventured into the camp of the enemy to propose an accommodation, but were seized and made prisoners. Herod escaped from Jerusalem just as the Parthians entered it. Antigonus was established upon the throne, and Hyrcanus and Phasæl in chains put into his hands. Phasæl being of foreign extraction, was condemned to death; but to avoid a public execution, he dashed out his own brains against a wall. Antigonus spared the life of his uncle, Hyrcanus; but to render it impossible for him again to serve in the capacity of high priest, he smote off his right ear, as that blemish, according to the Mosaic law, rendered him unfit for the office. Hyrcanus was carried a captive into Parthia, where he remained, in Seleucia, many years. Herod fled first to Egypt, then to Rome. Cæsar was dead; his murderers were absent, and bold, blunt Marc Antony was then the ruling spirit of that nation. Herod was immediately taken under his protection, and treated with honor, considering that he was a poor boy, the son of Antipater, an Idumean exile. He had not himself expected to be promoted to power; but, like his father in the preceding reign, he desired some branch of the family of Hyrcanus to be restored to the throne, that he might serve under him. Hyrcanus had a daughter, Alexandra, who had been married to Alexander, the son of Aristobulus, who escaped on his way to Rome a prisoner. By this marriage they had a son, also called Aristobulus. He was thus the grandson of both Hyrcanus and Aristobulus II., who had been sent to Rome. Herod put forward the claims of young Aristobulus III. But the Roman senate, under the influence of Marc Antony, did more than he requested, for they declared Herod himself king of Judea. Herod was only seven days in Rome, and accomplished more than all he intended, and returned hastily into Judea.

• Two years of vigorous effort were required for Herod to displace Antigonus, and gain for himself the gift of the Roman senate. He had to besiege Jerusalem in due form, and, after a great struggle against a desperate rival, he ultimately took the city, only by the aid of the governor and army of the city, and after six months' siege. Having at length triumphantly entered the city, his soldiers put great numbers of the Jews to death, and caused the streets to flow with streams of human blood. The fate of Antigonus is to be deplored. Seeing that all was lost, he went out to Socius, the Syrian governor, and implored mercy. He was put in chains and sent to Antioch, where Antony had just arrived. He visited the prisoner, and intended to take him to Rome to adorn his triumphal procession. But Herod could never rest easy so long as a rival to the throne existed. He therefore caused the unfortunate prince to be proceeded against as a common criminal, and condemned to be put to death by the barbarous execution of lictors and axes. Thus perished the last king of the descendants of Judea.

Hyrcanus still lived a prisoner in the East. While Herod was prosecuting the siege of Jerusalem, he went to Samaria and married Mariamna, the sister of Aristobulus III., and grand-daughter of both Hyrcanus and Aristobulus II. She was the sister of that Antigonus against whom he was then at war, and whom he afterward caused to be put to death in the manner above related.

Under favor of the Parthians, Hyrcanus was at length set at liberty and made high priest in that country, and treated with distinguished honor. But the love of his native country induced him to forego all these honors, and revisit Judea, where Herod caused him to be seized and put to death, notwithstanding he was the grandfatner of his wife. Herod reigned thirty-nine years. The last of the Jewish rulers had gone down to the grave by violent death. An Idumean sits undisturbed on the throne of that nation. The scepter of Judah has departed forever, and the kingdom from that time groaned under the reign of Herod the cruel, until the Shilo of promise came.*

PTOLEMY PHYSCON, B. C. 145.

Ptolemy Philometor had a brother, subsequently called Physcon, who at this time was a king of Cyrenia. Some of the nobility persuaded him to visit Alexandria, with the intention of placing him upon the throne of his late brother; but Cleopatra, the widowed queen, was not disposed to acknowledge his claim. She endeavored to raise her son, the son of Philopater, an infant, to the throne. Each party had control of an army, and there was prospect of a civil war. By the influence of Flamminius, a Roman officer, this war was delayed for a time, although it did not save Egypt from some most bloody scenes. A compromise was effected. Physcon was to marry Cleopatra, educate her son, and finally transmit to him the crown.

Their marriage was celebrated and the crown placed upon the head of Physcon, and, on the same day, he murdered the child of the queen in its mother's arms.

The first seven or eight years of the reign of Physcon were marked by excessive debauchery and horrible acts of cruelty. His prime minister, Hierax, a native of Antioch,

* Wise men of the East came to Judea to seek for him that was born king of the Jews. Not forty years before that event, the Parthians, who were the wise men of the East, had invaded Judea, captured Jerusalem, and carried the high priest captive into the East, where, doubtless, he had taught all around him of the expected coming of Shilo, as an event near at hand. Some of these wise men might have listened to the teachings of Hyrcanus on that subject, while a captive among them.

a faithful, brave and talented officer, was barely able to prevent his being dethroned and expelled. After the year 136, we hear no more of Hierax. Physcon, as if abandoned to all that is evil, caused the murder of almost all the men who had elevated Philopater to the crown, or had held office under him. He surrounded himself with a foreign soldiery, whose brutal and frequent murders caused great numbers of the inhabitants of Alexandria to flee from the city. These were generally the best, the most learned and most useful citizens. Alexandria became almost a desert. To repeople the desolate city, he sent proclamations to different countries, offering great advantages to those who should settle there. Multitudes of strangers flocked in, to whom he gave the deserted houses of the inhabitants; thus making this band of foreign adventurers dependent upon himself.

Cleopatra, the queen and sister of Physcon, had a daughter by her first husband, Philopater, also called Cleopatra. Physcon having taken a disgust at his sister-wife, became enamored of her child. In the year 130 B. C., he first ravished and subsequently married the younger Cleopatra, and repudiated the elder.

His repeated acts of monstrous cruelty, caused him soon to be as much hated by his new subjects, whom he had invited to Alexandria, as he had been by the former inhabitants. Fearing some outbreak, he determined to put it out of their power to do him harm. He resolved to murder all the young men of the city, supposing thereby he should render the rest too feeble to resist him. On a day of public exercise, when the multitude were assembled, he ordered his foreign soldiery suddenly to surround the people, and murder the youth. Many were slain; but this act threw the populace into great confusion and madness. They ran to the royal palace and set it on fire, hoping to consume the tyrant in it, but he had just effected his escape.

He fled with his wife and his young son, Memphitis, to the island of Cyprus. The people immediately put the government of Egypt into the hands of Cleopatra, the elder. The fugitive king prepared to make war upon Alexandria and the queen.

Physcon had an elder son in Alexandria, to whom he had given the government of Cyrenia. Fearing that the Alexandrians might make him king of Egypt, he sent for this son to visit him. The jealous father, to prevent a danger which had no foundation, except in his own guilty conscience, caused this son to be murdered. The barbarity of this act greatly increased the fury of his enemies, and caused many of his friends to forsake him. In Alexandria, they destroyed his statues, and added every possible insult to his name. Physcon believed that the elder Cleopatra had incited the Alexandrians to these deeds. He therefore determined upon a strange and unnatural revenge. Memphitis, his own son, was then with him in exile. He was the much beloved son of the elder Cleopatra. Physcon caused the throat of Memphitis to be cut, his body chopped to pieces, but his face to remain unmutilated. Then placing the mangled body in a chest, he sent it to Alexandria. The queen's birthday was approaching. When it arrived, it was celebrated with great pomp and splendor. Just in the midst of the rejoicing, the agent of Physcon presents the chest. It is opened, and the queen, in the midst of her festivity, beholds the face and the mangled body of her much loved boy. Grief and lamentation succeed to the voice of mirth. The corpse was exposed everywhere in the streets to the gaze of the multitude, who became greatly excited, and declared that Physcon should never more rule in Egypt. An army was raised to resist him, and committed to the care of Marsyas.

In 128 B. C., Physcon also raised an army, committing it to the command of Hegelochus, and sent him against Alexandria. A bloody battle was fought, the army of Physcon was triumphant, and the queen's soldiers were mostly cut to pieces, their general taken prisoner, and sent to Physcon.

Whether the bloody passions of Physcon had exhausted their energies and become quiet, or whether he had grown wiser by sad experience, we can not tell; but he seems, at this time, to have abated somewhat of his ferocious disposition. He gave Marsyas his liberty, without any penalty whatever.

The army of Cleopatra being greatly reducea, snc applied to Demetrius, king of Syria, for aid, promising him the crown of Egypt as his reward. Demetrius had married another Cleopatra, the eldest daughter of the queen of Egypt, by Philometor. Demetrius immediately marched an army into Pelusium; but trouble at home soon recalled him again. Cleopatra, of Egypt, being now absolutely destitute of aid, fled to Syria with her daughter, with whom she remained till the end of her life.

The next year, 127, Physcon entered Alexandria, and recovered his throne and kingdom. To be revenged upon Demetrius for attempting to aid the Alexandrians, he meddled with the affairs of Syria, by setting up an imposter, Zebina, in which he was for a time successful, and Demetrius lost his kingdom and his life. Subsequently, Zebina not-being willing to pay to Physcon the homage which he demanded, the king of Egypt again interfered in the affairs of Syria, and deprived Zebina of his ill gotten throne.

Physcon died 117 B. C., after a reign of twenty-nine years, subsequent to the death of his brother. Years marked with such horrible atrocities, that we look upon them amazed and are unable to make comment.

DEMETRIUS NICATOR AND THE SYRIAN CLEOPATRA, B. C. 145.

We have seen that Demetrius Soter lost his life in war with Alexander Bala, the imposter, and that Bala had been defeated by the present monarch.

Soter left three sons, two of whom, Demetrius, afterward called Nicator, and Alexander, had been sent to Cnidus, where they were at the time of their father's death. The younger was put to death by Bala, but the older somehow escaped his enemy. In the year 147, Demetrius II., (Nicator), left his retreat, and, gathering an army, contended for the throne of his father. After several vicissitudes of fortune, Bala was defeated, and fled to Arabia, where he was treacherously murdered, and the body sent to Philopater, king of Egypt, and Demetrius became king of Syria 145 B. C. Cleopatra, the daughter of Philometor, and wife of Bala, was given as a wife to Demetrius Nicator.

With the king of Egypt as a father-in-law, with the friendship of the Romans, and with the affection of his own people, who had been terribly oppressed by the rigor and maladministration of Bala, a judicious king might expect a prosperous and peaceful life on the throne of Syria. But all such indications soon vanished. All external circumstances are of no value, when indolence and debauchery reign at home. Demetrius was still young, unaccustomed to business, inexperienced in the affairs of State, and more devoted to pleasure than to the duties and responsibilities of office. He committed the care of all business to Sosthenes, the man in whose house he had found shelter in the days of his father's calamity. Gratitude to a benefactor is commendable; but the prime minister was a foreigner, having no sympathy with the people, and exercising no judgment, justice or discretion in the discharge of his official duties. His maladministration alienated the affections of the people from the government. He had disarmed all the native soldiery, and surrounded the throne with a foreign guard, mostly Cretans. Nicator devoted himself to debauchery, while his people were suffering from the extortions of his minister, and the butchery of all those who opposed his measures.

What else could be expected than that aspirants would avail themselves of the general discontent to grasp at the crown? Tryphon, who had been a minister of State under Bala, began to figure. Bala had left a son, Antiochus, afterward called Theos, in Arabia, in the care of a prince of that country. To him Tryphon repaired, obtained the young Antiochus, brought him to Syria, and through the aid of the people, who were wearied with the evil administration of Demetrius, declared him king of Syria, and placed him on the throne—not long there to remain, but simply to form a stepping-stone for his protector, who intended to murder him in due time, and take the crown to himself. All this was accomplished the next year, (143 B. C.), and the throne was filled by Tryphon, whose cruelty and maladministration were equal to that of his predecesssor.

EXPEDITION OF DEMETRIUS NICATOR IN THE EAST, B. C. 142.

The extensive plains on the banks of the Euphrates and the Tigris, with their cities, once forming the kingdom of Babylonia, and afterward subject to Persia, had, in the partition of Alexander's empire, fallen to Syria, and had been governed by officers appointed at Antioch. Thus they became the captives of those whom they had carried captive, as foretold by Isaiah. Many Macedonian families were also merged with the inhabitants of this district.

A little further east was Parthia, at this time a powerful kingdom. During the commotion of several preceding reigns in Syria, the Parthians, availing themselves of the embarrassments of their neighbors, had subdued Mesopotamia and attached it to their own empire. The Syrians were so much occupied with other matters that since the days of Antiochus the Great, or, perhaps, of Seleucus Callinicus, they had not been able to reclaim them. The Parthian yoke, however, was exceedingly severe, and the inhabitants desired a change of masters.

Tryphon, having brought Antiochus Theos, the youthful son of Bala, out of Arabia, and driven out Demetrius, first placed Theos on the throne, and then murdered him; after which he placed the crown upon his own head, and reigned at Antioch. Demetrius, defeated and repulsed from Antioch, had retired to Seleucia, where, depressed by misfortune, he devoted his time to debauchery and sensuality. Thus stood affairs in 142 B. C. The people of Mesopotamia sent him an invitation to repair thither and assist them in throwing off the Parthian yoke. He hears and responds to the call. Ambition rouses him from his indolence, and paints future scenes of glory. Could he subdue the Parthians and place himself at the head of the eastern provinces, he might, with their aid, expel Tryphon and regain the throne of Syria.

To the East he repairs; the Elamites, the Persians, the Bactrians and the mingled people join his standard, and the gathering hosts swell into a large army. In several engagements he repulsed the enemy, and all his bright anticipations gave promise of being realized. How delusive are the hopes of man! how inconstant the smiles of fortune! The Parthians, under pretense of negociating a peace with Demetrius, decoyed him into their power, and made a prisoner of him, and cut to pieces his entire army.

Let us look back upon Syria. Although Tryphon had expelled the preceding king, murdered the last one, and usurped the throne, it must not be supposed that he had undisputed possession of all Syria. During these events, two distinct factions, with their governments, ruled in Syria at different places. Cleopatra, the daughter of Philometor, the former wife of Bala, and afterward of Demetrius, still lived, a woman, proud, resolute, determined to rule, and not easy to be subdued.

Many of the generals and princes of Syria adhered to her, and even many of Tryphon's men went over to her standard. She held her court at Ptolemais.

When Cleopatra heard that her husband was taken captive, she sought new alliances to sustain herself against the usurper. There was at this time one Antiochus, afterward called Sidetes, a brother of Nicator; to him she sent an invitation to marry her, and offered him the crown, to the exclusion of her sons by Demetrius. This offer was accepted, and the new couple ruled for a time in Syria. In the spring of 139 B. C., Sidetes made war upon Tryphon, drove him out of his possession, and shut him up in the castle of Dora, from which he escaped, first to Arthesia and then to Sidon, where he was taken and put to death. In 138 B. C. we find Sidetes and Cleopatra in possession of the throne of Syria, which they held until 130 B. C.

But Demetrius Nicator still lives, although a prisoner. Let us return to him. His imprisonment had not been severe. He had been sent to Hyrcana, where, except his liberty, he received all the attention due to a king. Rhodaguna, the daughter of the king of that country, was given him in marriage, and for about ten years, the days passed cheerily along. Twice, however, Demetrius attempted his escape, but was retaken. The Parthian kindness to Demetrius originated in selfish policy. That people contemplated the invasion of Syria, in which event Demetrius was to be used as the rival of his brother, to divide and diminish the strength of Syria. Sidetes, suspecting their purpose, did not wait to be invaded. Having crushed his enemy at home, he marched, in 138, an army of eighteen thousand soldiers to the banks of the Euphrates, and commenced war to recover possession of Mesopotamia; this expedition was at first successful, in three engagements he defeated his enemy, and recovered all the provinces of the East that had formerly belonged to Syria. But the winter came and nipped his prosperity in the bud. The winter came, and to supply his army with food, it was necessary to divide it. In this divided condition, the enemy fell upon them, and defeated the whole army. Sidetes, in attempting to relieve the party nearest him, was slain. Thus terminated in defeat the entire expedition.

Before the defeat of Sidetes, the Parthians, fearing the results of this war, had set Demetrius at liberty, that he might, by returning to Syria, and reclaiming his wife and the throne, cause the return of Sidetes. Demetrius had set out, but when Sidetes was slain, the Parthians having no further need of that assistance, sent a dispatch to retake and bring him back again. But he was already far beyond their power. During that year he arrived safely at Syria, remarried his Cleopatra, and assumed once more the government of Syria, amid great rejoicings and celebrations, while his people were overwhelmed in the deepest mourning for the loss of their friends in the war.

ANTIOCHUS SIDETES

Was the younger brother of Demetrius Nicator, and was

sent with him into Caria in their youth by their father, Demetrius, before he was slain in the war with Bala. He seems to have been a moderately good king, and avoided the excesses either of cruelty or debauchery, for which so many of the kings of Syria were notorious. He was exceedingly fond of hunting, on which account he received the name of Sidetes, which, in Syriac signifies a hunter. In his war with Tryphon he exhibited skill and decision, which was speedily crowned with success. In his expedition to the East he also exhibited military talent. But one defect was manifest in his arrangements, which was probably the cause of his ruin; that defect was the large number of useless and effeminate persons that accompanied the army, and the extravagant luxury which exhausted their provisions. This army is thus described by Rollin:

"His army consisted of upward of eighty thousand men, well armed and disciplined. But the train of luxury had added to it so great a multitude of sutlers, cooks, pastry-cooks, confectioners, actors, musicians and infamous women, that they were almost four times as many as the soldiers, for they were reckoned to amount to about three hundred thousand. There may be some exaggeration in this account, but if two-thirds were deducted, there would still remain a numerous train of useless mouths. The luxury of the camp was in proportion to those that administered to it. Gold and silver glittered in all parts — even upon the boots of the private soldiers. The instruments and utensils of the kitchen were silver, as if they had been marching to a feast and not to war."

Cleopatra, although a second time married to Demetrius, did not surrender her share in the government, and held her court still at Ptolemais, while her husband, with the army, remained at Antioch. Being at war with Ptolemy Physcon, Demetrius was defeated in battle, and fled to Ptolemais, but the unkind queen, who never forgave his marriage with the princess of Bactriana, shut the gates against him, and he was compelled to retire to Tyre, at which city he was overtaken and murdered. Cleopatra thus became sole possessor of the crown of Syria. About the year 127, Physcon, out of revenge for Demetrius having invaded Egypt many years before, sent an imposter, Alexander Zebina, to claim the throne. This Zebina was a native of Alexandria, but he pretended to be the son of Alexander Bala, whose melancholy fate in Arabia some years before, we have given. It was in this war that Demetrius was defeated and compelled to fly to Tyre. The kingdom thus became divided between Zebina at Antioch, and Cleopatra at Ptolemais. The queen had sons by Demetrius. The oldest, Seleucus, now began to entertain a hope of gaining the throne of his father. He was declared king in 124, but his mother was more anxious to rule alone than to advance his interests. She also feared that, should Seleucus become fully established in the kingdom, he might avenge the death of his father, which, it was generally believed, was effected by her instigation. Within one year thereafter, in 123, she, with her own hand, plunged a dagger into the heart of her own royal son.

About this time three of the principal officers of Zebina revolted from him and joined the standard of Cleopatra. The queen fearing to be left quite alone, caused her second son to be proclaimed king. But he was quite young, and she therefore retained all the power. This son was called Antiochus Grypus, the latter name referring to his great nose. Physcon having been the agent by whose means Zebina had risen to power, demanded courtesy and service of him, which Zebina refused to yield. On this account Physcon determined to destroy him whom he had first elevated to power. He therefore settled all difficulties with Cleopatra, gave his own daughter, Tryphena, in marriage to Grypus, and aided him in a contest for the throne of Zebina, who was defeated and deprived of power. He retired to Antioch, where he formed a design of plundering the temple of Jupiter, which, being discovered, so exasperated the people that they furiously ran upon him and murdered him. Thus ended the life of the second imposter, and Grypus took the government of Syria.

Cleopatra, still unwilling to divide the power between herself and any one, once more prepared to murder her royal son, and confer the title of king upon another younger child, the son of Sidetes. To accomplish that purpose, she prepared a bowl of poison, which she presented to Grypus one day as he returned hot from some exercise. That prince having somehow been apprised of her design, very respectfully requested his royal mother first to drink; but, as she positively refused to do so, he called in witnesses, and, after charging her with the crime of intending to murder him, compelled her to swallow the draught, which took immediate effect, and ended the life of one of the worst of women, whose unparalleled crimes had been the destruction of her family and the scourge of the state. She had been the wife of three kings of Syria, and the death of two of them she had occasioned. She was the mother of four kings, one of whom she slew with her own hand, and attempted to destroy another. She died in the year 120 B. C.

PTOLEMY LATHYRUS, B. C. 117.

All the sons of Physcon, by his first Cleopatra, had been slain by himself. By the second, who was the daughter of the first, he left two sons, Lathyrus and Alexander, and three daughters, Cleopatra, Selene and Tryphena. He had also an illegitimate son, Apion, to whom he gave the kingdom of Cyrene, and who, at his death, willed his crown to the Romans.

Physcon, by his will, left the kingdom of Egypt to his queen, Cleopatra, and to whichever of the two sons she might choose. Of the wife of Physcon we know but little until after her husband's death. Left alone and clothed with the royal authority, she exhibited all the enormity of an adept in crime and cruelty. She had long entertained an implacable hatred to her eldest son. Before his father's death, Physcon, through her influence, had banished him to the island of Cyprus. The queen-mother preferred to associate with herself, in the government, her younger son, Alexander, because he was of a mild and peaceful spirit, and she could better control him than a prince who had energy to claim his share in the administration. The people of Alexandria were not disposed to acquiesce in this arrangement. They therefore disregarded the condition of the will, and, recalling Lathyrus from Cyprus, placed him on the throne to reign jointly with his mother. In these days it had become quite common for the princes of Egypt to marry their own sisters. The eldest widow and mother of the queen, it will be recollected, had been the wife of two of her brothers. Lathyrus was greatly attached to his elder sister, Cleopatra; but the imperious mother compelled her royal son, before he could share in the government, to renounce all claim to her, and marry his second sister, Selina. This arrangement proved a very unhappy one, as will be seen in the result. Tryphena, the third sister, had married Grypus, king of Syria. Cleopatra being at liberty, also married a prince of Syria, and both of these daughters were ultimately put to death in the most violent and brutal manner, for which their monstrous mother seemed not to grieve, so intent was she upon ruling absolute and alone. To her son Alexander, she gave the government of Cyprus, that she might rely upon him and his army for aid to check the measures of Lathyrus, her associate on the throne.

In the year 109 B. C., the Jews being at war with their near neighbors, besieged Samaria. The inhabitants of that city, in their distress, sent to Lathyrus for aid, and he promptly sent them six thousand soldiers. Cleopatra was under the influence of the Jewish counsellors, who had built a temple in Egypt. She disapproved of this measure, and threatened to deprive him of his share in the government for having encroached upon what she deemed her prerogative. In the year 107, she took from him his wife, Selene, by whom he had already two sons, both of whom died when quite young. Lathyrus, by his mother's authority, was banished from Egypt. He took charge of the little kingdom of Cyprus, and Alexander, who was the king of that island, was recalled, to take the throne of Egypt. This had been the original intention of Cleopatra, whose purposes had been frustrated by the people some ten years before.

The manner in which the imperious queen effected this change, was a fair specimen of woman's wiles and intrigue, showing how little credit ought to be given at any time to the testimony of designing women, when they complain of violence or insult. In a vast majority of cases, such accusers, fired with passion, or having some secret object to gain, are utterly unworthy of credit. Cleopatra caused two eunuchs, by whom she was attended, to be wounded and then exhibited to the populace, asserting that Lathyrus had committed violence. They declared that he had attempted to murder his mother, and that they had received these wounds in her defense. The fiction succeeded. The undiscriminating populace, who never weigh carefully the circumstances, and always give heed to tne complaint of woman, becomé enraged at the victim of her false accusations. Let it not, however, be forgotten that there is a just God, who declares that with what measure you mete, it shall be measured again, as we shall see in the fate of that false accusing woman.

The people were so excited, they would have torn Lathyrus to pieces had he not made a hasty retreat to Cyprus. Here he had lived before his father's death. The wrongs he had previously received from an imperious mother, were known, and the people gave no credit to the fictions of the queen. Lathyrus reigned on the island of Cyprus from that time, 107 B. C., until 99 B. C., about seven years, and Alexander, son of Physcon, became king of Egypt.

The Jews and the more northern people of Palestine and Samaria were still engaged in war with each other. Ptolemais was besieged by the Jews. The inhabitants sent to Cyprus for aid, which Lathyrus promptly furnished them. The opposite party sent to Cleopatra, in Egypt, to which call she also responded, and thus mother and son were ranged on opposite sides, and kept up the war in Palestine against each other, from 105 to 101 B. C. After shedding a vast amount of blood, they each retired, leaving the field of controversy about as they found it.

At this time, two brother princes were contending for the throne of Syria — Antiochus Cyzicus and Antiochus Grypus — each of whom had married a sister of Lathyrus, and both of whose wives had been murdered by the opposing factions. Lathyrus now entered into a confidential arrangement with Antiochus the Cyzicenian, with the hope of so strengthening himself as to regain the throne of Egypt. A knowledge of these facts aroused the ire of Cleopatra. She therefore took her daughter Selene, the wife of Lathyrus and gave her in marriage to Grypus, the opponent of the prince with whom Lathyrus was in alliance. She also furnished him treasures to carry on the war. The war between the two brother princes of Syria, prevented Lathyrus from receiving aid from that source, so that he was compelled to abandon, for the time, the hope of regaining the throne of Egypt.

But light arose in another quarter. Ptolemy Alexander, the brother of Lathyrus, whom the queen-mother had placed on the throne, was touched with some feelings of compassion for the exile, as well as disgusted with the conduct of his mother. He saw that he only had the title, and not the authority of a monarch. He saw that all these persecutions of his brother arose from his having dared, in one instance, to act for himself. He also saw that no crime restrained his mother when she had a favorite scheme to accomplish, and he feared that whenever he should be in her way she would not hesitate to sacrifice him. These feelings were completely roused when his mother took the wife of his brother and gave her to his enemy. Alexander, disgusted with the court, determined to resign and retire into peaceful obscurity. For this act of justice he deserves our highest esteem, although he may have been afterward guilty of an offense for which there was great provocation. Alexander retired; but the people, who had witnessed the conduct of the queen, and her dreadful temper, were determined she should not rule alone. With the utmost effort and the greatest entreaty, they persuaded Alexander to return and resume a share of the government. Ten years more rolled along, when Cleopatra, unwilling to share the government with any one, determined to murder Alexander. He became aware of her intentions, and, to save himself, put her to death, in the year 89 B. C. Thus the vile woman, who, to raise Alexander to the throne, falsely accused her son of an intention to murder her, is finally put to death by a son. Lathyrus did not avenge the wrong he had received; but God poured upon her the curse which her false accusation merited. Worthy to die was this monster in wickedness. Let us review the principal acts of her life. She had married her mother's husband, banished that mother from her home and her kingdom, and, as some authors say, subsequently murdered her. She had heard with indifference of the murder of her two daughters. She had compelled her eldest son to marry his sister, against his will, and then rudely tore that very wife away from him and gave her to his enemy, and now sought to slay her youngest son. What judgment shall calm, sober reason pass upon Alexander? He was King of Egypt; it was his duty to execute the laws. He caused the execution of his mother in self-defense, for she was plotting against his life. Her crime was one for which, by all just law, she had forfeited her life, and if capital punishment be justifiable, she ought to die; and Alexander was the proper person to order her execution. His act, therefore, though awful, can scarce be called a crime. But the unthinking populace judged not so. They knew and detested the old queen for her vice and cruelty; yet they were thrown into a panic of madness because Alexander had slain his mother. In a violent and turbulent manner they expelled him from the kingdom, from which they would not, a few years previously, permit him peaceably to retire. Lathyrus was now recalled to the throne of Egypt, to which he had a just title, although the treatment of Alexander was most unrighteous. He retired to foreign countries, and made, subsequently, several efforts to return to Egypt, in the last of which he perished, leaving a son of the same name, Alexander I. Lathyrus recovered the throne and held it about seven years.

In the year 81 B. C. the people of Thebes, a splendid city of upper Egypt, which had long before been desolated by Cambyses the mad, and which had, in some measure, revived, refused to pay tribute to Lathyrus, and broke out in open rebellion. The cause of this outbreak is not distinctly known. Lathyrus marched against Thebes, subdued the rebellion, wreaked his vengeance upon the people, and desolated the city, mutilating many of its ancient temples. In the latter part of the same year Lathyrus died, leaving his throne and kingdom to Cleopatra Berenice, his only legitimate child, the daughter of Selene.

Cleopatra Berenice, by the voice of the people, ascended the throne of her father in the year 80 B. C.

Alexander II., son of him who slew his mother, had experienced great vicissitudes of fortune, had received an excellent education under Grecian masters, had traveled in many foreign countries, and had secured the friendship of Rome. On the death of Lathyrus, Sylla, the dictator of Rome, sent Alexander to Egypt to take the throne of his late uncle. Cleopatra, his cousin, had now been reigning about six months. The nobles of Egypt, not disposed to yield up her claims to the throne, and yet not daring to offend Rome, determined that Alexander should marry the queen, and that they should reign jointly. But either he did not fancy his cousin for a wife, or perhaps was ambitious of reigning alone. He was displeased with the arrangement, but acquiesced. The marriage was celebrated, and nineteen days afterward he caused the queen to be put to death, thus securing to himself the entire possession of the government, which he held fifteen years. After a reign of seven years, he was annoyed by pretenders to the throne. In the year 73 B. C., Selene, once the wife of Lathyrus, and afterward of Grypus, of Syria, being the daughter of Physcon, began to claim Egypt for her sons. They visited

Rome, and after two years of ineffectual effort to induce the Romans to declare them heirs to the throne of Egypt, they returned disappointed into Asia. Eight years more Alexander continued to reign in Egypt, when, in 65, his mal-administration so exasperated the people that they took up arms against him and expelled him from Egypt.

After an ineffectual appeal to Pompey for aid, he retired to Tyre, where he died in the year 63 B. C., having bequeathed, by will, his kingdom and treasures to the Romans. Lathyrus had an illegitimate son, Auletes, who was immediately called to the throne of Egypt.

THE DECLINE OF THE EMPIRE OF SYRIA, B. C. 120 TO 65.

Actors.—Antiochus Grypus, son of Nicator; Tryphena and Selene, his wives; Seleucus, Philip, Demetrius Eucerus, and Antigonus Dyonysius, his sons; Antiochus Cyzicus, son of Sidetes; Cleopatra, his wife; Antiochus Eusebus, their son; Selene, his wife; Tigranes of Armenia, Antiochus Asiaticus, and Seleucus, sons of Selene.

The Syrian Cleopatra, preëminent for her crimes, had been the wife of three kings. In each case the subsequent marriage preceded the death of the former husband, and after the death of the third she re-married the second, whose death she afterward effected. She was also privy to the murder of the first. These three husbands were: Alexander Bala, who was betrayed and murdered in Arabia; Demetrius Nicanor, who was murdered at Tyre; and Sidetes, who was slain in battle with the Parthians. She subsequently murdered, with her own hands, her eldest son by Nicanor, and afterward attempted to poison the second, who compelled her to drink the draught which caused her immediate death.

This brings us to the date of our present subject, B. C. 120. On the death of Cleopatra, her second son Antiochus ascended the throne, and received the name of Grypus, on account of his great nose. Some three years previously he had married Tryphena, the daughter of Ptolemy Physcon, king of Egypt. Cleopatra had another son Antiochus, by Sidetes. On the death of Sidetes, when she re-married Nicanor, fearing for the safety of this child, she sent him into Asia Minor—in the city of Cyzicum, where he remained and received what in those days was deemed an excellent education. From the name of the place of his exile, he was ever after called Cyzicus, or the Cyzican. After the death of Nicanor, he returned, but his presence became obnoxious to his royal brother, and Grypus, who had been trained in his mother's school in the art of removing rivals, attempted to poison him. Cyzicus escaped from Antioch, and the administration of Grypus glided smoothly along for about six years, when the sea of political life became again tempestuous, and granted no calm to Syria for many years. Grypus, pursuing the indiscreet policy of his predecessors, since the days of Antiochus Epiphanes, undertook to conquer and exterminate the Jewish nation.

Accordingly, in 114, he marched with a large army into Judea. This was the time for the fugitive, who felt that in self-defense he must retaliate. He had spent years of his exile in secret, but not in idleness. The place of his retirement is not known. While Grypus was marching along the defile of Judea, intent upon conquest, intelligence reached him that Cyzicus was near Antioch with a large army. Grypus now found something else to do than fight the Jews. He hastened home to defend his throne and kingdom from the grasp of his brother. Cleopatra, the widow of Ptolemy Physcon, now ruled with despotic sway in Egypt, in connection with her son Lathyrus. She had three daughters—Cleopatra, Tryphena, and Selene. Tryphena had already married Grypus, Selene was the wife of Lathyrus, and Cleopatra remained unmarried. Just as the two brothers were engaging in this war, Cleopatra the younger, through her mother's influence, married Cyzicus, bringing as her dowry a large number of soldiers, many of whom, through the influence of the elder queen, had deserted Grypus, and joined the standard of the daughter, and with her united their interest with Cyzicus. The two parties were now about equal in strength—one being commanded by the king, the other by his rebel brother, their wives being sisters.

In the year 113 the combatants met in the plains, and engaged in battle. The king was victorious. Cyzicus fled into Antioch, and leaving his Cleopatra, as he supposed, in safety in that city, departed to raise additional forces to try again the field of battle. Grypus besieged and captured Antioch; Cleopatra fled to Daphne, and sought for safety in the temple—the same retreat to which, many years before, the unfortunate Berenice, sister of Evergetes, fled from the wrath of Loadicea. We might have expected kindness and sympathy among the female members of the royal household toward each other, even if their husbands from state policy were rivals; but this was practically an age of woman's rights, or, at least, of woman's authority in government, and we are abundantly taught in history that lovely as woman is in her appropriate sphere, when clothed with power and instated into the rough ways of the world, females are by far less humane and more implacably cruel than the sterner sex ever became. Tryphena urged her royal husband to put Cleopatra to death, even though she had taken shelter in the sanctuary. Grypus had more humanity. He urged that she was under the special protection of the gods, whose temple must not be profaned—

Death of the Syrian Cleopatra, at the Altar of Daphne.—See page 267.

that it was never honorable in war to put to death innocent women, however offensive might be the conduct of their husbands—and, above all, that she was the sister of the queen, and, finally, that her death would be of no avail to the stability of his throne. Alas, how often in this malignant world humanity is deemed an offense, and kindly feelings of compassion for the unfortunate—feelings which ought to do honor to him in whose breast they dwell—are made the occasion to blacken the character and traduce the fair name of her who possesses these virtues! The kindly feelings of Grypus for the unfortunate wife of his brother roused the jealousy of Triphena against her sister, lest Grypus should have a more ardent regard for her than mere compassion. She hated Cleopatra for having married their rival, but still more for having found compassion in the breast of Grypus. Against the orders of Grypus, and without the knowledge of that monarch, Tryphena, with a band of soldiers, repaired to Daphne, and attempted to force the fugitive from the temple. Cleopatra grasped the altar, and refused to loose her hold, and the soldiers cut off her hands. Holding up the bloody stumps, she implored the gods to avenge the wrong she had suffered, and the sacrilege committed in their holy temple, whose altars no longer protected the victim. The sister, unmoved by the spectacle, ordered the soldiers to despatch her, which was immediately done.

Thus, after but one year of connubial felicity, perished the daughter of the queen of Egypt, by whose intrigue she had been prevented from marrying the object of her choice, and compelled to marry this prince of Syria, for whose sake she lost her life in a most barbarous manner. Little, however, did that mother regard the fate of her daughter, nor that of Tryphena, which happened about one year after, so intent was she upon her own schemes of ambition against her sons in Egypt. Our sensibilities would be shocked at a recital of the barbarous deeds, were not the whole history of these times replete with instances of fearful cruelties and monstrous barbarities, the exhibition of which blunts our finer feelings. We learn here that where the gospel has not been taught, with its golden rule, the human race are without natural affection—implacable, unmerciful.

The next year after this terrible butchery of Cleopatra, 112 B. C., Cyzicus, having been absent raising troops, returned to Syria, fought a second battle, defeated Grypus, and captured Tryphena, and put her to death by torture, in revenge for the murder of his wife. Thus perished the two sisters whose ambitious mother had entangled them in the affairs of Syria, without consulting their wishes.

The fate of Tryphena may have been merited, although its severity seemed to have done no good. When will the possessors of temporary power learn the divine truth so often taught in the history of the world, that a day of retribution will surely overtake them—that "with what measure ye mete, it shall be measured again." It was now the time for Grypus to fly, and leave Cyzicus to take the throne. He retired to Aspendus, in Pamphilia, and remained a number of months. But the following year, he returned to Syria, at the head of an army, prepared to renew the war. The brothers appear now to have opened their eyes to the result of their quarrels. They had butchered each other's wives—they had desolated the country—they had alienated their people, and exhausted their treasury—they had not enjoyed their possessions, nor could either of them, if successful for a time in expelling the other, enjoy any permanent peace. After learning so costly a lesson, they agreed upon terms of peace, by dividing the kingdom. Cyzicus possessed Phœnicia, Celo-Syria, and the plains of the south, with Damascus for its capital; while

Grypus remained at Antioch, and ruled the rest of Syria—a finale to a long war, which might have been obtained as well without it, and presenting a strong argument in favor of modern doctrines of peace.

For a short period of time, now, there was a Syria north and a Syria south. These arrangements were not, however, of long duration. For the following ten years, Syria was the theater of no remarkable event, except the siege of Samaria by the Jews, in which Grypus participated. Of this siege an account is given in a separate article. About this time, Egypt was the scene of royal family quarrels. The old mother queen had driven her son Lathyrus from the throne, who had fled to Cyprus, where he still ruled.

In the year 101, Lathyrus, anxious to regain his throne and kingdom, formed an alliance with Cyzicus, of Damascus, who repaired to aid him in the undertaking. Cleopatra aware of that fact, and a more sagacious diplomatist than either of them, found means to prevent Lathyrus from receiving the expected aid. Selene, the third daughter of the queen, yet lived; she had been the wife of Lathyrus, by whom she was the mother of two sons, who died in infancy. When Lathyrus was deprived of the throne by his ambitious mother, Selene was taken from him and retained in Egypt. To prevent the king of Damascus from aiding Lathyrus, Cleopatra brought forth Selene and gave her to Grypus, with assurances of aid in carrying on the war against his brother, in the attempt again to recover the government of Syria. This, as Cleopatra expected and desired, employed the king of Damascus, so that he could afford no aid to Lathyrus, who was compelled for the present to abandon his expectations.

After an unsuccessful struggle between the two brothers, lasting nearly four years, with no definite result, Grypus was assassinated by one of his officers, Herocles by name, leaving at his death the country still engaged in civil war. Grypus had reigned twenty-seven years from the death of his mother. The crown passed to his oldest son. He left five sons by Tryphena. These were Seleucus Antiochus, Philip and Echelus (who were twins), Eucerus Demetrius and Antigonus Dionysius. On the death of Grypus, Cyzicus invaded Antioch; but, though he took the capital, he could not subdue Demetrius, who had succeeded his father, and was at the head of an army. The uncle and nephew engaged in battle. Seleucus was victorious. Cyzicus was captured and put to death, and the quarrel of the father's brothers descended to their sons. Thus, in the first year after his father's death, Seleucus found himself at the head of all Syria — not however to hold that position in peace. Cyzicus had left a son Eusebes, who retired from Antioch, eluding Seleucus and escaped to Aridas, an island on the Phœnician coast, north of Berytus. Returning the next year, 93 B. C., with a large army, he attacked his cousin Seleucus, defeated him, and regained the throne at Antioch.

Seleucus fled from that city and fortified himself in one of his other cities, where, with a few soldiers, he estabtablished himself. But he levied so great a tax upon the people to support him, that they became enraged, rose in revolt, surrounded his house and set fire to it, and Seleucus and all his men perished in the flames. The twin brothers, Antiochus and Philip, were still near Antioch. Exasperated at the fate of Seleucus, they determined upon revenge; they raised a small army, proceeded to Cilicia, invaded the guilty city and burned it to the ground, putting most of its inhabitants to the sword. On their homeward route, they met, on the banks of the Orontes, a detachment of soldiers from the army of Eusebes, who gave them battle and defeated them. Philip made a good and safe retreat, with part of his army; but Antiochus, in attempting to swim the river, perished. Thus ended the campaign of 92 B. C.

SELEUCUS.

Selene, the wife of Grypus, after his death, was so fortunate as to retain the government of a part of Syria, during all this struggle and conflict between the family of Cyzicus and Grypus. Eusebes, after the battle of Orontes, in which one of his opponents was killed and the other retreated with his army, did not feel entirely safe from his enemies, and desired to strengthen his cause. He therefore married Selene, the stepmother of his rival, and attached her possessions to his own. Lathyrus, her first husband, still lived. She had been forcibly and unjustly taken from him and given to Grypus. The second act, of marrying Eusebes, exasperated him, and he determined to give the new couple trouble. Demetrius Eucerus, the fourth son of Grypus, was at Cnidus, in Caria. Lathyrus sent for him, and while Eusebes and Philip were occupied in a war with each other in the north, Eucerus was crowned king of Damascus and the south of Syria, thus bringing a third competitor in the field. During the same year, Philip and Eusebes engaged in battle, in which Eusebes, with all the auxiliary forces obtained by marrying his rival's stepmother, was defeated. He fled to the Parthians, where, for a number of years, he remained an exile.

The empire was now divided between Philip and Demetrius. But this was not the end of strife. Antiochus Dionysius, the fifth son of Grypus, began to attract attention. He suddenly appeared in Syria at the head of an army, marched against and defeated his brother Eucerus, and established himself on the throne in his stead, which he occupied three years.

In 90 B. C., Eusebes returned from Parthia with a large

army, marched once more against Philip and contended for the throne of Syria. Strife, conflict, battles, cruel murders, barbarous wars, and no definite result, accompanied by all the distressing calamities of a cruel war, raged throughout all Syria for the space of seven years. The people became exasperated under their calamities. Their patience became exhausted; they determined to deliver themselves from the yoke of all the race of the Seleucidæ, and seek for themselves a foreign master, who should not be subject to the quarrels of these native princes.

Some were disposed to give all Syria to Egypt, but it was remembered that the Ptolemys had ever been the enemies to their country. Some thought it best to offer the crown to Mithridates, king of Pontus, but he was then engaged in a war with the Romans. None thought of a republic. That form of government was almost entirely unknown in Asia, and the people of Syria were illy prepared to exercise the duties of such a state. After much debate, it was agreed to call to the throne of Syria, Tigranes, king of Armenia, and he, either in person or by deputies, ruled them eighteen years.

THE FALL OF SYRIA, B. C. 65.

The land of Laban and Bethuel, of the Benhadads and the Zæl, had been subjected to the power of Nineveh, of Babylon, and of Persia, and with the latter country had been conquered by Alexander the Great, and, after his death, formed one of the four heads into which his empire was divided, according to the words of Daniel. After the short, but tempestuous reign of Perdiccas and Antigonus, Syria fell to the lot of Seleucus, in whose family the crown remained, until, by the invitation of the inhabitants, Tigranes, king of Armenia, took the throne, 83 B. C.

Whatever of irresistible pressure from a foreign foe, or

of heroic deeds of unsuccessful valor against superior forces, may be attendant upon the fall of a republic, in a kingdom it will uniformly be found that public vices and maladministration at home prepare the way for that fall, just as intemperance and inattention to the laws of animal life invite the disease which destroys the body.

The history of the world already demonstrates that the great ambition of nations ever holds the people responsible for the conduct of their rulers, as honor makes it the duty of each individual, instead of shrinking from politics, because of the ignominy attached to that subject, to read in the very ignominy the evidences of approaching evil, and with pure hearts and clear minds to understand the designs of government, and aid in correcting error, before the remedy is too late. The malignant hatred and leopard-like treachery of the Seleucidæ is manifest in these wars. Fighting, one branch of the family against the other, they diminished their numbers, exhausted their treasuries, and alienated their subjects, until they were an easy prey for any enemy. The products of the plains, raised by the industry of the inhabitants, instead of storing their barns and feeding their children, were consumed by the soldiery. The fine groves of figs and grapes, the mulberry and olive, had been destroyed by soldiers of hostile factions. The authors of all these calamities disregarded the interests of their quiet subjects, and were only intent upon their personal preferment. But their evil deeds disgusted the world, and when the time of necessity was upon them, none sympathized with them, demonstrating to princes and to presidents, to noblemen and republicans, to men in public life and to private individuals, that he who would have friends must act righteously.

The administration of the Armenian, either in person or by his deputies, was no less terrible or oppressive upon

Syria, than upon many other provinces. The people changed masters, but not burdens.

Except Selene and her two sons, the Seleucidæ were hunted out of Syria, and never more heard of. About 80 B. C., a long and distressing war was commenced by the Romans against Mithridates, king of Pontus, a state lying south of the Black Sea. A full account of this invasion is reserved for another work on Asia Minor, and only so much of that matter is here spoken of as involved the fate of Syria.

Tigranes had long before married a daughter of Mithridates. Although bitter quarrels existed between them, the son-in-law could not withhold aid from the father in his extremities. Mithridates, being defeated, fled to Armenia, and found protection with Tigranes. This event caused the Roman army, under Lucullus, to march into Armenia. After various successes, both Pontus and Armenia, with their kings, were finally subdued by Pompey, who had succeeded Lucullus in command, and Tigranes purchased an ignominious peace, and was permitted to hold a nominal government over Armenia, on condition of surrendering to the Romans Syria and Mesopotamia, with whatever claim he might have upon Judea. About 70 B. C., Tigranes having occasion to recall his deputies from Syria, to aid him against the Romans, Antiochus Asiaticus, eldest son of Selene, emerged from obscurity, and ascended the throne of his ancestors. He was the eldest, and, except one brother, the only known survivor of the Selucidæ.

There being no opponent, he reigned about three years, the country being crossed and re-crossed continually by the Roman armies, in their war with Tigranes and Mithridates. But on the final overthrow of these princes, in 65 B. C., he sought the friendship of the Romans, and their acknowledgment of his rights to the throne of his fathers. He had taken no part in the recent war; he had in no way forfeited his claim, which was just, if the claim of kings can ever be just. Why ought not his right to have been respected? Pompey declared that, by right of conquest, Syria belonged to Rome, and, having an army flushed with recent victory to sustain him, he dismissed Antiochus, without title or kingdom. The people, who, for several successive reigns, had received no protection from their sovereigns, were not disposed to aid him in defending his throne. Indeed, it mattered little to the multitude who ruled, whether native prince or foreign tyrant.

Thus by conquest and usurpation the third head of the third beast passed to the Romans, the fourth beast, dreadful and terrible; for what God by the mouth of His prophet has ordained shall surely come to pass.

From this time the history of Syria is blended with that of Rome, until the great partition, when it fell to the lot of the eastern empire, whose capital was Byzantium, now Constantinople. About 632 A. C., Syria was conquered by the Saracens, and has been in possession of some branch of the great Mohammedan family until the present time. Previous to the conquest of Alexander, the language of Syria had been native and peculiar, with no admixture of Persian, but after that event the Greek language gained gradually the ascendancy, and, in common with many nations at the time of Christ, was the principal language spoken, which greatly facilitated the spread of the Gospel, as most, if not all of the disciples, spoke that language. At the once proud capital of Syria the disciples were first called Christians.

SYNOPSIS OF THE KINGS OF SYRIA.

Seleucus Nicator was assassinated by the ungrateful Ptolemy, whom he assisted. Antiochus Soter died; the manner of his death is not given. Antiochus Theos, poisoned by his wife, Laodicea. Seleucus Callinicus died a prisoner in Parthia. Antiochus Ceraunus, poisoned by his officers, in Asia Minor. Antiochus the Great, slain by the inhabitants of Susiana, for attempting to rob their temple. Seleucus Philopater, poisoned by his officers. Antiochus Epiphanes died a distressing death, by worms, on his return from Persepolis. Antiochus Eupator, slain by his brother, Demetrius Soter. Demetrius Soter, slain by Alexander Bala, the imposter. Alexander Bala, beheaded in Arabia, by king Demetrius Nicanor, who was in turn assassinated at Tyre, by order of his wife. Antiochus Eutheus, slain by his minister, Tryphon. Tryphon, captured and put to death in a war with Sidetes. Antiochus Sidetes, slain in battle with the Parthians. Zebina, expelled and slain for attempting to rob the temple at Antioch. Seleucus V., slain by his mother, Cleopatra. Grypus, assassinated by his officer, Herocles. Cyzicus, taken prisoner and slain by Seleucus VI. Antiochus, drowned in the Orontes, in flying from battle. Seleucus VI., burned in Cilicia, for extortion. Philip died in exile, but is supposed to have been killed by Tigranes. Eusebes, expelled and died in exile. Demetrius Eucerus, slain in war with Tigranes. Dyonisius, expelled by Tigranes; manner of death unknown. Antiochus Asiaticus, defeated by Pompey; manner of death unkown.

PTOLEMY AULETES, B. C. 65

ALEXANDER II. having been banished from Egypt, on account of his cruelties, had retired to Tyre, where he soon after died. He left no heirs, and indeed, we might almost say that there lived not at this time a legitimate offspring of the Ptolemys. Alexander, at his death, bequeathed his kingdom and all his property to the Roman Senate.

The Egyptians were not disposed to acknowledge so readily a foreign master. They therefore raised to the throne Auletes, and made one of his brothers governor of Cyprus. Auletes was anxions to defeat the will of Alexander, and to be acknowledged king of Egypt by the Romans. To accomplish this, he bribed Julius Cæsar and the Roman Senate, with the promise of large sums of money. To raise this money, he levied exhorbitant taxes upon the people, which caused a rebellion, and in 58 B. C., he was compelled to fly the land. So secretly did he conceal his route, that the Egyptians either believed or pretended to believe, that he had perished. They therefore raised to the throne his eldest daughter, Berenice. But Auletes was not dead; he had made his way to Rhodes, where he met Cato, a distinguished Romans, who advised him to return to Egypt, and to take care of his kingdom. Cato urged him not to think of buying the friendship of Rome, "for," said he, "if you give them ever so much, their greediness will demand more, and take all you have." Auletes was convinced, and was disposed to return, but the friends he had with him, being in the service of Pompey, had interested motives in persuading him to proceed to Rome, and he yielded to their persuasion. At Rome, by the aid of Pompey, he presented to the Senate his complaints against his subjects, and demanded to be restored to his kingdom and government. The Egyptians, learning that the exiled king was at Rome, also sent an embassy of one hundred men, the most respectable princes and nobles, to plead their cause before the Roman Senate. Most of these men were secretly destroyed, either by poison or the dagger, at the instigation of Auletes. After three years' maneuvering, Rome finally restored Auletes to the throne of Egypt. Meanwhile let us observe a few things in regard to

BERENICE, B. C. 58:

This princess ascended the throne at the time of her father's banishment, and reigned three years. The Egyptians feared the growing power of Rome, and desired to strengthen the throne of their female sovereign. Antiochus Asiaticus of Syria, was of Egyptian extraction, his mother Selene being the daughter of Physcon. To Antiochus the Egyptians sent embassadors, offering him the queen in marriage, and the throne of Egypt, as her dower. But the embassadors found, on their arrival, that Antiochus was dead. He, however, had left a brother, Seleucus, as his successor. To him they made the same offer, and he accepted. He came to Egypt, and became the husband of Berenice, but not the king of Egypt. He was a man of very sordid, groveling spirit, so devoted to obtaining money by mean artifices, that he became an object of contempt to all. The queen abhorred him, and caused him to be strangled. Subsequently Berenice became the wife of Archelaus, high priest of Cumæ, in Pontus.

The Romans established Auletes in power by force of arms, which the Egyptians resisted, and in that resistance Archelaus was slain. Auletes would have put all the Egyptians to the sword, had he not been subdued by Antony. Egypt was soon reduced and compelled to receive an uninvited master, B. C. 55.

Almost the first act of Auletes, after his restoration, was to put to death his daughter, Berenice, for having worn the crown during his absence. He also caused the death, by poison and assassination, of nearly all the chief men of Alexandria who had been opposed to his restoration. His only other act worthy of note was the manner of paying his debts. One Rabinus, a Roman, had lent Auletes money, in the time of his troubles. Part of this money had been used in bribing the Roman officers and senate to reëstablish him on the throne of Egypt. Auletes being now in prosperity, Rabinus came to Egypt to obtain payment of this debt. Auletes told him he had no means of paying except to appoint him to take charge of the treasury, out of the receipts of which he might, from time to time, pay himself. The creditor, having no other means of securing the debt, accepted the offer; but as soon as he entered upon its duties, Auletes raised a pretext to accuse him of fraud, and the unfortunate creditor with difficulty escaped with his life, losing the entire debt. When Rabinus arrived at Rome, he met with new trouble, for he was there prosecuted for lending money to Auletes with which to commit the crime of bribery.

Ptolemy Auletes continued to reign in peace four years after his restoration, and the payment of his debts, and the persecution of his creditors. He died, and was succeeded by the famous

CLEOPATRA, B. C. 51.

When Ptolemy Alexander ascended the throne of Egypt, he was sustained there only by the favor of the Roman senate. Alienated by domestic feuds from his own kindred, he bequeathed his throne and kingdom to the Romans, his benefactors. By many he was deemed incapable of disposing by will of that which could scarcely be called his own. Auletes succeeded Alexander, and purchased back his kingdom from the Romans, by bribing Julius Cæsar and Pompey, then the two great men of the world; he also promised great sums to the senate, which were, however, never paid. These large expenditures of money exhausted the treasures of Egypt, and gave great offense to the people. They at last rebelled, and Auletus was driven into exile. The statesmen and counselors of Egypt rallied around Berenice, a young and beautiful princess, the eldest daughter of Auletes. Berenice assumed the crown and administered with regal authority for a short time, during her father's banishment; but ultimately, Auletes was restored to his throne and kingdom, and for the filial act of preserving the throne for him, Auletes caused his daughter to be beheaded; so lost had the Ptolemys become to all ties of affection, to every sense of honor and justice.

Auletes left four other children, two sons, both of whom were called Ptolemy — no other name having been transmitted to us by historians — and two daughters, Arsinoe and Cleopatra; the oldest of these was the far-famed queen, whose fortunes were coupled with those of Julius Cæsar and Marc Antony.

Cleopatra was born 68 years before the birth of Christ, and was ten years old when her elder sister, Berenice, was executed, leaving herself the oldest child, and heir apparent to the throne. Six years after this act of barbarism, Auletes was called before the judge of the quick and dead to meet in the other land the spirit of his murdered child. Auletes left a strange and unreasonable will; a legacy of trouble to his children, by which every one of them came to a violent death. By that will Cleopatra and Ptolemy, her eldest brother, were jointly to possess the throne and kingdom of Egypt, on the express condition that they should marry each other. Such incestuous marriages, though abhorred by us, and contrary to nature, were not uncommon in those days; but in this case it was an extremely unfortunate arrangement. These children entertained a great aversion to each other, which gradually ripened into the most deadly hatred. There were no points of affinity between them: she a maiden of nearly seventeen years, of beautiful form, possessing a high order of intellect and profound education—he a child of eleven years, mulish, stupid and slow of apprehension, and with a mind which future years failed to improve. To the charms of an exceedingly beautiful person, Cleopatra had added the much more valuable charm of a highly cultivated mind, and, for aught that appears at that time, a pure heart. She had studied philosophy under the best masters. She was well versed in the poetry and legends of the Greek authors. She understood chemistry and the sciences generally. She not only read, but wrote poetry. She was master of a great number of languages, and conversed freely and fluently with the embassadors from India, Persia, Rome, Syria, Macedon, and from the wilds of Arabia, in their own native tongues. She was well skilled in the arts and intrigues of diplomacy. At first glance we suppose that in her were united all the virtues of her predecessors—the first three Ptolemys, Soter and Philadelphus, who had gathered the great library and translated the Bible into Greek, and all the ardor and domestic affection of Evergetes and his wife, Berenice, whose golden locks had been translated to the skies—all the suavity of manners of the first of the early Ptolemys.

Take a second look at her history, and we will almost conclude that all the vices of the Ptolemys had been distilled into this, their last representative. Cleopatra was of a robust, vigorous constitution, ardent and impulsive. She was a specimen of what we sometimes, though rarely see, a combination of the highest order of intellectual development and mental culture, with the most complete development of the animal propensities, and a generous, good nature, which, under more favorable circumstances, might have been coupled with moral qualities, so as to have produced a triple compound of the most perfect human being: animal, intellectual, moral, each aiding, controlling and perfecting the other.

In the school in which Cleopatra was born, and influenced by the pressure of surrounding circumstances during her whole life, the moral and the virtuous elements of her nature could scarce fail to sustain a severe injury, and thus mar the beauty of the whole structure of the most accomplished and conspicuous personage that ever presided over the plains of the Nile. Cleopatra detested the condition of her father's will, yet she virtuously acceded to the requirements of the State.

The empty form and ceremony of marriage was celebrated between Cleopatra, the wise and beautiful, and the child of eleven years. But the parties never came together practically. They were never really married—never cohabited together. It would have been a sin against Nature and Nature's God, that such a couple should live in wedlock, not only on account of the incest, but from the entire incompatibility of their natures. Married life, when not affection but interest governs, and force of circumstances compel their union, is but honorable, legalized adultery, nor can licentiousness be checked, until teachers and rulers take a more philosophical view of the nature and innocence of those relations. Cleopatra was disposed to be contented with her divided share of regal authority; but her brother was as yet represented by ministers and statesmen, himself being but a child, and these statesmen labored to increase the hatred already existing between the royal couple. They could not rule Cleopatra, for she had a mind and a judgment of her own; they could not defraud the people, for she was faithful; they could not deceive her, for she was a diplomatist, and vastly their superior. What could they do? Just what little, narrow-minded souls always do to those who are of superior intelligence, hate and abuse the excellence which they did not themselves possess, and which, in others, was a standing reproach to their stupidity and depravity. They roused the prejudices of the people against a female sovereign, and persuaded the boy king to deny his sister any share in the administration, thereby hoping to have everything their own way. But Cleopatra was not thus easily to be disposed of by their stupid maneuvring. She refused to resign her claim to the throne to which she had a title. She had paid the unreasonable condition imposed upon her by an unwise father, and she would not surrender the reward. In a public assembly an attempt to dethrone her was made. With a loud voice she declared, "I am the princess of Egypt, the daughter of the Ptolemys. I am the eldest survivor of a long and illustrious line, whose administration has blessed this land. By the will of my father, I am entitled to half of the throne. But for that will I should have right to the whole. If that will be broken, I am sole queen. I am the sovereign of Egypt. I will not surrender its crown." Such talent, such boldness, such a heroic appeal would, in almost any other land, have roused a chivalry that would have defended her claim, and hurled her oppressors in the dust; but the ministers, with much effort, quieted the people, and banished Cleopatra. They shall see her again.

Let us now pause to consider the social, moral and religious aspect of Egypt at the time of the events above described. I have elsewhere said there were many points of similarity between the Egyptian and the Grecian. There were also some striking points of dissimilarity. Egyptian paganism partook of the sublime—the Grecian of the beautiful. Egyptian gods represented the hidden powers and mysteries of Nature. Clothed in obscurity, they were embodiments of the secret influence of the sun in governing the lesser bodies in some unaccountable manner, dispensing life and warmth to all things, giving the earth capacity to bring forth vegetable and sustain animal life. The Grecian Deities represented the more manifest, the beautiful and less secret works of Nature; the winds, the groves, the waterfalls, the waves of the sea—revealing themselves to the material sense—were the images of their poetic fancy; and there was more of the gentle, soothing contemplation—less of the dark profound. It must be admitted, however, that sometimes their theology rose to the sublime, as in the thunderings of Jupiter, the boisterous tread of Mars, or the surges of Neptune; yet even in these instances it was the manifest, not the hidden, which they interwove with the fictions of the Gods. While Egypt seemed to hold converse with the invisible, the unsearchable, yet powerful workshop of the universe, the Greek was like the cloud when the saffron tints of morn hang its tapestry around the borders, intimating joyous hope and bright tokens of future pleasure, as the evening cloud, illuminated with the golden hue of the declining sun, gorgeous, tasteful in every form, and hue, and tinge. Egypt was like the thunder pillar, rising majestically, and uttering its deep voice, rolling portentously high in the heavens, and intimating that within its dark folds, unseen by mortals, lie the elements in labor which ever and anon give but a moment's flash of light, half revealing its profound capacities. Hence the temples of Egypt, like the Gods that dwelt within them, were grand and imposing, covering acres, and reaching far into the sky—built for endurance, but not graceful in proportion. Grecian temples were not of great magnitude, which would be of little use amid their mountains, but they were graceful in form, well proportioned, and adapted to please the eye, rather than strike with awe. *They were intended to be the embodiment of* their own favorite motto, that "a thing of beauty is a joy forever." The pagan mysteries also represented the human passions. The Egyptians those of a mother who makes no display, whose affection is lodged deep in her bosom; while the Grecians sung of the passions, pride, lust and revenge, which openly manifest themselves.

Cast of mind and state of society favored these peculiarities. The Egyptians were austere, grave, deep thinkers, abounding in emblems of death and vast eternity; the Grecians were more voluptuous, and their emblems were more of present pleasure than of future retribution. They thought more of Bacchus and the Muses than of Pluto and Hades. The Egyptians were, in some measure, the prototype of our stern Puritan Fathers, two hundred years ago, while the Greeks resembled the graceful gayety of the fashionable Christians of the present day. This character of the Greeks, however, applies chiefly to the times after the fall of the Persian empire. During the entire reign of the Lagidæ, the Grecian type had been impressed upon the Egyptian mold; the two had become blended, and the gracefulness had, in no small degree, supplanted the austerity of the Egyptian, and under Cleopatra's future influence, the finishing touches of voluptuous refinement were applied to the sterner cast of earlier times. But I am anticipating. We will follow our heroine. The provinces of Phœnicia and Palestine had once been subject to Egypt. To them Cleopatra, in her banishment, retired. She appealed to their inhabitants to defend her rights. To this appeal they readily responded. The cities of Phœnicia, the hills of Palestine, poured forth their hardy soldiery, to rally round the standard of the queen, who now contemplated returning to Egypt, and with the sword defending her crown. But she was spared the necessity of such a measure. Another party appears in the field.

Rome had long been meddling with the affairs of the East, and most of the provinces of Alexander's empire had submitted to her sway. The Roman Senate thought it their duty to interfere in the affairs of Egypt, and settle the succession to the crown. For this purpose Julius Cæsar, with a small army, visited Alexandria, to summons the claimants before him and decide their fate. The absent queen was to be heard by a representative. This was in the year 48 B. C. Cleopatra knew too well the intrigues of courts, and the probable influence of a king at home, over that of a helpless queen abroad. She foresaw the probability that any counselor she might send, if not bribed to betray her cause, would but half defend her rights. With a courage and heroism rarely displayed by the sterner sex, she determined to be her own advocate. While the great sea was tossed by tempests — its surges so boisterous that no vessel dare leave the harbor, she, in an open boat, and with but one confidential friend, commits herself to the care of Neptune, pushes her way across the deep, and enters the outer harbor of Alexandria.

Julius Cæsar was then in Alexandria. The next day was set to hear the case. There was no time to be lost. The faithful attendant had prepared cloths of the richest kind. He spread them out, and the heroic Cleopatra allowed herself to be rolled in them, and bound up in the form of a bale of goods. Borne upon the shoulder of her friend, she was thus carried through the streets of Alexandria. When hailed by the sentinel, the bearer replied that he bore a present to Cæsar. He was permitted to pass. To the apartment of Cæsar he proceeded, and deposited his present. Cæsar unrolled the rich cloths, when, to his surprise, forth sprang from the bundle, a beautiful, youthful female.

Cleopatra related her adventures, and plead her cause before her judge. Cæsar was now about fifty years of age, a stern old Roman; but his heart was touched with sympathy for a defenseless queen, and a still warmer affection than that of pity moved the old hero. Cleopatra passed that night in the house of Cæsar. In winning his heart, she had already won her claim to her crown. There is, however, no evidence that there was at that time any criminal intercourse between them. The day dawned, a day that was to decide the title to the crown of Egypt. Ptolemy and his courtiers were in high hope, as they repaired to the hall of audience. But what was their surprise when they learned that the banished sister was then in the apartment of Cæsar? Indignation, rage and fury burst forth. But what could they do? The stern Roman had an army to sustain him. He declared that Cleopatra should be restored to her joint partnership in the throne. To this Ptolemy affected to agree, but a few days after his counselors and the officers of his army refused to abide by the decision. A tumult and riot was the result. The Roman soldiers put down the Egyptian faction. Ptolemy was slain, and the rebellion quelled. A part of the great library in the Bruchion was accidentally burned. The death of Ptolemy gave Cleopatra not half but the whole throne. From that time Cæsar and Cleopatra lived as husband and wife. Together they ascended the Nile, halting along its banks, and holding sumptuous festivals under gorgeous pavilions of silk. After having surveyed the most important coast of the country, they returned to Alexandria, still continuing to dwell together. Cæsar was at length called home to Rome. After some years Cleopatra followed her lover to the seven-hilled city. In Rome she again occupied the apartment and the bed of Cæsar, to the exclusion of his

Roman wife. Thus stood matters when Julius Cæsar was assassinated in the Senate Chamber. Cleopatra immediately returned to Egypt, a widow indeed, and there for a number of years she ruled with moderation, wisdom and ability. Her kingdom was prosperous, and her people happy. During this period no blemish stained her character.

During these years great events were transpiring in the Roman empire. Macedon, Thrace and Syria had already been added to their possessions. But the Parthians, a powerful nation in the East, were the enemies of Rome, and continually harrassed the eastern portions of Syria. Marc Antony, the avenger of Cæsar's death, the enemy of Brutus and Cassius, was commissioned to march to the East, to regulate affairs in Macedon and Asia Minor, and then proceed to check the Parthians. Antony was a great warrior, a bold unpolished man, and eminently luxurious and licentious. His journey was marked with every excess of debauchery. Jenkens thus describes it:

"His progress was one continued triumph; not such as best became a conquerer, but dishonored by the most shameful debauchery and excess. Kings bent before him, in humble obeisance, and laid their hoarded treasures at his feet. Queens rejoicing in wealth and beauty, sought his presence eagerly, and yielded every favor that he could ask. Never was the gross sensualism of his character more glaringly exhibited. The wealth of Crœsus filled his coffers; but it was needed to furnish new pleasures for his jaded appetite.

Sycophants and flatterers shared his gold, and partook with him in every vice and folly. Dancers and buffoons were his companions and attendants—the creatures of his bounty, and the ministers to his passions. Rumors of the sports and revelry, the riot and feasting, in which he delighted, went before him. Cities sent forth their entire population to greet his coming. His followers called him

Bacchus—a name that pleased him—and men and boys, disguised as Pans and Satyrs, and women, dressed as Bacchanals, in loose Asiatic robes, with vine wreaths about their heads, and fawn skins on their shoulders, ran before him, swinging their thyrsi, crowned with accanthus leaves and the foliage and berries of the ivy, beating their drums and shouting, "Iò Bacche! Io Bacche!"

This was Antony, brave but effeminate—talented and eloquent, but coarse by nature—generous in disposition, but often cruel and unforgiving—sometimes abandoned, as it seems, to the lowest of vices, and then breaking loose from his degradation, and exhibiting his character glowing with its old light. This was the Antony who, history tells us, was ruined by the arts of Cleopatra.

Antony halted at Tarsus, in Cilicia. Rome had long coveted Egypt, and Antony now aspired to the honor of adding it to her provinces. He therefore sought a pretext to quarrel with Cleopatra. A governor from Phœnicia, without orders from his queen, had given shelter to some of the party by whom Cesar was slain. Antony seized upon this fact, and sent positive orders for Cleopatra to appear before him at Tarsus. Was it her fault that she yielded to his demand?—she, the queen of a small kingdom, and he clothed with all the power of invincible Rome. What could she do other than to obey—yet, with womanly modesty, she delayed, deferred and postponed as long as possible. She at length set out to comply with the demands of Marc Antony. To do justice to her character we must take into view her circumstances—a queen without alliances, without foreign aid, and in danger of being seized by that all-absorbing Roman power. For her there was but one alternative—she must either win Marc Antony or lose her kingdom, and perhaps her life. Let us not judge too harshly of her. Force, not choice, directed the journey, but expediency decided the style and manner of it. She went with all the attending allurements which might gain the heart, and take captive her captor. One author thus describes her journey:

"It was a glorious pageant. The richest carvings adorned her barge, which fairly blazed with gold and splendor. Its sails of brightest purple swelled gracefully with the soft south winds that strained its silken cordage. Its oars, both blade and handle tipped and bound with silver, moved in harmony with the voluptuous music of the flute, the pipe, and the cithern. Above it floated the mystic ensign of the Egyptian monarchs, and from the burning censers on its prow, clouds of odorous perfume were wafted to the shore. Upon its deck was raised a lofty canopy of cloth of gold, beneath which, on a cushioned couch, with ivory and tortoise shell inlaid, reclined the dark-eyed queen of Egypt. She was robed like Venus, in a purple mantle, glittering with diamonds, and its border ornamented with threads of gold and silver intertwined. Roses and myrtles were wreathed about her brows, her ears were pierced with rings of pearl, a necklace of precious stones encircled her swan-like throat, the golden cestus clasped her waist, and golden sandals incased her tiny feet. Beautiful boys, disguised as Cupids, stood beside her and fanned her with their wings. Damsels, among the fairest at her court, whose houried beauty could not be surpassed, were habited as Nereides and Graces, in loose, transparent robes, and waited to do her bidding, or managed the helm and sails with great dexterity and skill.

"The shore was lined with people, who watched the barge laden with so much beauty, with straining eyes. As it moved along, the cry was raised that Venus had come to feast with Bacchus. From mouth to mouth it passed until it reached the market-place in Tarsus. All hastened forth to witness her approach—all save Antony, who, deserted by suitors and attendants, remained alone on the tribunal where he was seated. Immediately upon her landing, he sent an officer to her, with his greeting, coupled with the request that she would come and sup with him. 'Go, tell your master,' was her reply, 'that it is more fitting he should come and sup with me.' "

This assumption of social superiority put an end at once to all the dignity which Antony purposed to assume. He accepted the invitation of Cleopatra, and thus, at the very outset, exhibited a deference toward her, by which she did not fail to profit. For luxurious magnificence, and costly and profuse extravagance, the entertainment provided by Cleopatra had never yet been equalled. Her tents and pavilions, hung with cloth of gold, or silken tapestry from the looms of Tyre and Sidon, were pitched beside the sparkling waters of the Cydnus, in a noble grove of spreading plane trees and stately laurels. Lamps of bronze and gold, suspended by gilt chains, or supported by lofty candelabra, arranged in squares and circles, and raised or depressed at pleasure, shed their perfumed light around. Blazing censers, filled with choicest spices, loaded the air with fragrance. There were long rows of marble tables and silver tripods, covered with tureens and urns, and vases of gold and silver, fashioned with elegance and taste. Large silver vessels or chargers, splendidly embossed, contained the juicy meats, the fish, the hares, and the pheasants. The bread and fruited cake were brought in silver baskets. Bronze dishes, with ornaments inlaid, were filled with eggs and roes of fishes, with oysters from the Hellespont, with fresh and pickled olives, with radishes, dried dates and raisins; mulberries, newly gathered; almonds and confections. Banqueting cups, of most exquisite workmanship, were wreathed with garlands, and poured brimming full of the rich juice of Chios, or the produce of the Egyptian soil, not the mild wines of Thebais and Coptus, but the light, fragrant Narcoticum, and the oily and aromatic Læntoticum.

Upon the ornamented seats and couches reclined the guests, with chaplets of violets and roses, myrtle and ivy bound about their temples. Their ears were charmed with soft strains of music, and buffoons amused them with their droll tricks and pleasantries. Attending servants cooled them with fans of peacock feathers, while they listened to the mythological love stories which the pantomimists related, or watched the dancing girls, who, clad in the gossamer robes of Coa with golden bangles upon their feet, and emerald bracelets upon their arms and shoulders, moved with airy steps before them.

High above them all was Cleopatra, with Antony reclining near her. Upon her head the diadem of Egypt, with the asp — the emblem of divinity — on it, flashed with rarest gems. Her tunic glittered with all the colors of the East, and was overspread with rich embroidery. A Babylonian shawl of finest tissue was thrown around her shoulders, and at her side gleamed a Persian dagger, whose hilt was pearls and diamonds. Cushions of crimson damask rose invitingly about her swelling limbs. Her full lips parted but to utter honeyed words. The glow of satisfaction was on her cheek, and in her eye the light of triumph."

Such was the first meeting of Marc Anthony and Cleopatra. She came, she saw, she conquered. Antony was completely captivated with the charms of the Egyptian queen, and she, in turn, realized that she held her kingdom only as she held the Roman in the net of her bewitching charms.

Day after day was spent in fond dalliance. They sailed along the Phœnician coast to Tyre; it was then the intention of Antony to have left her and proceeded against the Parthians. But so irresistible was her attractive influence that Cleopatra drew him into Egypt. Here time rolled on, and voluptuousness drowned all recollection of his duty to Rome or resistance to the Parthians.

Meantime, that enemy was gaining victory after victory on the plains of Mesopotamia. Affairs at Rome now demand a passing notice. Marc Antony was now the most distinguished Roman commander, and aspired to imperial power. All this time, while he was lost in fond dalliance with Egypt's queen, he had a wife, Fulvia, in Rome, who, with her friends, was endeavoring to raise him to the imperial dignity. She was faithful to her lord, who was unfaithful to himself.

Octavius, another distinguished Roman, had become the rival of Antony, and, during his absence, had taken rapid strides toward absolute power. Fulvia and her friends defended the cause of Antony, and had raised an army to resist Octavius, but were defeated, and compelled to flee from Italy. She proceeded toward Phœnicia to meet Antony, but died at Sicyon. Antony left Egypt and proceeded to Phœnicia. Here he received letters from Fulvia, which induced him to leave Syria to its fate and turn westward. After the death of Fulvia, Antony proceeded to Rome. The two political parties, of which he and Octavius were the leaders, were, for a short time, reconciled by the marriage of Antony with Octavia, the sister of Octavius. The marriage was based upon political considerations alone, and could, of course, produce no great domestic felicity.

Octavia was indeed mild, gentle and winning, and she labored to refine the rough nature of Antony. Some years passed along with comparative quiet, but Antony could not entirely efface from his heart the impressions of the queen who ruled on the banks of the Nile.

The provinces of Rome were committed to the care of the different triumvirs, and to Antony fell the region lying east of the Ionian sea. The Parthian war made it necessary that he should revisit the scenes of his former pleasure; he therefore repaired to Cilicia with a large army. Cleopatra had remained for some years in Egypt. She was now the mother of three children — Cæsaron, the son of Julius Cæsar, and Alexander and Cleopatra, twin children of Marc Antony. She had been left in Egypt during the late changes in Rome. Antony, now again in the East, revived his attachment for Egypt's queen.

He requested her to meet him in Phœnicia, with which request she cordially complied, not without some chiding for his having deserted her and married Octavia.

Scenes of luxury and debauchery were again revived. To pacify her for his past neglect he gave her several territories that had fallen to Rome, among which were Phœnicia, Lower Syria, Cilicia, Cyprus and part of Palestine. At length Cleopatra returned to Egypt, and Antony proceeded against the Parthians; but the delay had given the enemy powerful advantages over him, and he returned to Phœnicia with the mere shattered remnants of a well disciplined army. They were only saved from entire destruction by the timely aid of Cleopatra, who met them at Sidon with supplies of food and clothing. From this time Cleopatra seemed to have the entire control of Antony. He appears to have lost all independence, energy and promptness of character. His Roman wife, Octavia, started to meet him in his distresses, and proceeded as far as Athens, when, through the influence of Cleopatra, Antony sent her back with cruel and bitter reproaches. Antony spent the winter in Alexandria. In the spring he again proceeded to the East, subdued the Armenians, captured their king and dragged him a prisoner into Egypt.

After another season of riot, he once more marched against the Parthians. Cleopatra accompanied him, determined not again to lose sight of him. But news from Rome changed his course, and turning westward, he proceeded as far as Ephesus.

QUARREL BETWEEN AUGUSTUS CÆSAR AND MARC ANTONY.

To the history of Rome properly belong these Roman quarrels. It is only the intention to introduce here so much of those matters as particularly explains the history and fate of Egypt.

Marc Antony, who wept and made political speeches over the dead body of Julius Cæsar, had been victorious in arms against the Eastern nations, had greatly enlarged the Roman Empire by subduing the rebellion of Syria, Judea and other provinces, and had done the State good service. For these reasons he deserved their highest esteem. But Rome had another favorite son. This was Octavius, subsequently called Augustus Cæsar. Each aspired to be the first man of Rome. Each had his partisans; but the great services of Antony stood a rebuke to the less active Augustus. This rivalship had led to an enmity which both professed to have extinguished by the marriage of Antony with Octavia, the sister of Augustus. This marriage was consummated, expressly and without disguise, for political purposes—was not sought or especially desired by Antony, but was concocted by the professed political friends of both, who thus hoped to unite their interests, while they had their own private ends to gain.

But Antony was already practically wedded to Cleopatra, the Egyptian, and that queen ever claimed him as her husband. By the Roman law and religion, the marriage of two wives at the same time was prohibited, while that of Egypt did not condemn such marriages. Which then was the greater sinner, the Egyptian first wife, or the Roman second? Yet the Romans attach all the criminality of subsequent events to the Egyptian queen, and all the suffering innocence to the Roman wife.

It can not be doubted that all parties acted with impropriety and unrighteousness. Let it be remembered, that Rome was aspiring to grasp the crown of Egypt, and sought an apology for gratifying that desire. Roman intrigue invented circumstances, and perverted facts, to misrepresent the character and intentions of Cleopatra, and justify themselves; and Roman historians, ever partial to their own country, have recorded the misrepresentations and perpetuated the slander, while Egypt, crushed beneath the iron heel of Roman despotism, was not permitted to be heard in defense of her latest queen and her prostrate throne. Antony still thought more of his Cleopatra than of his Octavia. He had spent some time in idleness in Rome with the latter; he had traversed mountains and deserts, on fatiguing campaigns, with the former; by each he was the father of two children. Why should he not still continue his fond regard and constant affection for her, the older of the two wives, the one chosen from affection, not from policy, the companion of his toils as well as of his leisure. If Cleopatra and Antony spent hours in luxury and debauchery, they also accompanied each other in the fatigues, marches and storms of war; nor did the queen of Egypt shrink from participation in his hardships, toils and dangers. How unjust are the insinuations of the Roman writers, that she was inconstant and treacherous to him, and desired to do him harm. With all the prejudice of her Roman biographers, they have not failed to record in her favor facts, which, if not sufficient to acquit her of all wrong, are abundantly ample to diminish her guilt and extenuate her faults, while they fully convict her accusers of gross misrepresentation. But whatever might be the right or the wrong, by any code of morals, the neglect of Octavia, and the tender regard for Cleopatra, and the stimulus of unbounded ambition, roused anew the hatred of Augustus and his partisans against the absent Antony. Many Romans, however, adhered to the latter ; many brave men left their homes in the imperial city to join his standard, when these two great commanders prepared for, and finally engaged in war against each other.

Cleopatra was still the true wife and faithful friend of Anthony. She joined him with all her Egyptian forces, and notwithstanding Roman misrepresentation, manifested a commendable sincerity in her attachment.

PREPARATIONS FOR WAR BETWEEN THE TWO GREAT ROMANS.

Antony and Cleopatra had been spending some time at Ephesus, but hearing of the movements of Augustus against him at Rome, he prepared for defense.

However innocent Octavia might have been, Antony believed that she was the occasion of these movements. He therefore divorced her and declared war against Augustus. He then removed to Samos, where his armies were concentrated.

Rollin, upon the authority of Pliny, the Roman historian, relates the following as having occurred at this place :

"Whatever passion Cleopatra professed for Antony, as he perfectly knew her character for dissimulation, and that she was capable of the blackest crimes, he apprehended, I know not upon what foundation, that she might have thought of poisoning him, for which reason he never touched any dish at their banquet till it had been tasted. It was impossible that the queen should not perceive so manifest a distrust. She employed a very extraordinary method to make him sensible how ill-founded his fears were; and if she had so had an intention how ineffectual all the precaution would be. She caused the extremities of the flowers to be poisoned, of which the wreaths worn by Antony and herself at table, according to the customs of the ancients, were composed. When their heads began to grow warm with wine, in the hight of their gayety, Cleopatra proposed to Antony to drink off those flowers. He made no difficulty, and after having plucked off the end of his wreath with his fingers, and thrown them into his cup filled with wine, he was upon the point of drinking it, when the queen, taking hold of his arm, said to him, 'I am the poisoner against whom you take such mighty precautions, as if it were possible for me to live without you. Judge now whether I wanted either the opportunity or means for such an action.'

"Having ordered a prisoner condemed to die to be brought thither, she made him drink that liquor, upon which he died immediately."

We may now ask, of what black crime had Cleopatra as yet been guilty, that Antony knew her character for dissimulation? Simply, that she had loved and united her person and fortune with that of the Roman officer with whom she had a perfect right to wed, and whose kind regard she had retained by firm attachment and kindness in return; while Octavia, forced upon him for mercenary purposes, whatever of meekness and commendable virtue she might have possessed, had not succeeded in retaining or exhibiting the same regard.

What had Cleopatra to gain by his death? What advantage was it to her to follow his standard from land to land, and engage in distant wars? Could she not at any time, if she chose, depart—retire to her own kingdom and dwell in quiet? No other explanation of her conduct can be given than to admit her firm, true and virtuous attachment to him whom she esteemed her rightful husband. It is not even pretended by her Roman accusers that, at this time, or any other subsequent to her first interview with Antony, he had any rival in her affections. Is it not much more probable that the fears and unjust suspicions of Antony were roused by the secret emissaries of Augustus, who, under color of friendship, were trying to alienate Antony and Cleopatra, the easier to conquer both, and rob the queen of her kingdom. The friends of Antony having departed from Rome to join his standard, Augustus easily induced the Senate to declare war—not, indeed, against Antony, although he was the victim intended, but against Cleopatra, queen of Egypt.

What had she done? Antony was a Roman officer, commissioned and sent forth by Roman authority to conquer and govern the eastern nations. He still held that commission. Cleopatra, by following his standard, had aided a Roman in doing what Rome commanded to be done. Whatever might have been her social misdeeds, this was the extent of her political offense. If Antony had exceeded his authority, or was guilty of mal-administration, Rome should have canceled his commission, and recalled him from service.

But what justification is there for making war upon his ally, who had no reason to suppose her acts were adverse to the will of Rome. Behind all these pretexts lay the insatiable thirst to add Egypt to the number of Roman provinces, and for this purpose the character of its talented queen must be traduced, and she be made the victim of war.

BATTLE OF ACTIUM, B. C. 31.

War having been formally declared, Antony with his army left Samos, sailed along the coast, and encamped near Corcyra. The forces consisted of five hundred ships, two hundred thousand foot soldiers, and twelve thousand horse. In his company were five kings from Lybia, Cappadocia, Paphlagonia, Comegera, and Thrace. Others, who could not attend in person, sent their troops, from Pontus, Judea, Lycaonia, Galatia and Media.

Rollin thus describes the navy of Antony: "These ships of war were of extraordinary size and structure, having several decks, one above another, with towers upon the head and stern, of a prodigious hight, so that those superb vessels upon the sea might have been taken for floating islands. Such great crews were necessary for completely manning those heavy machines, that Antony, not being able to find mariners enough, had been obliged to take husbandmen, artificers, muleteers, and all sorts of people, void of experience, and fitter to give trouble than do real service."

"A more splendid and pompous sight could not be seen than this fleet when it put to sea, and had unfurled its sails. But nothing equalled the magnificence of Cleopatra's galley, all flaming with gold its sails of purple, its flags and streamers floating in the wind, while trumpets and other instruments of war made the heavens resound with airs of joy and triumph."

Augustus now sailed out and encamped at Brundusium. His army was far inferior in numbers to that of Antony, but was more choice, and his navy was much better disciplined. It consisted of two hundred and fifty ships, of less size but more agile and easily managed, than Antony's. He had eighty thousand footmen, and about twelve thousand horse. But the season was far advanced, and the rigors of winter now set in, and hostile operations were deferred until the next spring.

The vessels sought commodious harbors, and the land forces reposed in their winter quarters. Thus ended the year 32 B. C.

Early in the ensuing spring the opposing forces were put in motion. But nothing decisive occurred until late in the season. Considering the superior force and greater experience of the army, and the undisciplined character of the newly enlisted sailors, the officers in Antony's staff advised him not to engage in a naval battle, but to fall back and fight upon land, or invade those portions of Macedon and Thrace that favored Augustus. They further advised that as Cleopatra's forces were mostly naval, and as women were timid in time of battle, it would be better to dismiss her, and let her retire to Egypt. Besides other advantages, this would be a gain of moral force. The formal declaration of war was against Egypt, not Antony. If Egypt retired, Augustus would be clearly in the wrong, warring against a Roman army, under the command of a Roman officer, attended by a Roman consul—while Egypt, separate from Antony, had committed no offense against Rome.

This was wise counsel, and, had it been observed, might have changed the results; but the most high God ruleth in the nations of the earth, and his counsel had determined to dispose of the last head of the Kingdom of Brass.

Cleopatra, from the number and splendor of ships and men entertained no doubt of their triumph, and indulged high hopes of yet being Empress of Rome, when Antony should have subdued Augustus, and made himself master of the seven-hilled city. These delusive hopes were like the bright rays of the setting sun bursting through the clouds for a moment, after a tempestuous day, then retiring shrouded into the darkness of the night.

Antony could not be persuaded to separate from her who had followed his fortunes, and in whose smiles his soul seemed to have its entire existence. At this critical juncture, his decision was impolitic, but impulse and passion, not judgment, ruled the Roman. So the adverse forces prepared for action on the sea.

Near the head of the Ambracian Gulf stands a promontory at whose base was then the city of Actium. On opposite sides of this strait stood the two armies, arranged in order of battle, to be spectators of a conflict which, as they supposed, was to decide the fate of two great men. But, as God designed, and history proves, to decide the fate of two great kingdoms.

On the second of September, in the early part of the day, the fleets in the mouth of the Gulf engaged in action, and so continued until the darkness of night suspended their operations. For a time victory seemed doubtful to which side to lean. Antony's superior navy, although his inexperienced sailors managed badly, appeared to be the more successful. Cleopatra, seeing the unskillfulness of Antony's ships, and the clashing and terror of his arms, although not in the least danger herself, was overwhelmed with confusion and alarm. She therefore turned her vessel and fled, drawing after her the entire Egyptian fleet of sixty ships.

This action of hers has been greatly censured as the result of treachery, but it is far more probable that confusion and womanly fear inspired the queen—that she acted more from momentary impulse than from any settled design, or any intelligent purpose. Her conduct, although unpardonable in a warrior, does honor to her womanly timidity. Had she, the learned, skillful diplomatist, been also the corrupt, treacherous, intriguing courtezan that her enemies represent her, she would not thus have yielded to fear. So intelligent a bold, bad woman would have been reckless and undismayed by blood and carnage. Her act was a cowardly blunder rather than a crime. Her desertion threw everything into confusion, and decided the fate of the day against Antony, who, seeing her depart, lost all courage himself.

Forsaking his faithful officers who continued the conflict until night, he fled in an open boat, with but few attendants, overtook Cleopatra's flag-ship, and was taken on board by the fugitive queen. The next day, Augustus, perceiving the victory to be complete, despatched vessels in pursuit of the fugitives, but being unable to overtake them, returned again to the main body.

The land forces of Antony, being deserted by their commander, voluntarily surrendered, and were engrafted into the army of Augustus.

Humbled, mortified and disheartened by his defeat, Antony at first refused to see Cleopatra, but took his station on the forepart of the vessel, with his elbows upon his knees and his face buried in his hands, resigning himself to moody reflections. What thoughts revolved in his breast during those three long days! How memory must have brought up the scenes of the past—the recollection of his first wife Fulvia—the resentment of his neglected Octavia—the joyous hopes when he was first sent out with the Roman army—the conquest of so many nations—the humiliation of so many men of renown—and now had come his own downfall, occasioned, in no small measure, by his passions and his blind attachment to Cleopatra, whose weakness, not to say duplicity, had ruined him. In such reflections as these, three days passed. The vessel, coasting along the shores of the Peloponnesus, arrived at Tænarus. Here an interview was had, and Cleopatra and Antony were reconciled, and again lived together. What was now to be done! A last and ineffectual struggle was yet to be made to avert impending fate. Antony had left an army in Africa to guard the coast of Lybia. To Lybia, therefore, he sailed, hoping, by their aid, to mend his waning fortunes. But tidings of his dishonor had preceded him, and Scarpus, the commander of that army, had declared for Augustus.

Antony was now alone. To him the world was as bleak, as barren, and as uninviting as the desert sands before him. But for the earnest persuasion of a few friends, he would have committed suicide. From that time, we find him frequently contemplating that step as a last resort, rather than be taken to Rome and exposed to the scorn of Augustus and Octavia. From Lybia Antony proceeded to Egypt, where Cleopatra had gone, having sailed from Tænarus directly to Alexandria. Of her arrival there, Rollin thus speaks: "When she approached that port, she was afraid if her misfortunes should be known, that she would be refused entrance. She therefore caused her ships to be crowned, as if she was returning victorious, and no sooner landed than she caused all the great lords of her kingdom, whom she suspected, to be put to death, lest they should excite seditions against her when they were informed of her defeat. Antony found her in the midst of these bloody executions. Is it not probable that Cleopatra was informed that her capital was filled with time-serving officers, seduced by Roman bribery, and traitors to their sovereign, only waiting opportunity to declare against her: and that, after having landed, she fereted out their treason, or that some overt act betrayed them, and that, as they deserved, they were executed according to the laws of nations; and further, that the Roman sympathy for them originated in the fact of their secret understanding with Augustus?

CLOSING EVENTS IN ALEXANDRIA.

Cleopatra rightly apprehended that Augustus would pursue her to Alexandria. She had a small fleet on the Red Sea. To prepare for the worst, she contemplated transporting her vessels in the Mediterranean to them, over the isthmus, about ninety miles, that she might be in readiness to escape to India, or elsewhere, if Alexandria should be taken by the enemy. How these ships were to be transported over land, we do not know; but it is certain that such things were anciently done.

In the spring of 30 B. C., the Romans, according to expectation, invaded Alexandria, and the Arabs, taking advantage of her misfortune, robbed and burned her ships on the Red Sea, and thus caused her to abandon the project of transporting the others. Stripped of nearly all her means for military defense, the energetic queen was yet not driven to despair, but next resorted to negotiation, which she managed with admirable diplomatic dexterity. Rollin, upon the authority of Roman historians, informs us that she thought only of gaining Cæsar and of sacrificing to him Antony, whose misfortunes had rendered him indifferent to her. Subsequent events demonstrate that, so far from being indifferent, their mutual misfortunes cemented more fondly their mutual attachment. Rollin's next words are, "she loved even to madness." How then could she be indifferent? She counseled him to send embassadors to Cæsar to sue for peace, and she joined her own embassadors with his for that purpose. In their extremities, this was certainly wise and judicious; but she gave her embassadors instructions to negotiate separately for herself. This is taken by Rollin and others as evidence of an intention to betray Antony. But it proves no such intention. How much easier could negotiation be conducted separately. She could then plead that she was a queen of royal descent; that she was the independent sovereign of Egypt; that she had only assisted Marc Antony while he was a Roman officer under commission, and doing the bidding of the Roman senate; that she had done nothing against Rome; that if Rome had repudiated Antony, she also had withdrawn from his standard, and ought to be left in the quiet possession of her kingdom. These most reasonable propositions being granted, she might claim immunity for Antony, not as a Roman officer, nor a Roman rebel, but as an Egyptian subject and the husband of an independent queen. While Antony's friends might urge in his behalf, that although he had acted under Roman authority, as his commission was recalled and he had no command of any Roman army whatever, he ought to be permitted to retire as a private citizen; that the war was declared not against him, but against Egypt; but negotiating separately from Cleopatra, he would cease to be a party in the war. The instructions, therefore, of Cleopatra, to treat separately, instead of being injurious to Antony, would have been advantageous to both.

But neither justice nor equity had any place in the council of Augustus. He refused to see the embassadors of Antony, but dismissed those of Cleopatra with encouragement.

Rollin says, he gave reason to conceive great hopes in case she would sacrifice Antony to him. Here, then, the secret comes out; the wish is the father of the thought. It was Augustus, and not Cleopatra, that proposes to betray

Antony: it is the temptation of the Roman which the Egyptian queen rejected.

Deputies were sent a second time to Cæsar with no better results. Time rolled along, and Cleopatra was trying experiments with various poisons, to ascertain by which she could most easily end her own life. Driven to desperation and contemplating suicide, what possible motive could she have for betraying Antony?—what possible gain could his destruction be to her? She well knew that the avaricious Roman cared less for one fallen, wretched man, than for the crown of Egypt; that not Antony, but herself and her treasures were the prize, and she would sooner perish than see herself dragged, like a beast, to Rome.

Anticipating the worst, she caused splendid tombs to be erected, adjoining the temple of Isis, to which she removed her treasures, and where she might bury herself within the walls and await the result. Augustus, fearing she might burn these treasures and commit suicide, and thus rob him of the glory of carrying them and her captive to Rome, sent daily messengers to deceive her with false hopes.

Having landed his army, he marched hastily upon the city. Antony, although told of Cleopatra's intrigueries, credited them not. Gathering the few forces in the city, he made a vigorous sally, cut to pieces many of the enemy, pursued them to their very camp, and returned victorious into the city. He hastened to Cleopatra, and the remainder of the day was spent in feasting, while the whole palace resounded with acclamations of joy.

It is said by historians, that Cleopatra, who had no thoughts but of amusing Antony, ordered a magnificent feast to be prepared, at which they passed the rest of the day and part of the night together. What else had she to do but to amuse him? Did he not deserve her kind regards, after the glorious achievement of the day in her defense? The Roman historians are determined to find fault with her. If she smiles, she is deceiving and treacherous; if she does not smile, she has deserted, and is false. The next day, Antony determined to pursue his advantage. He assembled the army upon an eminence, and sent his ships and galleys against the Roman fleet. While all eyes were gazing upon the movement, what was Antony's astonishment to see the flag drop from Cleopatra's admiral's ship, and the whole fleet surrender to Cæsar! This treason the Romans charge to Cleopatra, although there is no evidence she had any knowledge of it: it was more probably effected by Roman bribery.

Antony next sent a challenge to Cæsar to fight single-handed, which Cæsar, with words of contempt, declined.

Deserted by all his land forces, ridiculed by Cæsar, and by false representations made to believe that his beloved queen had betrayed him, he returned to the city, full of rage and madness, and hastened to the palace to wreak his vengeance on his betrayer. But the bird had flown. Cleopatra learning the fate both of the army and navy, anticipated the worst results, and fled to the tombs. Probably contemplating the act of suicide, she sent a messenger to Antony to inform him that the deed was already done.

This intelligence converted his rage and madness into commiseration for her fate, and excessive grief for their mutual calamities. He determined not to survive her. Retiring to an apartment with but one faithful slave, he laid aside his armor, and commanded him to plunge a dagger into his breast. The slave, more courageous than his master, stabbed himself and fell dead at Antony's feet. Encouraged by his example, Antony thrust his sword into his own body, and fell fainting, while streams of blood, from both their wounds, flowed over the floor.

A messenger arrived and announced that Cleopatra still

lived. Antony hearing her beloved name, revived, permitted his wounds to be dressed, and requested to be carried to her presence. Borne upon the shoulders of his attendants, he arrived at the tombs. Cleopatra not forgetting the device by which, years before, she had gained access to Julius Cæsar, was fearful that some stratagem was concealed in that burden, or that the attendants might be the emissaries of Augustus, coming to capture her. She would not unbolt the doors, but from her window dropped down chains and chords, which were passed around the body of Antony; then, the queen, with two female attendants, the only persons in the castle, drew him up. Dangling in the air, with garments streaming with blood, and drawn up by female hands, he arrived at the window. He was taken in and laid upon a bed. Cleopatra stripped the clothing from her own body, and wiped the blood, oozing from his wounds. Few words of mutual counsel and kind regard passed between them, when, clasped in the arms of Cleopatra, Antony expired. And this was the scene of mutual, constant, connubial love in the day of calamity, love even unto death, worthy of all praise from the pencil and pen of the artist and the historian, which the Roman writers have stigmatized as false, treacherous and licentious.

Thus perished, in Egypt, by Roman ungrateful intrigue, two great Romans, Pompey and Marc Antony, who had done more to extend the empire of Rome than the united con quests of all her other generals.

Cleopatra, by permission of Augustus, caused Antony to be buried with all honor, and according to the most splendid Egyptian customs; thus again by her action, contradicting the false accusation of treachery to him. By deception and artifice, unworthy of a hero, the servants of Augustus gained possession of the apartments of Cleopatra. Rollin says: "Cæsar did not think it proper to see Cleopatra in the first days of her mourning." But if Cæsar knew that she was false to Antony, how could he suppose her grief so great? Soon, however, he visited her, under pretense of great friendship, but full of hypocrisy, designing to seize her person and treasures, and carry them captive to Rome.

She was too sagacious not to detect his purpose, and withhold her confidence. That interview, as described by Roman writers, reveals her dreadful anguish and inconsolable grief. She made the most pathetic appeals to Augustus for compassion, but that hard-hearted warrior was unmoved by her calamities. He retired, intending soon to secure his prey. But she preferred death to captivity by the rival and enemy of her beloved husband. She deceived Augustus, it is true, as she had a right to do. We again quote from Rollin: "The better therefore to cajole him, she sent to desire that she might go to pay her last duty to the tomb of Antony, and take her leave of him. Cæsar having granted her that permission, she went thither accordingly, to bathe that tomb with tears, and to assure Antony, to whom she addressed her discourse as if he had been present before her eyes, that she would soon give him a more certain proof of her affection."

Had Cleopatra been that corrupt, deceitful, treacherous woman that the Romans describe her, ready to betray Antony, his tomb would not thus have been visited by her, while contemplating her own departure to the spirit land. The troubled, guilty conscience of a bad person, would above all other places upon earth, avoid the tomb of its victim.

Returning from these sad ceremonies, she wrote a letter to Augustus, requesting to be buried in the same tomb with her beloved Antony. Evading the watchful guards, she received in a basket of figs, the fatal Asp, which she applied to her arm, where its poisonous bite infused into her veins the deadly fluid, and Cleopatra, the learned, the talented, and the calumniated queen of Egypt, the last of the Lagidæ, after a reign of twenty-two years from her first coronation, and in the thirty-ninth year of her age, was wrapped in the sleep of death.

A few words tell the remainder of the story. Cæsar, on receiving the letter, hastened to the tombs to secure his victim, but she had escaped his grasp. He carried off her treasures, made Egypt a Roman province, and thus terminated the last branch of the KINGDOM OF BRASS.

THE END.

TABLE OF RULERS

IN THE

KINGDOM OF BRASS,

ARRANGED IN

CHRONOLOGICAL ORDER.

KINGS OF MACEDON.

	B. C.		B. C.
Cassander,	317	Sosthenes,	280
Philip IV.,	298	Antigonus Donatus,	278
Alexander and Antipator,	297	Demetrius,	242
Demetrius,	294	Antigonus Doson,	232
Lysimachus,	288	Philip V.,	220
Ptolemy Ceraunus,	282	Persus,	178
Meleager,	280	The Romans,	168

THE LAGIDÆ.

	B. C.		B. C.
Ptolemy Soter,	306	Ptolemy Lathyrus,	117
Ptolemy Philadelphus,	285	Ptolemy Alexander I.,	107
Ptolemy Evergetes,	248	Ptolemy Alexander II.,	81
Ptolemy Philopator,	221	Ptolemy Auletes,	65
Ptolemy Epiphanes,	204	Ptolemy Berenice,	58
Ptolemy Philometor,	180	Ptolemy and Cleopatra,	51
Ptolemy Physcon,	145	The Romans,	30

THE SELEUCIDÆ.

	B. C.		B. C.
Seleucus Nicator,	300	Antiochus V., (Eupator)	164
Antiochus Soter,	280	Demetrius Soter,	162
Antiochus Theos,	278	Alexander Bala,	150
Seleucus II., (Callinicus),	246	Demetrius II., (Nicator,)	145
Seleucus III., (Ceraunus),	226	Antiochus VI., (Eutheus),	144
Antiochus III., (the Great),	223	Zebina,	130
Seleucus IV., (Philopator),	187	Several kings at a time,	
Antiochus IV., (Epiphanes),	175	The Romans,	64

www.ingramcontent.com/pod-product-compliance
Lightning Source LLC
LaVergne TN
LVHW020226110826
845151LV00003B/836

9781425532635